D1555210

Poe, Fuller, and the
Mesmeric Arts

•

Poe, Fuller, and the Mesmeric Arts

TRANSITION STATES IN ● THE AMERICAN RENAISSANCE

Bruce Mills

UNIVERSITY OF MISSOURI PRESS
COLUMBIA AND LONDON

Library of Congress Cataloging-in-Publication Data

Mills, Bruce, 1958–
    Poe, Fuller, and the mesmeric arts : transition states in the American
Renaissance / Bruce Mills.
        p. cm.
    Summary: "Examines how the writings of Edgar Allan Poe and Margaret
Fuller draw from representations of and theories concerning animal
magnetism, somnambulism, or hypnosis rendered in newspapers, literary
and medical journals, pamphlets, and books, and also includes discussion of
Ralph Waldo Emerson, Lydia Maria Child, and Walt Whitman"—Provided by
publisher.
    Includes bibliographical references and index.
    ISBN-13: 978-0-8262-1610-6 (alk. paper)
    ISBN-10: 0-8262-1610-2 (alk. paper)
  1. American literature—19th century—History and criticism.
2. Mesmerism in literature. 3. Poe, Edgar Allan, 1809–1849—Knowledge—
Psychology. 4. Fuller, Margaret, 1810–1850—Knowledge—Psychology.
5. Mesmerism—United States—History—19th century. 6. Mesmer, Franz
Anton, 1734–1815—Influence. 7. Altered states of consciousness in
literature. 8. Animal magnetism in literature. 9. Sleepwalking in literature.
10. Hypnotism in literature.   I. Title.
    PS217.M47M55 2005
    810.9'353—dc22

                                                                            2005021968

∞™This paper meets the requirements of the
American National Standard for Permanence of Paper
for Printed Library Materials, Z39.48, 1984.

Designer: Kristie Lee
Typesetter: Crane Composition, Inc.
Printer and binder: Thomson-Shore, Inc.
Typeface: Veljovic Book, medium and bold.

For

Jacob, Sarah, and Mary

Contents

Preface

A higher philosophy must teach us that the senses are but the instruments, the mind the power, of knowledge. The development, indeed, of its immortal stores may depend upon some external touch, which unlocks the treasures of the casket, and one by one exposes them to the light; but, as a seed includes potentially the future plant, leaf, blossom, and fruit, so too does the mind contain within itself its own capacities of expansion.

Chauncy Hare Townshend, *Facts in Mesmerism* (1841)

WRITING RALPH WALDO EMERSON in February 1844, Margaret Fuller jests over his apparent reluctance to join in a mesmeric evening with the clairvoyant Anna Quincy Thaxter Parsons: "Sarah Clarke had fully intended to invite our new Ecstatica for Monday Evening, and submit to your eye the same revelations as to ours, when she was informed by Caroline [Sturgis] that you had spoken of such experiments as 'peeping through the keyhole,' and such like." In January of the same year, she had written a letter that, along with remembrances of Emerson's son, Waldo, contained a lengthy description of one of Parsons's abilities: that of holding a letter whose author was unknown to her and "reading" the character of the writer while "under Mesmeric influence." In a real-world predecessor to Hawthorne's fictional Priscilla in *The Blithedale Romance,* the "ecstatica" Anna Parsons offered what were considered surprisingly accurate features of individuals ranging from Aaron Burr to Harriet Martineau to Emerson himself. Unlike her serious and quite thorough record of the evening in January, however, Fuller's later and much briefer epistle to her friend quickly moves from playful monologue to a comic-serious dialogue between Sarah Clarke and herself over whether to extend an invitation to Emerson: "M[argaret]. I do not like to have Mr E. deprived of the opportunity. Shall I write to him, and ask him if he can go to look, believing the actor, as all law divine or human demands, innocent until proved guilty?"

To which "Sarah" replies: "And make him aware that she neither makes a show of herself, nor seeks excitement, but comes to our house as to that of a friend, where she may expand, and give pleasure by the use of what seem to us real and uncommon powers."[1]

In the intimate exchanges between figures like Fuller and Emerson, it would not have been uncommon to hear such conversation. Whether witnessing or reading of these "uncommon powers" in a friend's parlor, at a public lyceum, or in newspaper accounts of somnambulists, individuals living in the 1830s and 1840s would have been inundated with reports of a science delineating the expansive powers of the mind and the imagination. For modern readers who look back on Franz Anton Mesmer's theory of animal magnetism and nineteenth-century studies of mesmeric consciousness as "pseudo"-science, it is easy to fall into the kind of skepticism that Emerson apparently felt and to attribute evidence of inexplicable powers to both skillful trickery and self-deception. However, as recent scholarship has demonstrated, the findings assigned to the science of animal magnetism in its first half century can be better understood not as a kind of evolutionary dead end in psychology and neuroscience, but as evolving conceptions of the unconscious.[2]

This study, then, is not meant to be a quaint tour in the sideshow of literary lost arts. While certainly fascinating in and of itself, the mesmeric literature also offers insights into theoretical or philosophical models behind antebellum notions of the writing and reading process. As manifested in the writings of Edgar Allan Poe and Margaret Fuller, an understanding of animal magnetism initiated se-

---

1. Margaret Fuller, *The Letters of Margaret Fuller,* ed. Robert N. Hudspeth, 3:181, 177, 182. It is possible that Hawthorne drew from knowledge of Fuller's interest in these mesmeric readings when composing *The Blithedale Romance.* When holding a letter that the fictional Coverdale had just received from Margaret Fuller, the "Veiled Lady" Priscilla takes on Fuller's mannerisms. In her own way, then, Priscilla embodies some of the specific abilities of the "ecstatica" Parsons. See chapter 7, "The Convalescent," in Hawthorne's romance.

2. One of the most exhaustive and informative studies of the emergence and development of the science of animal magnetism is Adam Crabtree's *From Mesmer to Freud: Magnetic Sleep and the Roots of Psychological Healing.* See also Robert C. Fuller, *Mesmerism and the American Cure of Souls;* Maria Tatar, *Spellbound: Studies on Mesmerism and Literature;* Robert Darnton, *Mesmerism and the End of the Enlightenment in France;* and Henri F. Ellenberger, *The Discovery of the Unconscious: The History and Evolution of Dynamic Psychiatry.*

rious speculation on the relationship between language and sensation. In especially respected studies of this science, Poe and Fuller read theories on the relationship between physical/verbal "gestures" and the faculty of the imagination. Consequently, they considered ways in which to understand the connection between words and the psychological states of readers. Rather than tracing a "sideshow," or peripheral influence, this book maps out a constellation of literary and scientific texts that reveal foundational concepts for Poe and Fuller. While reflecting the assimilation of numerous literary and philosophical influences, the work of Poe and Fuller betrays a critical vocabulary and conceptual framework rooted in the debate over the precise meaning of mesmeric phenomena and thus in the era's emphasis on interior states.

Moreover, this study suggests that, rather than being figures who are less easily positioned within the "renaissance" of American literature, Poe and Fuller are writers/critics who articulate definitive elements of this period of artistic flowering. That is, they formulate a creative and critical practice that shifts the emphasis from constructing a national literature responsive to historical and geographical realities (such as the vast American landscape and the contact between settlers and the "Indian") to developing literary forms alert to the fluidity and dynamic qualities of inward perception. To frame this in a suggestive though simple way, they move from an ontological orientation to an epistemological one, from what might be considered an "American" knowledge toward an "American" way of knowing. In essence, through an understanding of the physics and metaphysics of perception, they reflect a literary theory and practice that absorbs (and responds to) the expansiveness of democratic conditions.

Considering how the era adjoined an understanding of the imagination and animal magnetism illuminates why writers such as Poe and Fuller would have turned to notions of mesmeric consciousness in their work. By the third and fourth decades of the nineteenth century, the definition of the imagination reflected an interesting convergence of metaphysical, medical, and literary influences. To engage deeply in the creative process, then, invited a simultaneous investigation into the divine, the physiological, and the psychological dimensions of the mind. According to Abraham Rees's first American

edition of *The Cyclopaedia,* the imagination is "a power or faculty of
the soul, whereby it conceives and forms ideas of things, by means
of impressions made on the fibres of the brain, by sensation." While
the first paragraph of the definition briefly introduces the distinction
between the passive imagination ("retaining the simple impression
of objects") and the active imagination (the dimension of the faculty
that "arranges" and "combines" images "in a thousand ways"), the
bulk of the entry is devoted to the suggestive connection between
the operations of the organs of our senses and the soul. Composed
of little fibres, the article argues, the sense organs are moved either
at the fibres that terminate in the brain or at the outward parts of
the body. Significantly, the encyclopedia entry distinguishes between effects evoked by inward, or immaterial, causes and those introduced by outward, or material, ones:

> Now the agitation of these fibres cannot be communicated to the
> brain, but the soul will be affected, and perceive something. If then
> the agitation begins where objects make their first impression, *viz.*
> on the external surface of the fibres of our nerves, and is commu-
> nicated thence to the brain[,] the soul, in that case, judges that what
> she perceives is without, that is, she perceives an external object
> as present; but if only the anterior fibres be moved by the course
> of the animal spirits, or in some other manner, the soul then imag-
> ines, and judges, that what she perceives is not without, but within
> the brain; that is, she perceives an object as absent: and herein lies
> the difference between sensation and imagination.[3]

As will be explored in Chapter 1, this emphasis on an interior process
and on the power of the imagination to evoke images of absent objects echoes the scientific evidence that invisible forces can indeed
affect bodies from a distance. In other words, just as the movement
of distant celestial bodies reveals the invisible but powerful influence
of gravitational forces, so too do the interior "motions" of the mind
(and their visible effects) suggest a model for understanding the
imagination and the relationship between words and readers' responses. In the instance of the imagination, however, man, not God,
serves as the primary mover, that is, the consciousness whose will
sets in motion distant sensations. Writers need only look inward in

---

3. Abraham Rees, "Imagination," in *The Cyclopaedia* (1810–1824), vol. 19, n.p.

an effort to understand how to select, arrange, and combine the language symbols that are most evocative to readers' souls and thus call forth powerful effects or impressions.

Perhaps most remarkable in the speculation that finds a place under the *Cyclopaedia* heading "Imagination" is the extensive treatment of the "influence of [the imagination], on the corporeal Frame." In fact, of the fourteen pages in the entry, the authors devote almost half to the history and effects of animal magnetism. Drawing from Franz Anton Mesmer's *Memoir on the Discovery of Animal Magnetism* (1779), the article characterizes this magnetic "agent" as a "fluid universally diffused, and filling all space, being the medium of a reciprocal influence between the celestial bodies, the earth, and living beings;—it insinuated itself into the substances of the nerves, upon which therefore it had a direct operation;—it was capable of being communicated from one body to other bodies, both animated and inanimate, and that at a considerable distance, without the assistance of any intermediate substance." In their synopsis of Mesmer's principles and their summary of the report of a French commission appointed by the king in 1784 (whose members included Benjamin Franklin) to assess the merits of Mesmer's ideas, the authors underscore a central finding: "Great and extraordinary as the powers of this new agent seemed to be, the phenomena were proved to be referrible solely to the *imagination* of the parties magnetised."[4] By centering the effects within the imagination rather than in the influence of a material (though invisible) fluid upon the nerves, they further manifest the era's transition from an emphasis on external, or material, causes to internal, or immaterial, ones. Though "debunking" Mesmer's belief in the presence of an actual physical fluid, then, the commission unexpectedly gave legitimacy to theories that underscore the special power of the imagination.

By the 1830s, most practitioners of mesmerism accepted such findings and dismissed Mesmer's early notion that the effects observed while patients were in a magnetic state resulted from the manipulation of an unseen but physical agent through the passing of hands along the body; rather, they increasingly explored how to "touch" or "move" the inward faculty through the artful method of the magnetist. In the decades after Mesmer introduced his findings, instruction on

4. Ibid.

the practice of inducing a magnetic state drew attention to the artful exertions of the mesmerist upon an attentive and willing patient.
Typically, doctors or practitioners of the science sat with subjects'
legs between their knees or with patients sitting quite near them; in
that position, they fixed their gaze upon their subjects, began a series of physical gestures or hand passes (sometimes accompanied by
verbal cues), and, as a result, produced a sympathetic relationship
or rapport with their patients. In *Facts in Mesmerism, with Reasons
for a Dispassionate Inquiry into It,* a text read by both Poe and Fuller
and widely cited in studies of animal magnetism during the era,
Chauncy Hare Townshend quotes from the French commission's
findings as powerful evidence for the existence of animal magnetism: "That which we have learned, or, at least, that which has been
proved to us, in a clear and satisfactory manner, by our inquiry into
the phenomena of mesmerism, is, that *man can act upon man,* at all
times and almost at will, by striking the imagination; that signs and
gestures the most simple may produce the most powerful effects;
that the action of man upon the imagination may be reduced to an
art, and conducted after a certain method, when exercised upon patients who have faith in the proceedings."[5] In the investigations into
the phenomena of magnetic and electrical forces, then, we repeatedly witness a coming together of terms and concepts that are as applicable to literary creation as to medical practice or social reform.
For many in the era, in fact, the implications of Mesmer's initial discoveries pointed toward foundational principles, precepts that discerned underlying laws of creation as applicable to the motion of the
stars as to the subtle workings of the mind. For some, these insights
resulted in new paradigms for the creative process; they began to believe that the ideal artist should attend less to classical models than
to emerging conceptions of the imagination and interior states. To
affect the reader demanded that the writer understand the inward
causes of certain effects.

In light of this mesmeric or inward turn, it is striking but not unexpected that the *Cyclopaedia*'s extensive discussion of the imagination fails to mention by name the writers that we might most
associate with Romantic conceptions of the artist. Instead, the ar-

5. Commission of the French Academy of Science, quoted in Chauncy Hare
Townshend, *Facts in Mesmerism,* 18.

ticle turns to the medical and philosophical speculations that informed the notions of such figures as Coleridge and Wordsworth. In my study, I trace the evolution of this understanding and application of animal magnetism in order to capture how medical study of healing at a distance (that is, the ability of material "bodies" to have an unseen effect on distant animate and inanimate objects) progressively shifted from conceptions of sympathetic joining of atoms or gravitational movement of planetary bodies to the effects of such immaterial causes on the human will and imagination. In other words, I survey the steady journey toward this preoccupation with inward states. That the effects of animal magnetism increasingly began to be understood in terms of the will and imagination rather than the actual manipulation of a material fluid points toward the path from medical to literary practice. In seeing that their "cures" did not necessarily depend upon the actual manipulation of an external or "animal" fluid, physician-magnetists began to shape a method applicable to the art of writing. The evolution of the method of inducing the magnetic state is a study in the psychology of signs and the power of such signs upon the imagination of the patient/reader.

Reaching artistic maturity in a decade that saw the introduction and intense exploration of animal magnetism in the United States, both Edgar Allan Poe and Margaret Fuller betray a direct awareness of the findings that profoundly influenced the imaginative arts and become case studies in the impact of evolving medical practices and conceptions of human psychology. Rather than see both figures as atypical, however, I contend that their assimilation of insights associated with animal magnetism embodies the era's central shift from "historical fiction" toward an emphasis on inner states, character psychology, and formal/genre choices that best encompass "renaissance" texts. Understanding the ways in which Poe and Fuller accommodated the mesmeric "arts" introduces a conceptual lens from which to reconsider writers such as Emerson and Whitman.

Again, given that both writers have typically been excluded from or are marginal figures in influential paradigms of antebellum literature, such a claim invites a reconsideration of the underlying assumptions that shaped more writers than Poe and Fuller. As J. Gerald Kennedy argues in his introduction to *Romancing the Shadow: Poe and*

Race, Poe has in fact existed in an "anomalous position in both old
and new" canonical configurations and has been excluded from some
especially influential "nationalist critical paradigms from F. O. Matthiessen to Sacvan Bercovitch." Revealingly, he adds,

> Evincing little sustained interest in the frontier, the natural land-
> scape, the Puritan past, the settlement of the colonies, the Revo-
> lution, or democracy itself, he seems in many ways the most
> un-American of our early writers. Many of his narratives (and
> poems) depict not native scenes but the fantastic, half-remembered
> landscape of the England he had seen in childhood. Perhaps not
> coincidentally, Poe has won greater acclaim in Europe, where read-
> ers and critics have either detached his work from its historical
> contexts or assimilated it into Continental intellectual traditions.[6]

What I would argue, however, is that Poe's "American" tendencies
exist not in the outward signs of national identity, but in the critical
and creative practice that resonates with the democratic act of privileging individual consciousness. Such tendencies reside not so much
in product as in process. What remains consistent between Poe and
Hawthorne and even Poe and Emerson is a foundational "faith" in
the inward as a means to generate form or reform. Whether in fiction or essay, these writers share the belief that the "rules" of one's
art and the precepts for one's life are discoverable through intensive
attention to the microcosm of the individual mind.

Just as Poe articulates a particular literary practice consistent with
this centripetal-centrifugal dynamic (that is, the generation of larger
truths through preoccupation with the individual self), so too does
Margaret Fuller engage in the era's emphasis on the generative nature of the inward gesture. As I will explore in the later chapters,
Fuller's self-conception and early critical perspective draw in inci-
sive ways from the magnetic and medical texts. It is revealing that
Fuller termed herself a "somnambulist" at a time when newspapers
and journals included accounts of the remarkable actions of women
somnambulists in New England. (While *somnambulist* refers simply
to an individual who walks in his or her sleep, the popular and scientific literature of the period often used the word to describe peo-

---

6. J. Gerald Kennedy, introduction to *Romancing the Shadow: Poe and Race,*
ed. J. Gerald Kennedy and Liliane Weissberg, xiii.

ple who demonstrated clairvoyant abilities while in a dreamlike or unconscious state.) Perhaps more significant, however, are the ways her critical values as well as her notions of reform and gender reflect a study of the mesmeric literature and personal experience with animal magnetism. In her effort to discern the especial genius of woman in *Woman in the Nineteenth Century,* Fuller herself announces the relevance of the electric or magnetic, two terms used to name an invisible, all-pervading energy or force that affects material bodies and/or connects the material with the spiritual. In turning to ways in which Lydia Maria Child's *Letters from New-York* and short fiction develop Fuller's ideas, I strive to trace gendered interpretations inevitable in mesmeric principles. I suggest the consonance between Fuller's and Child's views at a time when both women lived in New York and, as evidence suggests, engaged in conversation about the "feminine" in the context of mesmeric findings.

Admittedly, my ongoing fascination with Poe and Fuller emerges from the degree to which these writers—so central in theorizing and establishing the short-fiction genre (Poe), in more directly conceptualizing gender in the context of a democratic culture (Fuller), and in describing aesthetic principles or social visions that embrace centripetal and centrifugal forces (Poe and Fuller)—trouble some popular configurations of the literary period. In many respects, as a teacher and a scholar, I found it easier to set them up as marginal figures. Working with Emerson, Whitman, Hawthorne, and Melville provided a kind of coherence that Poe—and Fuller, to a lesser extent—disrupted. The more that I taught and read around their work, however, the more clearly did I come to discern the broader impulses of the period. Certainly, their writings grow out of the peculiar biographical realities of their "genius," to use the term of the era. Perhaps it can be said, however, that their uncharacteristic literary journeys (and particular personal struggles) served as catalysts, as the unique blend of circumstances that motivated a more direct and enduring desire to integrate the truths of mesmeric consciousness and that initiated the occasions for clarifying a critical framework for the inward life. In part, I came to recognize that their imaginations led them to wrestle more explicitly with the science of the mind and the relationship between language, sensation, and those higher states of perception evoked by art.

Placing the work of Poe and Fuller in the context of an overlooked and evocative cultural dialogue (and thus drawing extensively from the vast medical, psychological, and philosophical orientations toward mesmerism) enabled me to trace critical issues and points. Given the place of Poe and Fuller in the canon, I decided that a certain coherence emerged in considering figures whose work, as already noted, fell less easily within critical efforts to provide a "unified" vision of the era. It is my hope that this selective focus might initiate the kind of rediscoveries (in Poe, Fuller, and other writers) that lead readers toward new insights and that continue the work of seeing Poe and Fuller in fresh and vital ways.

Acknowledgments

IN MY FIRST senior-level seminar at Kalamazoo College, one of my students, Virginia Lautzenheiser, wondered why Margaret Fuller used the term *electric* in conceptualizing the feminine in *Woman in the Nineteenth Century.* This study arises from the seed of this encounter. My student's curiosity and the lingering sense that behind this one term there existed a rich set of cultural assumptions concerning gender, reform, and the capacities of the human mind led me to the shelves of countless libraries and years of research and writing. To Virginia Lautzenheiser (now Eifert) and the students who have been part of my ensuing seminars on mesmerism and nineteenth-century literature, I offer my heartfelt thanks. Without our conversations, my own reflections would have remained indistinct and incomplete. Finally, for their work in helping prepare the manuscript for final submission, I thank Will Miller and Paul Lewakowshi.

I owe a special debt of appreciation to Ellen Caldwell, now at the University of California, Fullerton, for close readings of major portions of my early drafts and for her ongoing interest and support of my research. Her acute insights and careful editing helped me see how to return to various sections with a more critical eye. In addition, I have drawn in central ways from the careful reading of my fellow Kalamazoo College Americanist, Amelia Katanski, as well as former colleague Cari Carpenter. Their reading of my chapter on Margaret Fuller's early writings was critical in its development. To *all* my colleagues within the English Department, however, I owe thanks for their continued support. I have also benefited from the support of Kalamazoo College; without grants for research trips and a sabbatical leave, I would not have had the opportunity to devote intensive time early in the project to archival research. Finally, my ability to do extensive archival research benefited immeasurably from a summer stipend provided by the National Endowment for the Humanities.

In my teaching, I remind students that new insights always emerge from the foundation of others' works. To Joel Myerson,

xix

Richard Hudspeth, Jeffrey Steele, Christina Zwarg, Charles Capper, and the many others who have made essential primary work available to other scholars or who, in their own writings, have provided specific insight or support to this book, I offer a humble sense of thanks. And, while I am years away from their early mentoring, I still wish to thank Kathleen Diffley and Ed Folsom at the University of Iowa for inculcating essential skills as a scholar and setting in motion my own contribution to the field.

Without the assistance of the various staff at the following libraries, the book would also have been incomplete: Houghton Library, Harvard University; Radcliffe Library; the Countway Medical Library; the Massachusetts Historical Society; the National Library of Medicine; and the Library of Congress. I especially wish to thank Stephen Greenway at the National Library of Medicine for his gracious assistance. For last-minute assistance in relation to the project, I am indebted to Nancy Bagnasco at Madonna University and Kathy DeMey at Calvin College. Finally, and closer to home, I want to thank Robin Rank and Stacy Nowicki, reference librarians at Kalamazoo College, for their help with the continual requests of a colleague and friend.

To Clair Willcox and Jane Lago at the University of Missouri Press, I offer my appreciation for your commitment to the book and your careful attention to all aspects of its publication. The manuscript also benefited from the copyediting of Gloria Thomas Beckfield.

Excerpts from Margaret Fuller's unpublished manuscripts have been published by permission of the Houghton Library, Harvard University. Fuller's sketch, "Double Triangle, Serpent and Rays," from her 1844 journal, is reprinted courtesy of the Massachusetts Historical Society. I am grateful to the University of Georgia Press for allowing the reprint of excerpts from my introduction to Lydia Maria Child's *Letters from New-York*.

Finally, I wish to express my love for Sarah and Jacob, who have spent weekends waiting for me to return home and join in the more important play of their own imaginations. And, as always, I wish to thank my partner in life, Mary Holtapp, for her love and patience.

Poe, Fuller, and the Mesmeric Arts

•

Introduction

Toward an American Aesthetic

The Centripetal and Centrifugal Force of Mind

For the threshold of our modernity is situated not by the attempt to apply objective methods to the study of man, but rather by the constitution of an empirico-transcendental doublet which was called *man*. Two kinds of analysis then came into being. There are those that operate within the space of the body, and—by studying perception, sensorial mechanisms, neuro-motor diagrams, and the articulation common to things and to the organism—function as a sort of transcendental aesthetic; these led to the discovery that knowledge has anatomo-physiological conditions, that it is formed gradually within the structures of the body, that it may have a privileged place within it, but that its forms cannot be dissociated from its peculiar functioning; in short, that there is a *nature* of human knowledge that determines its forms and that can at the same time be made manifest to it in its own empirical contents. There were also analyses that—by studying humanity's more or less ancient, more or less easily vanquished illusions—functioned as a sort of transcendental dialectic; by this means it was shown that knowledge had historical, social, or economic conditions, that it was formed within the relations that are woven between men, and that it was not independent of the particular form they might take here or there; in short, that there was a history of human knowledge which could both be given to empirical knowledge and prescribe its forms.

Michel Foucault, *The Order of Things*

One of that centripetal and centrifugal gang,
I turn and talk like a man leaving charges before a journey.

Walt Whitman, "Song of Myself"

IN THE MINDS OF antebellum writers, the intensive focus on creating a national literature existed amid an ongoing dynamic

1

of centripetal and centrifugal forces. Not only did these powers of attraction and repulsion provide a visual representation of the material and spiritual universe, but they also embodied what might be termed the cosmology of a democratic culture. Set in motion through both the self-reliant and the expansive logic of democracy, these forces played themselves out in the simultaneous (and seemingly contradictory) emphasis on individual freedom and on political union. In addition to these manifestations of sociopolitical realities, however, the inner mechanism of the human mind betrayed the evidence of counterbalancing energies through the effects of some harmonizing agent or magnetic principle in the nature of all creation. Ultimately, as Foucault suggests, new conceptions of the human mind signaled a revolution in the various institutional and literary forms of mental cultivation and self-culture.

In the midst of this epistemological shift and evolving theories, genres, and vocabulary, writers sought to develop an aesthetic that would capture the dynamic nature of the mind. Thus, it can be expected that creative and critical "practices" reflected and harnessed the "anatomo-physiological conditions" of knowing. In these conditions, after all, writers could come to understand the link between outward effects and inward forces and, potentially, discern the material workings of spiritual laws. Significantly, the discovery of and speculation on these laws influenced a generation of writers who embraced the challenge of responding to Nature and nation. To capture the workings of the universe was to embody a democratic "state," that is, a condition that achieves a harmonious relationship between material and spiritual tendencies. In effect, writers such as Edgar Allan Poe and Margaret Fuller—as well as Emerson, Hawthorne, Whitman, and others—were inscribing the nature of the mind in their experimentations with narrative and poetic forms. Their central writings seem to address the question, How does one create an aesthetic that effectively explores, accommodates, and fosters the harmonious interplay of transition states (individual and national)?

In Poe's and Fuller's efforts to understand the nature of animal magnetism and mesmeric consciousness, we observe most directly how their theories and practices grew from an understanding of the relationship between mind and literature. In this introduction, however, I wish to preface the ensuing chapters' close attention to the case studies of Poe and Fuller with the suggestive dimensions of this epistemological shift. While later revealed in Poe's dialectic of the expansion and subsequent contraction of the universe or in Fuller's fluid notion of the "great radical dualism," the era's understanding of magnetic or electric forces reveals more than these particular authors' idiosyncratic "theories" of life and art. In these theories, we find the evidence of a shift in epistemological orientation that shaped American literary consciousness and, as a result, narrative and poetic forms. In short, we discover the ideas and language that mark the centripetal and centrifugal dynamic of a national aesthetic.

In an era that represented the world as the interplay between opposing energies, the intensive speculation on animal magnetism suggests more than a narrow attempt to describe effects ensuing from invisible and antagonistic forces. Rather, it signals a broader cultural desire to explain—even posit—a fluid energy whose active presence resists the impulse toward overly rigid (and destructive) oppositions and a divisive individualism. The Western democratic impulse and the enlightenment ideals that served as its foundation, in fact, predisposed writers to emphasize the centrality of fluid, not fixed, identities or concepts, that is, to imagine transition states, not static ones. (Among many of the era's texts that betrayed the influence of enlightenment values in their speculation on democratic realities, Hector St. John de Crèvecoeur's *Letters from an American Farmer* and Alexis de Tocqueville's *Democracy in America* offer some of the most enduring articulations of the kind of Promethean and protean energy arising from the elimination of traditional social structures.) In the study of mesmerism, people came to locate an "over-force"— what Lydia Maria Child and others called the "electric" and characterized as the "medium that puts man into relation with all things, enabling him to act on all, and receive from all."[1] While the observed effects of mesmeric forces led to a range of theories, they were consistently attributed to or explained by an energy that defied borders, even erased them. As we will see, Fuller associated this energy with an apprehensiveness, an ability to encompass or be receptive to seemingly antagonistic qualities and, in this receptivity, to foster a "state" that promised the possibility of a wholeness or

1. Lydia Maria Child, *Letters from New-York,* ed. Bruce Mills, 157.

unity. Such a "union" had implications for the state of both the individual and the nation (that is, the body politic) as well as the state of artistic practice.

For the artist, the mesmeric literature was evocative, for it provided ways in which to understand changing notions of individual consciousness and an evolving model for the relationship between writer and reader, words and effects. Because the study of human psychology and the nature of the unconscious was in its early stages, however, the very practical challenge for writers—that is, to develop a new mode of discourse that encompassed a new understanding of mind—seemed especially acute in the first half of the nineteenth century. Again, characterizing this shift from a classical to a modern sensibility, Foucault argues that the

> human sciences did not inherit a certain domain, already outlined, perhaps surveyed as a whole, but allowed to lie fallow, which it was then their task to elaborate with positive methods and with concepts that had at last become scientific. . . . The epistemological field traversed by the human sciences was not laid down in advance: no philosophy, no political or moral option, no empirical science of any kind, no observation of the human body, no analysis of sensation, imagination, or the passions, had ever encountered, in the seventeenth or eighteenth century, anything like man.[2]

In other words, antebellum writers were in the process of developing new disciplines of study in attempts to understand a categorically different way of knowing. In medical texts, philosophical treatises, cosmological theories, and metaphysical essays, the trained and untutored of the late eighteenth and early nineteenth centuries contributed the kind of speculation that laid the groundwork for current ideas regarding neuroscience, psychology, and the unconscious. And, in doing so, they introduced a discourse that shaped how writers saw the world and also shaped their art.

In his effort to assert how the human sciences embodied a dramatically new "episteme" that marked the transition to modernity, however, Foucault might overstate the degree to which people in the late eighteenth and early nineteenth centuries revised the way

2. Michel Foucault, *The Order of Things: An Archaeology of the Human Sciences*, 344.

they formulated knowledge. By the first three decades of the nineteenth century, in fact, writers could draw from a rich set of medical and philosophical texts whose reflections on the laws of motion generated an increasing understanding of inward, or psychological, "laws." So much so that, again by the late 1820s and early 1830s, standard definitions of *imagination* assumed a readership that accepted its physiological and psychological dimensions—or, in Foucault's terms, its "anatomo-physiological" aspects—and understood investigations concerning animal magnetism as providing central insights into the nature of a faculty especially important to writers.

If the centrality of this physical-metaphysical discourse on motion, inward states, and the nature of perception seems beyond the realm of the literary, it may be because literary study has tended to separate what was often the seamless connection between writers' theories of "life" and their literary theory. Tracing the "esoteric origins of the American renaissance," Arthur Versluis argues, "One major reason that Western esoteric traditions did not receive much academic attention until the end of the twentieth century, and the beginning of the twenty-first, is that these traditions are inherently transdisciplinary."[3] While undergoing some change, it is still a tendency of literary study to return to an era's literature and overlook the "nonliterary" material—either in the anthologizing of the period or in the privileging of only the poetic, dramatic, and fictional genres.

The selective representation of Samuel Taylor Coleridge's *Biographia Literaria* (1815) in prominent anthologies clearly exemplifies this tendency and, given Coleridge's revered place among those interested in the science of animal magnetism, can further reveal the correlation between notions of the imagination, magnetic forces, and speculation on the mind. In anthologies, the parts of *Biographia Literaria* most often excerpted deal with the "literary," that is, excerpts from beginning chapters on Coleridge's early education, reading interests, opinions on poets before and after Pope, thoughts on Wordsworth's poetry, and, importantly, distinctions between fancy and imagination. Typically, anthologies also include material from chapters 13 through 24 on the imagination, or "esemplastic power." Interestingly, Coleridge's response to the "law of association," or associative power (chapters 5 through 12), remains outside the

3. Arthur Versluis, *The Esoteric Origins of the American Renaissance,* 5.

purview of most texts and, as a result, the period. (According to the work of David Hartley, associationism could be used to "explain how the most complex mental processes—imagining, remembering, reasoning—might be analyzed into clusters or sequences of elementary sense impressions and that ultimately all psychological acts might be explained by a single law of association."[4]) However, like Poe's *Eureka,* Fuller's "Wisconsin" chapter, and Child's essay on the "electric," Coleridge's reflections in these middle chapters provide an extensive explanation for preceding notions of the imagination and ensuing assertions of its unifying power.

Coleridge begins his philosophical musings by drawing attention to the distinction between things and thoughts. In doing so, he establishes his affinities with idealists rather than materialists and asserts a position consistently underscored in studies of mesmerism, that is, that we "draw our sensations from the signs of things, and not the things themselves."[5] Noting the tendency of men in various ages to construct "tables of distinctions," Coleridge describes a finer difference, often asserted, that "[in] our perceptions, we seem to ourselves merely passive to an external power, whether as a mirror reflecting the landscape, or as a blank canvas on which some unknown hand paints it." Such a position, however, could not long be held, for these ideas, "concerning the mode in which our perceptions originated, could not alter the natural differences between *things* and *thoughts.*" He continues:

> In the former, the cause appeared wholly external, while in the latter, sometimes our will interfered as the producing or determining cause, and sometimes our nature seemed to act by a mechanism of its own, without any conscious effort of the will, or even against it. Our inward experiences were thus arranged in three separate classes, the passive sense, or what the school-men call the merely receptive quality of the mind; the voluntary, and the spontaneous, which holds the middle place between both.

Arising in his own day, Coleridge claims, the law of association offers new insight into the spontaneous sense. Significantly, in his re-

<hr>

4. *Encyclopaedia Britannica Online,* s.v. "Hartley, David," http://search.eb.com/eb/article?eu = 40213 (accessed July 30, 2003).
5. Townshend, *Facts in Mesmerism,* 233.

flections, Coleridge reminds us of the close relationship between psychological laws and the physics of planetary movement: "the law of association being that to the mind, which gravitation is to matter." Critical to any understanding of the plasticity of the imaginative faculty, then, is the recognition that, contrary to Locke's materialistic assertions and Hartley's refining of such assertions through his knowledge of the nervous system, the human mind constructs or shapes sensory data. The motion of the mind must be understood not as a manifestation (outcome) of the direct imprint or sensory impression of material *things* but as the active force that gives shape to sensation. Or, to paraphrase Emerson's distinction between the materialist and the idealist in *Nature,* the former conforms thoughts to things while the latter conforms things to thoughts.[6]

To posit the formative and plastic nature of the imagination relies on an understanding of the mechanism of knowing itself, that is, on what mediates the receptive and voluntary qualities of mind and on how this unconscious agency supervenes the conscious will. As we will see with Poe, this speculation on the nature of artistic power shifts attention from tuition to intuition, from an apprenticeship to past masters and forms to an attentiveness to the divine mechanism of the inner self and the nature of perception.[7] For Coleridge, this philosophical and aesthetic orientation finds expression in "Thesis X" in the twelfth chapter of *Biographia Literaria:*

> The transcendental philosopher does not enquire, what ultimate ground of our knowledge there may lie out of our knowing, but what is the last in our knowing itself, beyond which *we* cannot pass. The principle of our knowing is sought within the sphere of our knowing. It must be something therefore, which can itself be known. It is asserted only, that the act of self-consciousness is for *us* the source and principle of all *our* possible knowledge. Whether abstracted from us there exists any thing higher and beyond this primary self-knowing, which is for us the form of all our knowing, must be decided by the result.

6. Samuel Taylor Coleridge, *Biographia Literaria, or Biographical Sketches of My Literary Life and Opinions,* ed. James Engell and W. Jackson Bate, pt. 1, 90, 92; Ralph Waldo Emerson, *Nature,* in *Selections from Ralph Waldo Emerson,* ed. Stephen Whicher, 44.

7. For a fictional rendering of this shift, see Nathaniel Hawthorne's "The Artist of the Beautiful," in *Mosses from an Old Manse,* 447–75.

Coleridge's disinterest, so to speak, in the stable knowledge of tradition is replaced by the "fixt point" that *is* self-consciousness. In
other words, such inward faculties as the imagination provide stability and mediate the centripetal and centrifugal forces that Emerson
would later characterize in "Circles." Addressing the seemingly unsettling nature of the "endless seeker with no Past at [his] back,"
Emerson argues that "this incessant movement and progression
which all things partake could never become sensible to us but by
the contrast to some principle of fixture or stability in the soul." Not
surprisingly, in distinguishing between primary and secondary
imagination in a later chapter, Coleridge envisions this divine faculty in very active and dynamic terms:

> The primary IMAGINATION I hold to be the living Power and prime
> Agent of all human Perception, and as a repetition in the finite
> mind of the eternal act of creation in the infinite I AM. The sec-
> ondary I consider as an echo of the former, co-existing with the
> conscious will, yet still as identical with the primary in the *kind* of
> its agency, and differing only in *degree,* and in the *mode* of its oper-
> ation. It dissolves, diffuses, dissipates, in order to re-create; or
> where this process is rendered impossible, yet still at all events it
> struggles to idealize and to unify. It is essentially *vital,* even as all
> objects (*as* objects) are essentially fixed and dead.

Such a definition marks a dramatic transformation from a classical
and neoclassical sensibility and thus offers new terms for the creative process and product. Moreover, it implies and fosters a new
relationship between writer/text and reader. In a sense, each participates in the Emersonian truth that there are "no fixtures in nature,"
that the "universe is fluid and volatile," and that "[p]ermanence is
but a word of degrees." The poem or story, then, is ideally a formal
representation of the universe of a single perceiving consciousness;
the writing thus takes on the "psychological" orientation, content,
and form that distinguish groundbreaking nineteenth-century texts
and increasingly mark a "modern" sensibility.[8]

· · · ·

8. Coleridge, *Biographia Literaria*, pt. 1, 283–84, 304; Emerson, "Circles," in
Selections from Ralph Waldo Emerson, 176, 168.

Late-eighteenth- and nineteenth-century research on animal magnetism formed one of the central sites of cultural discourse that attracted writers. It provided suggestive speculation for figures such as Coleridge who were developing a "literary" theory consistent with new physical and philosophical truths. Before turning from the illuminating and influential reflections in *Biographia Literaria,* it would be useful to consider additional musings in Coleridge's *Theory of Life* as a means to distinguish another important element in this inward orientation, an element that suggests more directly the democratic affinities of this epistemological shift.

As noted earlier, the unifying aspect of the imagination (and the similar, harmonizing element of magnetic forces and/or consciousness) forms a necessary element in a world of opposing forces. In *Theory of Life,* Coleridge offers a common rendering of his era's dialectical grid in a way that anticipates Poe's efforts to delineate a theory of the universe: "If we pass to the construction of matter, we find it as the product, or *tertium aliud,* of antagonist powers of repulsion and attraction. Remove these powers, and the conception of matter vanishes into space—conceive repulsion only, and you have the same result." In further discerning the implications of only the operation of partial forces, he asserts an influential and widespread understanding of the material and spiritual universe: "For infinite repulsion, uncounteracted and alone, is tantamount to infinite, dimensionless diffusion, and this again to infinite weakness; viz., to space. Conceive attraction alone, and as an infinite contraction, its product amounts to the absolute point, viz., to time." It becomes clear that "life" embodies a synthesis of these forces, a counterbalance that, for Coleridge and others during his time, came to be depicted as opposing poles on the four distant points of intersecting axes.[9]

9. Coleridge, *Theory of Life,* in *Shorter Works and Fragments,* ed. H. J. Jackson and J. R. de J. Jackson, pt. 1, 522. Coleridge most likely composed *Theory of Life* in November through December of 1816. Interestingly, it was meant as a contribution to the debate between the Transcendentalist notions of John Abernethy (*An Enquiry into the Probability and Rationality of Mr. Hunter's Theory of Life* [1814]) and the materialist views of William Lawrence (*An Introduction to Comparative Anatomy and Physiology* [1816]). Both men were responding to the work of John Hunter. Coleridge was supportive of Abernethy, who had argued that "what Hunter had called *material vitae diffusa* ('the diffused matter of life') was something like electricity: 'a subtile substance of a quickly and powerfully mobile nature, seems to pervade everything, and appears to be the life of the

In the macrocosm and microcosm of material life, then, we observe principles fundamental to both physical and psychological
laws. Or, according to Coleridge, in the two poles between the "veg-
etable and animal creation" and the crowning entity of the human
body, we witness the "unceasing *polarity of life, as the form of its
process, and its tendency to progressive individuation as the law of its direction.*" Chief among the conceptions flowing from such a principle
is the "original fluidity" of the world. In such a view, chaos should
not be understood and represented as the conflict between opposing forces but as the "one vast homogeneous drop!" (One is reminded here of Melville's description of whiteness in *Moby Dick,*
that is, as an example of an evil or chaos gesturing toward the oblit-
eration of difference, heterogeneity.) And, in words that resonate
with the era's ongoing exploration of fluid states, Coleridge argues,
"The whole history of Nature is comprised in the specification of the
transitional states from the one to the other. The symbol only is fictitious: the thing signified is not only grounded in truth! it is the law
and actuating principle of all other truths, whether physical or intellectual." Turning next to his notion of magnetism as "the first and
simplest *differential* act of Nature," he configures this power as embodying opposite poles and, in the end, as a twofold power, thesis to
its antithesis. Within this flux or interplay between opposing forces,
we again arrive at an effort to describe or theorize magnetism as a
pervading and harmonizing presence. To posit a world of antagonistic poles is only a partial explanation. In a sense, we see in the observable effects of attraction and repulsion the necessary presence
of an all-encompassing power.[10]

Coleridge's distinction between the passive dimensions of fancy
and the active force of the imagination can be understood as the difference between a partial understanding of centripetal and centrifugal forces and a full comprehension and application of broader,
harmonizing powers. That is, the poet of the imagination sees *both*
oppositions *and* unifying principles and, as a result, can reflect those
harmonies in art. It is instructive to close this consideration of Cole-

---

world; and therefore it is probable that a similar substance pervades organized
bodies, and produces similar effects in them'" (Coleridge, *Theory of Life,* 482). For
Coleridge's "Compass of Nature," see *Shorter Works,* pt. 1, frontispiece, 602–3.
    10. Coleridge, *Theory of Life,* in *Shorter Works,* pt. 1, 533, 534–35.

ridge with one of his more revealing (and lengthy) harangues on the flawed nature of the fancy:

> But we cannot force any man into an insight or intuitive posses-
> sion of the true philosophy, because we cannot give him abstrac-
> tion, intellectual intuition, or constructive imagination; because
> we cannot organize for him an eye that can see, an ear that can lis-
> ten to, or a heart that can feel, the harmonies of Nature, or recog-
> nize in Her endless forms, the thousand-fold realization of those
> simple and majestic laws, which yet in their absoluteness can be
> discovered only in the recesses of his own spirit.

According to Coleridge, this shortcoming—and the inability to coerce a higher level of insight and imagination—arises from the ossification of imaginative powers "by the continual reaction and assimilating influences of mere *objects* on his mind." In other words, the "*passive* fancy" shackles individuals with external things and, through "habitual slavery to the eye, or its reflex," thus inhibits a capacity to transform objects. Throughout his reflections, Coleridge opposes such "ossifying" and "paralyzing" ways of perceiving the world with the vital power of a constructive imagination. He concludes with a telling lament for such a limited soul: "[H]e must be content, while standing thus at the threshold of philosophy, to receive the results, though he cannot be admitted to the deliberation—in other words, to act upon *rules* which he is incapable of understanding as LAWS, and to reap the harvest with the sharpened iron for which others have delved for him in the mine." Such thoughts cannot help but call to mind Poe's endeavor to capture the essential role of intuition in his delineation of the "laws of the heart divine" in *Eureka.* As Poe cautions, a person "must have a care, however, lest, in pursuing too heedlessly the superficial symmetry of forms and motions, he leave out of sight the really essential symmetry of the principles which determine and control them."[11]

That Coleridge follows his breathless critique of passive fancy with a paragraph pointing toward the importance of studies in magnetism and electricity further reinforces the centrality of such studies:

11. Ibid., 525–26; Edgar Allan Poe, *Eureka: A Prose Poem,* in *The Science Fiction of Edgar Allan Poe,* ed. Harold Beaver, 300.

> It is not improbable that there may exist, and even be discovered, higher forms and more akin to Life than those of magnetism, electricity, and constructive (or chemical) affinity appear to be. . . . But in the present state of science, the magnetic, electric, and chemical powers are the last and highest of inorganic nature. These, therefore, we assume as presenting themselves again to us, in their next metamorphosis, as reproduction (i.e., growth and identity of the whole, amid the change and flux of all the parts), irritability and sensibility; reproduction corresponding to magnetism, irritability to electricity, and sensibility to constructive chemical ability.

Clearly, how Coleridge comes to understand and apply the truths of magnetism or electricity may not always coincide with the thinking of later theorists; in fact, he seems in conflict at points as to the extent to which magnetism/electricity embodies antagonistic *or* unifying forces. Yet, with many writers of his and ensuing generations, he shared the belief that an understanding of universal laws is intricately linked to consideration of the relationship between magnetic forces and the mind. Moreover, it is essential that the individual start from within, that he or she "take up inwardly" this search for all-embracing laws.[12]

   The unifying agency of the inward life and the fluidity of the material world were what preoccupied writers of the American Renaissance. Ever in the process of becoming, the universe of the stars and the expansive nature of individual consciousness partake of this vital existence, this fundamental law, this magnetic essence. And, importantly, it is this attentiveness to the conditions of the mind—and an evolving democratic consciousness born from such conditions—that directly and indirectly shaped an aesthetic of the transition state. After all, if we extend the implications of Coleridge's logic, we can see that the literary form and content of the passive fancy not

   12. Coleridge, *Theory of Life,* in *Shorter Works,* pt. 1, 526. Coleridge expresses ideas that Emerson later echoes in "The American Scholar." According to Emerson, "The ambitious soul sits down before each refractory fact; one after another reduces all strange constitutions, all new powers, to their class and their law, and goes on forever to animate the last fiber of organization, the outskirts of nature, by insight" ("The American Scholar," in *Selections from Ralph Waldo Emerson,* 66).

only reflects an "ossified" imagination but also fosters a paralyzing perception. Not surprisingly, then, Poe, Fuller, and others became less concerned with creating a national literature out of the "things" of an American past and more concerned with how such materials might be taken up through the laws of the mind. They were concerned less with accommodating the past than with delineating the magnetic "motion" of the mind, that is, the state of consciousness that ameliorated antagonistic forces and offered the promise of a unifying self-culture. In effect, the national literature had to break out of the ossifying rules of addressing literary and cultural needs through historical fiction; paradoxically, it had to turn inward to create an authentic body of American literature.

That Poe and Fuller engaged deeply in this epistemological struggle is evident in their effort to attend to the truth of magnetism and thus notions of the unconscious or inward state that were available to them in the 1830s and 1840s. It is important to understand, however, that this fascination with mesmeric states signals more than a narrow or isolated attraction to what we might see as the mysteries of the unconscious. Instead, the speculation on somnambulism, magnetic states, electric forces, and the relationship between divine motion and the human will provided the conceptual foundation for an aesthetic of becoming and a deeper understanding of the imagination as a unifying faculty. Thus, as suggested by Coleridge's thinking, the era's discourse functions as a kind of shaping sensibility, one that facilitated an understanding of how the imagination *acts* and that fostered subtle and dramatic shifts in poetic or narrative forms.

Perhaps one of the most striking manifestations of a shifting aesthetic is the singing of the individual and national "body electric" in Whitman's "Song of Myself." In many ways, we can see the form and content of the work as a formal embodiment of the mesmeric consciousness. (Again, it is what Foucault termed the "transcendental aesthetic" emerging from a focus on "anatomo-physiological" conditions of knowledge.) To use Coleridge's words again here, the poem captures the "unceasing *polarity of life, as the form of its process, and its tendency to progressive individuation as the law of its direction.*" Paradoxically, the individuation in Whitman's poem is envisioned as the dialectic between the "I" and the "we," that is, between simultaneously single and collective identity. In other words, the fluidity of this individuating tendency suggests the transitionary nature of the self and, importantly, the responsiveness of this self to the centripetal and centrifugal conditions of democratic life. That Whitman saw this "procreant urge of the world" not as a threat to individual identity but as a vital element to a democratic self is confirmed throughout the entirety of the poem:

> Out of the dimness opposite equals advance . . . . Always
>   substance and increase,
> Always a knit of identity . . . . always distinction . . . . always a
>   breed of life.
>
> To elaborate is no avail . . . . Learned and unlearned feel that
>   it is so.
>
> Sure as the most certain sure . . . . plumb in the uprights,
>   well entretied, braced in the beams,
> Stout as a horse, affectionate, haughty, electrical,   `
> I and this mystery here we stand.

Returning to the seeming chaos and contradictions of his poetic "I," Whitman underscores what seems counterintuitive rather than intuitive: "Do you see O my brothers and sisters? / It is not chaos or death . . . . it is form and union and plan . . . . it is eternal life . . . . it is happiness."[13]

As will be examined more extensively in the conclusion of this study, Whitman's 1855 edition of *Leaves of Grass* can be understood as a work that grew out of the dialectical thinking rooted in both the era's philosophy and the diversity of American life. Even more importantly, it posited a kind of consciousness that resisted the rigidity of past poetic forms and fostered a generative transition state necessary to a democratic art and culture. In short, it found a form that held centripetal and centrifugal forces in harmony. Interestingly, while Whitman's innovative poetic form tested readers long educated in traditional rhyme schemes and rhythms, it clearly resonated with the period's notions of higher states of consciousness, especially as described in the mesmeric literature. (In fact, the poetic persona's transcendence of spatial and temporal boundaries complements the confessions of clairvoyants and, at the very least,

13. Walt Whitman, "Song of Myself," in *Leaves of Grass*, ed. Malcolm Cowley, lines 37, 38–43, 1307–8. I am using the 1855 edition of *Leaves of Grass*.

shares an affinity with the psychological states recorded in articles and books on animal magnetism.[14]) Moreover, it is arguably the case that the catalogues, to cite one groundbreaking feature of the poem, manifest a poetic state of mind consistent with mesmeric consciousness and, as a result, mirror the fluid nature of a perceiving "eye" that dissolves conventional boundaries.

The resonance between the era's notions of magnetic states and the elevated consciousness of Whitman's poetic persona is striking. In *Mesmerism and the American Cure of Souls,* Robert C. Fuller summarizes the characteristics of the highest state of mesmeric consciousness (often termed a clairvoyant state), which emerge in the period's literature: "Here the individual has come into direct contact with animal magnetic fluid, and his mind is temporarily imbued with its omnipresent and omniscient properties. At this deepest level of consciousness, subjects feel themselves to be united with the creative principle of the universe (animal magnetism). There is a mystical sense of intimate rapport with the cosmos. Subjects feel that they are in possession of knowledge which transcends that of physical, space-time reality."[15] Whether or not individuals accepted the actual existence of an animal fluid, Fuller offers a vocabulary as appropriate to this higher state as to "Song of Myself." Interestingly, as we will see in relation to Margaret Fuller and her own sense of the healing dimensions of magnetic "reform," such a state often led to harmony or healing.

Thus, at a very basic but important level, the things and people signified in the catalogues of "Song of Myself" become the "law and actuating principles" of all truth. Having absorbed his nation and formative notions of the age, Whitman "dissolves, diffuses, dissipates, in order to re-create." Whitman's willingness to reside in a transition state, defying the limits of time and space, contributes to the work's ultimate coherence. Clearly, it is hard to imagine that this identifiably "American" poem could have been written prior to the extensive research into the nature of perception, imagination, and mesmeric

14. The literature on animal magnetism records the ability of those in magnetic sleep to "travel" to distant places and describe the homes of observers. For one example of this defying of spatial boundaries, see William L. Stone, *Letter to Doctor A. Brigham, on Animal Magnetism: Being an Account of a Remarkable Interview between the Author and Miss Loraina Brackett While in a State of Somnambulism,* 19–31.

15. Robert C. Fuller, *Mesmerism and the American Cure of Souls,* 46.

consciousness that so influenced Romanticism and so pervaded the culture from the late 1820s through the 1840s.

In recent years, scholars have increasingly found themselves turning their eye toward mesmerism, for any close reading of the era's texts introduces terms and concepts that can only be understood within its theoretical constructs. Thus, Fuller's use of the word *electric* at a critical juncture in theorizing the nature of the masculine and the feminine and Poe's consideration of inward "effects" in his formulation of the short prose tale invite an attention to the mesmeric literature. For some scholars, the turn to this body of literature reflects a growing awareness of the "subversive imagination" of the period's canonical authors, that is, an appreciation of the way in which such figures as Poe and Hawthorne drew from their knowledge of the pseudosciences. In *Beneath the American Renaissance,* David S. Reynolds maintains that "[a]nimal magnetism and mesmerism seem to lie behind many of the subtler effects of Poe's early fiction, particularly the creative interpenetration of the spiritual and material in tales like 'Morella,' 'Ligeia,' 'The Fall of the House of Usher,' and 'The Masque of the Red Death,'" but that, "[a]s Poe progressively tried to identify earthly causes for the supernatural, his use of these pseudosciences became more explicit, to the detriment of his literary art."[16] The suggestion here is that the form of Poe's fiction arises from his understanding of mesmerism. At the same time, because it is not the focus of his study, Reynolds does not enter into the theoretical materials available to Poe enough to see the particular relationship between his success as an artist and his attentiveness to the nature of perception. This is the difference between attending to the content available to Poe (for example, in popular or sensational presentations of animal magnetism) and the theoretical or philosophical grounding to his artistic choices. It is possible to see Poe's fiction, whether judged as good or bad, as evolving from a conception of the mind and thus reflecting the ways in which writers might construct stories to create powerful effects.

In *Mesmerism and Hawthorne: Mediums of American Romance,* Samuel Chase Coale takes this next step in discerning the difference be-

---

16. David S. Reynolds, *Beneath the American Renaissance: The Subversive Imagination in the Age of Emerson and Melville,* 244.

tween using mesmerism for content and integrating its underlying principles for form. "Several critics," he points out, "have previously discussed the use of mesmerism as a theme in [Hawthorne's] work, but very few have discussed mesmerism as an influence on the very structure and texture of it." In his chapter entitled "The Mesmerist's Gaze and Hawthorne's Psychology of Idolatry in the Tales," Coale traces more extensively his argument that, despite Hawthorne's "fervent objections to mesmerism and spiritualism," the "shape and structure of his fiction parallels the three phases of the original mesmeric process: the transition, the trance, and within the trance."[17] Such an argument further suggests that, regardless of an author's acceptance of, indifference to, or resistance to animal magnetism, the physiological and philosophical underpinnings to this science reinforce Foucault's notion of a changing episteme. Thus, Hawthorne could shape his art within an understanding of the "anatomo-physiological conditions" that would affect the way his readers might respond to his writing. It is not surprising that Poe praised a writer who shared a similar artistic epistemology.

From Jeffrey Steele's suggestive consideration of Margaret Fuller's understanding of the electric to Arthur Versluis's connection between animal magnetism and the esoteric origins of the American Renaissance to Alison Winter's extensive examination of mesmerism in Victorian England, the landscape of scholarship now includes a serious reframing of how the era came to accommodate findings associated with magnetic states and the imagination.[18] Following the cues from these critics and the evocative panorama of the shift from a classical to a modern episteme traced in Foucault's *The Order of Things,* this study examines a new orientation to the period, one that, in effect, offers the vocabulary of the centripetal and centrifugal and the magnetic or electric as a way to conceptualize underlying affinities and unities. This paradigm of the transition state provides further clues to an aesthetic orientation that promises an "athletic" reading that the era's writers sought and shaped.

While Thoreau, Emerson, Fuller, and other figures central to

17. Samuel Chase Coale, *Mesmerism and Hawthorne: Mediums of American Romance,* 7, 28.

18. See Jeffrey Steele, *Transfiguring America: Myth, Ideology, and Mourning in Margaret Fuller's Writing;* Arthur Versluis, *Esoteric Origins of the American Renaissance;* and Alison Winter, *Mesmerized: Powers of Mind in Victorian Britain.*

American literary history voice such thoughts, they simply express views widely articulated and directly related to the confluence of conceptions of mind, of literary form, and of democratic expansiveness. In the opening essay "Influence of Free Governments on the Mind" from the April 1835 *Southern Literary Messenger,* we hear how calls for a national literature starting in the late 1810s evolved from asserting the use of distinctive history and geography to discerning the synergy between the limitlessness of mind and of free principles. Significantly, the article title seems to misname cause and effect, for its opening suggests that the mind rather than political institutions shapes society:

> Human society, from the nature of its formation, is governed in all its multifarious movements, however majestic or delicate, by mind. There are no changes, nor revolutions in society, that do not acknowledge its influence. It is the all-pervading, all-exciting cause of human action. Its power on the social system is similar to that of gravitation in regulating the magnificent and rolling orbs of space; the great centre of attraction, holding together and preserving in harmonious order the thousand relations of life.

Moreover, the article declares, "[a] ceaseless activity is the original characteristic of all material creation" and "[a]ll matter, whether on the surface, or in the centre of the earth, is imperceptibly undergoing a continuous change."[19] Though the writer clearly underscores the importance of the unique dimensions of the vast and diverse American landscape and peoples, he sees these realities (and imaginative resources) not as an end, but as a means to realize the very nature of an expansive mind. For those in the literary profession, the call for a national literature had evolved into an attention to the state of one's own mind, to those manifestations of the highest states of mind, and to the effects of literary choices on readers' psychological states. If material creation embodied a ceaseless activity and ever-changing nature, then it demanded an equally dynamic aesthetic. In the history and philosophy of mesmeric consciousness, Poe, Fuller, and others discerned those principles that offered the promise of accommodating transition states.

19. H. J. G., "Influence of Free Governments on the Mind," *Southern Literary Messenger,* 389.

1 . . .

Charting the Mesmeric Turn

Sympathy, Animal Magnetism, and the Motion of the Mind

First follow NATURE, and your Judgment frame
By her just Standard, which is still the same:
Unerring Nature, still divinely bright,
One *clear, unchang'd,* and *Universal* Light,
Life, Force, and Beauty, must to all impart,
At once the *Source,* and *End,* and *Test of Art.*
Art from that Fund each just Supply provides;
Works without *Show,* and without *Pomp presides:*
In some fair Body thus th' informing Soul
With Spirits feeds, with Vigour fills the whole,
Each Motion guides, and ev'ry Nerve sustains;
It self unseen, but in th' *Effects,* remains.

Alexander Pope, An Essay on Criticism

I prefer commencing with the consideration of an *effect.* Keeping originality *always* in view . . . I say to myself, in the first place, "Of the innumerable effects, or impressions, of which the heart, the intellect, or (more generally) the soul is susceptible, what one shall I, on the present occasion, select?" Having chosen a novel, first, and secondly a vivid effect, I consider whether it can be best wrought by incident or tone—whether by ordinary incidents and peculiar tone, or the converse, or by peculiarity both of incident and tone—afterward looking about me (or rather within) for such combinations of event, or tone, as shall best aid me in the construction of the effect.

Edgar Allan Poe, The Philosophy of Composition

DISTINGUISHING BETWEEN teachers literary and sacred, Ralph Waldo Emerson classes Alexander Pope among the poets and philosophers who speak *"from without,* as spectators merely, or perhaps as unacquainted with the fact, on the evidence of third persons" and not among those who speak *"from within,* or from experience, as parties and possessors of the fact." Placing Pope's "essay" beside Edgar Allan Poe's reflections on the writing process, it is possible to discern the differences that may have elicited such a judgment. An outward tendency pervades Pope's poetic lecture. Thus, while connecting *"Nature"* with *"Effects"* fed by the unseen wellspring of the informing soul, the starting point is not inward, but outward. To be a poet or critic is not to know one's own mind as much as it is to apprentice oneself to past models: "Those RULES of old *discover'd,* not *devis'd,* / Are *Nature* still, but Nature *Methodiz'd."* Or, as he would underscore not many lines later, "Be *Homer's* Works your *Study,* and *Delight,* / Read them by Day, and meditate by Night, / Thence form your Judgment, thence your Maxims bring, / And trace the Muses *upward* to their *Spring."*[1] It is not that Pope fails to discern the immaterial motions or unseen nerves that guide and sustain the muse; instead, to borrow Emerson's terms, he seems more like a spectator whose gaze is preoccupied with the evidence of third parties.

Whereas Pope's essay sees effects as dividends from the funds supplied by Nature, Poe's critical perspective conceptualizes "effect" quite differently. It is not the dividend, but the principal. Interestingly, his creative focus fosters an inward gaze, a gesture clearly underscored in his parenthetical correction "or rather within." Certainly, Poe's reflections do not mean that he is unaware of past models or that his choices in incident and tone are uninformed by a familiarity with literary heritage. Rather, they seem more concerned with how choices in language and form evoke a sensation or impression. Such a fact is confirmed later, when Poe admits that, after identifying his intention of "composing a poem that should suit at once the popular and the critical taste," he initially considered the

1. Ralph Waldo Emerson, "The Over-Soul," in *The Essays of Ralph Waldo Emerson,* 170; Alexander Pope, *An Essay on Criticism,* in *Eighteenth-Century English Literature,* ed. Geoffrey Tillotson, Paul Fussell Jr., and Marshall Waingrow (New York: Harcourt Brace Jovanovich, 1969), 556 (epigraph is from 555–56).

length of the work: "If any literary work is too long to be read in one sitting, we must be content to dispense with the immensely important effect derivable from unity of impression—for, if two sittings be required, the affairs of the world interfere, and every thing like totality is at once destroyed."[2] It would seem, then, that Poe's literary foundation is not rooted in the study of and delight in Homer's works, but in the examination of the muse traced from the mechanics of the mind.

For writers in the nineteenth century, Pope did in fact offer a striking foil to prevailing conceptions of artists and the creative process. Set beside the writing of Pope, Poe's critical vocabulary invites a number of questions. Why would he be more intently interested in reader psychology than past lyrical models? Why would an emphasis on impression or sensation figure so prominently in his literary choices? Answering these questions directs us toward discourse on the relationship between the mind and sensation that pervaded antebellum culture. In *Facts in Mesmerism, with Reasons for a Dispassionate Inquiry into It,* Chauncy Hare Townshend draws from an ongoing examination of animal magnetism in asserting that we "have followed sensation inward only to arrive at the mind itself, and to exhibit it as not the plaything of the senses, but their lord and master." In continuing, he turns to a Kantian notion articulated by Coleridge: "It is time that we who talk of the march of intellect at the present day should rise above the vulgar view of sensation, and, as Coleridge phrases it, endeavor 'to create the senses out of the mind, and not the mind out of the senses.'"[3]

In order to understand why Poe focused on the interior effects of a writer's "compositions," why Margaret Fuller integrated the vocabulary of magnetic states and the "electric" into her literary criticism and views on gender, and, more generally, why authors of the first half of the nineteenth century increasingly viewed imagination in the context of investigations into the mesmeric arts, we must turn

2. Edgar Allan Poe, "The Philosophy of Composition," in *Edgar Allan Poe: Essays and Reviews,* 15.

3. Townshend, *Facts in Mesmerism,* 251–52. Townshend slightly alters Coleridge's thoughts from *Specimens of the Table Talk of the Late Samuel Taylor Coleridge.* Coleridge had said, "The pith of my system is to make the Senses out of the Mind—not the Mind from the Senses, as Locke etc." (*Specimens of the Table Talk,* ed. Carl Woodring, pt. 1, 312).

to this discourse on the unseen but visible influence of magnetic or electrical forces. For the period, the terms *magnetic forces* or *electrical forces* refer to an unseen and all-pervading energy that affects material bodies (often with healing results) and connects the material and spiritual worlds. From medical journals to private diaries, from public demonstrations to intimate parlor gatherings, and from well-researched medical and philosophical treatises to magazine fiction, writings by Americans speculated extensively on the meaning of phenomena that seemed to offer insight not only into the connection between the material and spiritual worlds but also into the impact of linguistic signs and gestures on human physiology and psychology. If we start with the notions of sympathies and antipathies that would still have resonated during Pope's life and trace them to conceptions of mesmeric forces, the particular outlines of this inward tendency and its implications on the nature of the imagination emerge with greater clarity. In other words, by investigating the evolution of "sympathy" from medicinal texts of the seventeenth century to studies of animal magnetism within the late eighteenth and early nineteenth centuries, we gain insight into how writers imagined the relationship between their words and readers.

"What do we know . . . ," asks John Campbell Colquhoun in the summer of 1831, "of the real cause of the phenomena of mineral magnetism, of electricity and galvanism; of the susceptibility of disease in the animal organization; of infection; of the salutary operation of many medicinal drugs, &c.?"[4] Such a reminder that unseen causes exist behind observable effects—that bodies can act upon each other from a distance—formed a common refrain in the countless studies of magnetic phenomena. Often ridiculed for their "occult" interest in animal magnetism, scientists and scholars repeatedly reminded readers of the need to practice intellectual humility in the face of new and remarkable findings. In the responses to Copernicus and Newton, they argued, the history of science afforded countless examples of authoritative challenges to revolutionary discoveries and paradigms. Besides this effort to cultivate receptive readers, figures like Colquhoun carried the added burden of establishing a con-

4. John Campbell Colquhoun, introduction to *Report of the Experiments on Animal Magnetism,* 5.

tinuum between the old and new, of "translating" past scientific stories and theories into narratives that would resonate more convinc-
ingly within the milieu of the nineteenth century. In a sense, he
and others had to encourage readers to see the marginalia—the incomplete insights that had existed on the margins of preceding scientific discourse—as central to more enlightened understandings of
human will and the operations of the mind.

In Colquhoun's introduction to *Report of the Experiments on Animal Magnetism* (1833), we witness his desire to establish the particular legacy of animal magnetism, one that represents not a breach
from the past, but a bridge to it. Soon after quoting Father Lebrun's
injunction from *History of the Critique of Superstition* that "the opinion
of man cannot set limits on the operations of nature," Colquhoun
lists eminent seventeenth-century physicians and philosophers who
"assumed the existence of an universal magnetic power" that helped
explain "the dependence and reciprocal action of bodies" and who
claimed that the "will or imagination of man, when energetically
called into action, is capable of producing a perceptible effect" upon
others even from a distance. That Colquhoun describes the pre-
Enlightenment beliefs of his predecessors in ways consonant with
nineteenth-century views is revealing. By the 1830s, most apologists for animal magnetism understood the science in terms of
"reciprocal action of bodies" and of the central importance of the
magnetist's "will or imagination" in inducing healing.[5] Depending
upon the mesmeric practitioner or theorist, however, the specific
interest in the new science manifested itself through varying
though typically complementary emphases. While many physicians
underscored the healing dimensions of the invisible power, meta-
physicians turned to the illuminating insights that higher states of

5. Ibid., 6, 23–24. Colquhoun's list of respected sixteenth- and seventeenth-
century physicians and philosophers was consistently cited in the literature on
animal magnetism, especially those texts that sought to delineate the continuum from Renaissance thinking to findings of the antebellum period. Gesturing toward his predecessors, he observes that "there is a still more incredible
power noticed by many authors, which enables an individual, by an energetic
effort of volition, to produce very extraordinary effects upon the corporeal organism of others" (22–23). This text and his later publication *Isis Revelata: An
Inquiry into the Origin, Progress, and Present State of Animal Magnetism* (1836)
represent fully researched examinations of animal magnetism and include extensive reviews of published materials.

consciousness or clairvoyant abilities gave to the potential of the human mind and the nature of the spiritual. In the scientific and philosophical explorations surrounding animal magnetism, the era articulated its interest in better understanding the relationship between the material and spiritual realms.

In the emphasis on the reciprocity of physical bodies and the power of the imagination, we can discern preexisting conceptions that found their locus within the notion of the sympathies. In *The Order of Things,* Michel Foucault considers sympathy as one of four forms of similitude that inform the notion of resemblances and thus the "semantic web" that shapes the order of things up to the sixteenth century. Drawing from sources of the period, Foucault asserts the special importance of *sympathy* (in relation to *convenientia* [convenience], *emulatio* [emulation], and *analogy*) and its opposite, *antipathy:* "But such is its power that sympathy is not content to spring from a single contact and speed through space; it excites the things of the world to movement and can draw even the most distant of them together. It is a principle of mobility: it attracts what is heavy to the heaviness of the earth, what is light up towards the weightless ether; it drives the root towards the water, and it makes the great yellow disk of the sunflower turn to follow the curving path of the sun." Foucault goes on to argue that, "[b]ecause of the movement and the dispersion created by its laws, the sovereignty of the sympathy-antipathy pair gives rise to all the forms of resemblance," that the "first three similitudes are thus all resumed and explained by it," and, ultimately, that the "whole volume of the world, all the adjacencies of 'convenience', all the echoes of emulation, all the linkages of analogy, are supported, maintained, and doubled by this space governed by sympathy and antipathy, which are ceaselessly drawing things together and holding them apart." Again, a look at these theoretical precursors will underscore the degree to which Poe's poetic agenda marks a significant conceptual shift from the time of Pope and will suggest the importance of mesmerism in developing (and understanding) this inward turn.[6]

Sir Kenelm Digby's discourse on the "powder of sympathy," first published in 1658, a text Colquhoun cites in his 1833 report on animal magnetism, establishes an early explanation for healing at a distance and thus an understanding of the order of things resonant

---

6. Michel Foucault, *The Order of Things,* 23, 25.

with Foucault's summary of this sixteenth-century *episteme*. A respected physician of the period, Digby gained renown for his curing of a patient named Howel, a man whose hand had suffered severe cuts by a sword. The relief and eventual cure of Howel's pain ensued after Digby simply dissolved a "Powder of Vitriol" in water containing the man's bloody garter. According to the account provided by Digby, this combination of powder and cool water, even though it was not applied to the patient, immediately transferred to him a "pleasing kind of freshnesse, as it were a wet cold napkin [that] did spread over [his] hand." To explain this cure and others performed without direct contact with the patient, Digby relates a series of principles hypothesizing a preponderance of invisible atoms capable of registering movement across space:

> The *First Principle* shall be, that *the whole Orbe* or *Sphere of the Air is filled with Light.*

> The *Second Principle* shall be, that *The Light glancing so upon some body, the rayes which enter no further but rebound from the superfices of the body, carry with them some smal particles or atomes. . . .*

> My *Third Principle* shall be, that *The Air is full throughout of small Bodies or Atomes;* or rather that, which we call our air, is no other than a mixture or confusion of such Atomes, wherin the aereal parts predominate.

Central to his remaining four principles is the notion of sympathy. Citing evidence that various kinds of invisible attractions exist in the world (for example, "Magnetical," "Electrick," "Flame," and "Filtration"), Digby asserts that certain atoms are more inclined to "mingle more willingly with the body which draws them" because of "the Resemblance and Sympathy they have one with the other." The intermingling of the vitriol, water, and blood of the patient, then, sets in motion a chain of atoms that eventually attach themselves to the body that draws them. Through this sympathetic commingling, the body heals.[7]

While Digby's theories were not universally accepted, they still

---

7. Sir William Osler, *Sir Kenelm Digby's Powder of Sympathy: An Unfinished Essay,* 12; Sir Kenelm Digby, *Of Bodies, and of Mans Soul. To Discover the Immortality of Reasonable Souls. With Two Discourses of the Powder of Sympathy, and of the Vegetation of Plants,* 153, 159, 173.

signal the persuasiveness of "Resemblance" as a lens for understanding the world and an ongoing belief in some universal principle of attraction manifested in outward though unseen material
forces. Not surprisingly, physicians consistently conceived of curative
agents in terms of sympathy and the growing evidence of invisible
forces of attraction and repulsion. In *The Art of Curing Sympathetically, or Magnetically* (1700), H. M. Herwig argues that we "have in
our selves the whole Firmament, with the Planets and Stars, and as
heat penetrates an Iron Furnace, and the Sun Glass, so do the Stars
Men with all their properties." Though living in a time that saw the
transition away from the classical period's embrace of resemblances
as a way of organizing knowledge or knowing the world, Herwig
offers a definition of sympathy that encompasses or at least gestures toward what Foucault characterizes as the ability to draw even
the most distant of things together. "Sympathy," Herwig explains,
"is a mutual and natural affection and combination between natural things, arising from a peculiar and occult congation [sic]," or, to
define the idea using different terms, it is a "consent," a joining together "by a mutual marriage, as bound in a kind of league one to
another." Quite telling here is this idea that, for some authorities at
least, such a binding together seems consensual. This belief in "con-
senting" partners anticipates growing efforts to harness what previously had seemed outside the vision and volition of humankind. In
the relationship between mesmerist and patient, we will see the re-
quirement of mutual willingness by both parties as a vestige of this
belief in the "consensual" nature of sympathetic forces. That is, as
Joseph Philippe François Deleuze would later write in his *Practical
Instruction in Animal Magnetism,* for one individual to act upon another, "there must exist between them a moral and physical sympathy."[8]

Since this binding together formed a natural part of the human
condition, it became important for doctors to differentiate between
types of sympathy in order to understand and thus harness its powers. Such an enterprise fit well within the emerging sensibility of
the eighteenth century. In *A Treatise on Sympathy* (1781), Seguin
Henry Jackson distinguishes between mental and corporeal sympa-

---

8. H. M. Herwig, *The Art of Curing Sympathetically, or Magnetically,* 10, 21;
Joseph Philippe François Deleuze, *Practical Instruction in Animal Magnetism,*
trans. Thomas C. Hartshorn, 22.

thies: "The first arises from a sensation in the mind, determining to particular organs, or particular parts of the body, and raising in them certain feelings, actions, and inclinations, sometimes agreable, and sometimes disagreable." Including "longings" and "depressing passions," he terms this sort "sympathies of consciousness." A second kind of sympathy, "sympathies of impression," depends "upon the operation of external bodies, and the condition of the moving and sentient extremities of the nerves, and more generally occurs in diseased states of the system."[9] Jackson's desire to refine the manner in which sympathy might be classified signals a growing tendency to distinguish between the origins of certain bodily effects. In other words, a doctor might find a person's ailments to arise from interior causes or exterior ones, from a starting place within the mind or from without, through the physical senses. As a result, then, the doctor might see a mental or corporeal cause to an illness and, in response, employ a remedy that might affect the imagination and/or certain bodily functions. Thus, the physics and metaphysics of sympathy became increasingly configured in physiological and psychological terms. In addition to anticipating definitions of the imagination that differentiated between sensations produced from within and those induced from without, such an evolving understanding of "sympathy" increasingly suggested an alignment with Kant, not Locke, that is, with the belief that the senses are created out of the mind, not the mind out of the senses.

During the period when the notion of sympathy increasingly reflected an interest in the nature of inward faculties, the theory of animal magnetism emerged as a new way of conceptualizing this binding, universal force. Significantly, this theory draws from scientific findings on the motion of planetary bodies. Just as the sympathy-antipathy tension demonstrated some divine order in the universe, so too did gravitational forces and planetary motion reveal the imprint of divine will. If God or divine will could be seen as the first mover, then those creatures made in God's image could also participate in this celestial motion.

It is not surprising that Franz Anton Mesmer, the Austrian physician who named animal magnetism and for whom mesmerism is named, should have begun his conceptualization of the phenomenon

9. Seguin Henry Jackson, *A Treatise on Sympathy, in Two Parts,* 6–7.

with a publication entitled *Physical-Medical Treatise on the Influence of the Planets* (1766). Written to complete his medical degree, this thesis reflects a bridge between beliefs commonly articulated in writings on sympathies/antipathies and scientific findings on the gravitational properties of attraction and repulsion introduced by Sir Isaac Newton in the seventeenth century. Differentiating his views on the effects of celestial bodies from the ideas that formed the foundation for sympathetic cures, Mesmer nonetheless echoes earlier medical texts in linking animal health to the motion of distant spheres. According to Mesmer, it was Newton who "forced to our consciousness the structure of the world itself," "established the laws of attraction, by which the machinery of the universe is governed," and "clarified to the highest degree the reciprocal attraction of all things." Unlike Digby, who connected his findings to secrets learned in "oriental parts" and thus whose theories still retained the suggestion of mystic terms and causes, Newton substantiated his assertions through mathematical proofs. In significant ways, then, the numerical confirmation of observed planetary motion and gravitational laws gives a rational shape or visibility to the invisible.[10]

In Mesmer's writings, we see that notions concerning sympathy, though still lingering within medical training and claiming advocates during a period of transition, begin to be supplanted by the vocabulary of reciprocity and the motion of physical bodies. Where once had existed the language of sympathy and antipathy, there arose the concepts of attraction and repulsion. Mesmer explains:

> All bodies are mutually attractive or extend towards one another by means of a force which goes from individual particles of matter to all other individual particles. The force which one body has an effect on the others is accomplished by the union of the forces of the particles which compose the body. . . . One calls this reciprocal action GRAVITY or ATTRACTION, and one considers it as a universal and infallible law of nature which is expressed in this triple proposition: (1) All matter is mutually attractive. (2) This attraction is proportional to the quantity of matter. (3) At varying distances, it changes in proportion to the square of the distance.

10. Franz Anton Mesmer, *Physical-Medical Treatise on the Influence of the Planets*, in *Mesmerism: A Translation of the Original Scientific and Medical Writings of F. A. Mesmer*, trans. and ed. George Bloch, 5; Osler, *Digby's Powder of Sympathy*, 13.

And how does this predictable motion of distant bodies inform the medical concern for the smaller bodies of humankind? According to Mesmer, "There is a force which is the cause of universal gravitation and which is, very probably, the foundation of all corporal properties; a force which actually strains, relaxes and agitates the cohesion, elasticity, irritability, magnetism, and electricity in the smallest fluid and solid particles of our machine, a force which can, in this report, be called ANIMAL GRAVITY." Of particular note is how this physical force replaces the notion of the sympathies and appears to name a nearly immaterial power. Significantly, in relation to this animal gravity, the human body becomes a sensitive receptor: "In the animal machine, the part of the nervous system which is exposed to the emanating impressions of luminous matter is small, but it is sufficient to move the entire body and produce astonishing changes in the mind and the body." In effect, the grand scheme of the universe still has a quality so subtle that it can be received by and mapped within the interior mechanisms of the human body.[11]

Interestingly, in a discourse on magnetism published nearly twenty years later, Mesmer speaks directly of the relationship between earlier notions of sympathy and his own discovery of animal magnetism. "Since time immemorial," he notes, "one has spoken of sympathy, antipathy, of attraction, repulsion, of ethereal matter, of *phlogiston*, of subtle matter, of animal spirits, of electrical matter, and of magnetic matter." In listing past beliefs with emerging theories, he implies that earlier explanations represent attempts to describe natural laws that, with the discoveries of Newton, later theories more accurately delineate. The phenomenon of animal magnetism, then, "is no longer considered to be the action of an incomprehensible attraction completely similar to the occult faculties of Aristotle; it is a natural force, received equally by the senses and by reason."[12]

Arising in significant ways from Newton's theories on the motion of bodies, the formal study of animal magnetism, not unexpectedly, often began with speculation on the nature of movement and its inward effects on humankind. At meetings of the Society of Harmony,

11. Mesmer, *Physical-Medical Treatise,* 5–6, 14.

12. Mesmer, "Discourse by Mesmer on Magnetism," in *Mesmerism: A Translation,* 34, 36. In Bloch's glossary to "Discourse by Mesmer on Magnetism," *phlogiston* is defined as "the hypothetical principle of fire, regarded as a material substance."

a group formed in Paris in 1783 whose members paid to learn Mesmer's principles of animal magnetism, Nicholas Bergasse, a Lyon lawyer who supported Mesmer, lectured on the "three basic principles, God, matter, and movement; the mesmeric fluid's action among planets, within all bodies, and particularly within man" as well as "the techniques of mesmerizing; illness and its cures; the nature of instinct; and the occult knowledge obtainable through the fluid's action on man's inner sense." In *The General and Particular Principles of Animal Electricity and Magnetism* (1792), one of the first (and most influential) books on animal magnetism written in English, Dr. John Bell offers a representative example of the way students of these lectures assimilated the ideas. Prefaced with a copy of the certificate verifying his attendance at the June and July 1785 meetings, the book opens with a section entitled "General Ideas on Motion." According to Bell, "Motion exists in all parts of the universe: all bodies are endowed with a certain degree of it, in proportion to their different organizations." Such a fact of existence implies, of course, a First Mover, or God. That is, through divine will at the moment of creation, God invested the world with the principle of animation. While Bell does not directly name God as the First Mover, he clearly implies a primary action or cause and thus echoes Mesmer's assertion that, "[c]reated by the Supreme Being and put into action by His omnipotence, the form, existence, and exact and combined movement of the globes which roll in the ocean of space result, without doubt, from this universal source."[13]

First published in 1794, Dr. Ebenezer Sibly's *A Key to Physic and the Occult Sciences* further articulates the era's common practice of establishing a connection between vitality or movement and the divine will. As does Bell, Sibly links motion and thought. The book's subtitle asserts Sibly's intentions: *Opening to Mental View, the System and Order of the Interior and Exterior Heavens; the Analogy betwixt Angels and the Spirits of Men; and the Sympathy between Celestial and Terrestrial Bodies.* Sibly's book underscores the growing tendency to see an affinity between external and internal motion and thus fos-

13. Bergasse is quoted in Robert Darnton, *Mesmerism and the End of the Enlightenment in France,* 77; John Bell, *The General and Particular Principles of Animal Electricity and Magnetism,* 7; Mesmer, "Discourse by Mesmer on Magnetism," in *Mesmerism: A Translation,* 35.

ters an emerging emphasis on the study of internal states of mind. In his section "On God," speculation on the connection between thought and motion resonates with notions disseminated in the Society of Harmony. First breaking down beings of this world into cogitative and incogitative, Sibly asks, "Is it possible to conceive that [matter at rest] can add motion to itself, or produce any thing?" The answer: "Matter, then, by its own strength, cannot produce in itself so much as motion. The motion it has, must also be from eternity, or else added to matter by some other being, more powerful than matter." Consistent with many texts of the eighteenth and early nineteenth centuries, *A Key to Physic* clearly affirms the existence of God through a line of reasoning born from the divine blueprint of reasoning itself. The capacity to think distinguished humankind from "incogitative matter" and, by implication, linked human beings to the divine. And, importantly, the ability to reason could be seen as synonymous with motion, with action in the world, and thus with the visible effects of unseen forces linked to the human will and imagination. As asserted by many individuals supporting the validity of animal magnetism, the raising of an arm, after all, begins with thought or intention, that is, internal "movement." Without will or thought, there is no motion, there is no material change in state.[14]

Consistent with the lectures of Bergasse as well as the views expressed by Bell and Sibly, Marquis de Puységur, the individual credited with discovering magnetic somnambulism, or, as we term it now, the hypnotic state, offers revealing speculation on celestial motion and God as the primary mover. He writes that the "observation that I have made, that a ball rolls only when a hand, or agent, determines to it this movement, has brought me to the conclusion,

14. Ebenezer Sibly, *A Key to Physic and the Occult Sciences,* title page, 5. Interestingly, in a section entitled "Of Sympathy and Antipathy in Natural Bodies," Sibly contextualizes late-eighteenth-century notions concerning effects in nature and their occult or unseen causes within the writing of such figures as Digby and Paracelsus (a figure Foucault cites in his book): "The wonderful effects we see in nature, whose true and efficient causes are not easily found out, obliged philosophers heretofore to have recourse to occult causes, and to attribute all those effects to natural sympathy and antipathy." He would later note that from an "investigation of these properties in nature, medicine and the art of healing were first discovered" and that "sympathy and similitude are synonymous" (28, 33).

that since the earth and all the planets roll in space, it must be, like-wise, that some agent has communicated to them the impulse which determines their revolutions." Thus, the reality of God *and* his ac-tion—that is, "God, principle and cause; the existence of the uni-verse, his action"—provides the framework for the practice of medical magnetism. Applying these ideas more directly to the act of induc-ing a magnetic state, Puységur asserts that, during the process of mesmerizing a patient, "the compassion which a patient inspires in me, creates the desire, or the thought of being useful to him, and the moment that I determine to attempt to relieve him, his vital principle receives the impression of the action of my will." While God's will or actions cause unlimited motion in matter, however, the human magnetizer creates limited motion. In a question-and-answer "catechism" on the science, Puységur addresses a query that calls to mind the previous century's efforts to explain action from a distance, that is, the desire to understand, through the idea of the sympathies, gravitational pull, or magnetic attraction, how bodies can be "moved" across space. How does one explain, without a phys-ical intermediary substance, the ability to transmit an impulse? Puységur's reply: "Animal magnetism, is not the action of one body on another, but the action of thought on the vital principle of the body"; "we need not seek an explanation; *it is, because, it is; thought moves the matter.*" Such a notion again invites an orientation to in-ward, not outward or external, forces. In short, the will of the creator elicits the effect. Will, however, must be manifested in thoughts, motions (gestures), and words.[15]

Of even more importance, however, Puységur's records concern-ing his magnetizing of Victor Race, a young peasant on his estate, il-luminate the relationship between theories on the human will, thought, and motion and their actual applications in medical prac-tice. Understanding as Mesmer before him that magnets or other medical instruments were unnecessary, Puységur developed a heal-ing rapport through the imposition of his will upon a receptive pa-tient. Characterizing Puységur's description of Race's "magnetic somnambulism" or "magnetic sleep," Adam Crabtree identifies basic aspects of what we now term the hypnotic state: "a sleep-waking

15. John King, *An Essay of Instruction on Animal Magnetism; Translated from the French of the Marquis de Puységur*, 62, 63, 61.

kind of consciousness, a 'rapport' or special connection with the magnetizer, suggestibility, and amnesia in the waking state for events in the magnetized state." As Crabtree recounts in *From Mesmer to Freud,* these conditions—"along with paranormal phenomena (mental communication and clairvoyance)"—recur in the literature of the century. As a result of these findings, further studies of animal magnetism can be seen as forming two strands:

> Mesmer's approach to healing and his healing theory were physically oriented. His explanation of the phenomena of animal magnetism was consistently formulated in terms of matter and motion, and he believed that every aspect of animal magnetism could sooner or later be verified through physical experimentation and research. With his emphasis on magnetic sleep ("the gentle crisis"), magnetic rapport, and the place of the will in magnetic healing, Puységur turned animal magnetism in a new and clearly psychological direction. He explicitly opposed a materialist philosophy of nature and believed that the phenomena of animal magnetism provided strong evidence against it.

Thus Puységur believed that the insights gained from attention to the peculiar state of magnetic sleep led directly to the mind, not to the workings of the spheres.[16]

With growing frequency, then, the last half of the eighteenth century and first part of the nineteenth witnessed this emphasis on the similarity of the movement of physical bodies and the motion of thought. That which manifests the binding force formerly expressed in the notion of the sympathies moved from celestial motion to the movement of the mind. In the discourse on animal magnetism, we find this relationship between motion and thought most visibly articulated, for, in the remarkable effects of magnetic phenomena, the expansive potential of the mind most distinctly revealed itself. The step from this revelation to an assessment of the properties of the imaginative faculty is a short one. That the effects of animal magnetism increasingly began to be understood in terms of the will, the imagination, and, eventually, the power of suggestion rather than the manipulation of imperceptible atoms or material fluid demarcates a conceptual shift with profound implications on literary

16. Adam Crabtree, *From Mesmer to Freud,* 39, 51–52.

practice. In seeing that their "cures" did not necessarily depend upon magnets, touch, and/or the passing of hands near the body, physician-magnetists began to shape a method as applicable to linguistic gestures—to the art of writing—as to the art of healing. The evolution of the method of inducing magnetic states offered principles for creating more powerful effects within readers.

Two episodes in the history of animal magnetism illuminate this transition from emphasis upon physical fluid to one on an inward faculty (that is, the imagination) and the importance of effective methods in generating a stronger rapport between doctor and patient. In 1778, having arrived in Paris from Vienna, Franz Anton Mesmer set up practice and soon aroused the interest of doctors in the city. Though he offered at least two striking demonstrations of the phenomenon of animal magnetism, the majority of the members of the Academy of Science refused to accept his hypothesis of an actual physical fluid and instead attributed the effects to the patient's imagination. Despite resistance from the reputable medical and scientific societies in Paris, Mesmer did gain some powerful converts, including Charles Nicholas D'Eslon, a physician who had standing as a member of the Faculty of Medicine of Paris. D'Eslon witnessed a number of cures at the hands of Mesmer and came to his defense concerning the charge that the patient's imagination, not a physical fluid, led to apparent changes in condition. Discussing the healing of a boy who was near death, D'Eslon argued that Mesmer had no relationship with the child before visiting him: "At one time I had rashly decided that Mesmer really had no discovery at all, and that if he did extraordinary things, it was by seducing the imagination. I want to observe that this is not the case here. . . . But besides, if Monsieur Mesmer had no other secret than to be able to cause the imagination to act effectively to produce health, would he not have a marvelous thing? And if the medicine of the imagination is the better one, why are we not using the medicine of the imagination?"[17] In D'Eslon's argument, we can also hear both H. M. Herwig's and Seguin Henry Jackson's connections between sympathetic and magnetic cures and the growing distinctions between sensations (or effects) induced from without and from within.

17. Ibid., 17. For an informative overview of the reception of and challenges to animal magnetism in France, see *From Mesmer to Freud,* 12–37.

Ultimately, in 1784, the king of France appointed two commissions—one from the Academy of Science and the other from the Royal Society of Medicine—to consider whether animal magnetism exists. With Benjamin Franklin serving as the chair, the Academy of Science commission concluded that the phenomena attributed to animal magnetism ensued from patients' imaginations, for, "having armed themselves with that philosophic doubt which ought always to accompany enquiry," the investigators themselves experienced no measurable effects from private attempts by D'Eslon or his assistants to magnetize them.[18] Interestingly, in witnessing demonstrations of magnetism with patients who were in the same room and thus able to observe the behaviors of others and who were more susceptible to the effects (that is, members of the lower class, individuals with nervous dispositions, or people in ill health), the commissioners saw remarkable sensations.

As a result of their initial findings, however, the commissioners decided to test just how much the method affected patients' responses and the degree to which a more powerful effect ensued from the greater "art" of the mesmerist. In the words of the report, they focused a final set of experiments on determining "to what degree the power of the imagination can influence our sensations." In one such experiment, a woman who was led to believe that D'Eslon performed the "magnetical operation" upon her from the other side of a door, when he actually had not, fell into a magnetic crisis. Such an experiment, of course, simply tested whether or not certain effects could be elicited through appealing to the imagination. In order to study whether the degree of a magnetic response, or crisis, varied in relationship to the nature of the operations brought to bear

18. Benjamin Franklin et al., *Animal Magnetism; Report of Dr. Franklin and Other Commissioners, Charged by the King of France with the Examination of the Animal Magnetism as Practised at Paris,* 23. Townshend would later question this rationale: "Again: they who draw strong conclusions against mesmerism by affirming that it cannot take effect unless the imagination be prepared to receive it, should remember that they who, deeming they shall feel nothing under mesmerism . . . are both forewarned and forearmed *against* the influence in debate, and are thus themselves under the predisposing sway of the imagination as much as their opponents, only in a different manner; the one party believing they *shall,* the other that they shall *not,* experience certain effects. Under these circumstances, how the latter can pretend to a more accurate judgment on the point than the former, I confess I cannot perceive" (*Facts in Mesmerism,* 287–88).

upon the imagination, however, the commissioners devised a different experiment. With a young woman mesmerized by a doctor named
Jumelin, they conducted a series of tests. First blindfolded and made
to believe that she was being magnetized, the patient reported mod-
est effects. After the removal of the "bandage," or blindfold, and
thus seeing and hearing the magnetic operations, she indicated a
higher degree of symptoms. However, after a suggestion that Jumelin's hand should descend to a certain level of the nose as it had
done during a previous sitting, she experienced the most profound
response. This series of events confirmed the commissioners' suspi-
cions: "But it was not enough that she should be expressly informed
that she was magnetised, it was also necessary that the sense of seeing should yield her a testimony, stronger, and capable of greater effects; it was necessary that a gesture with which she was already
acquainted should reexcite her former ideas. It should seem that
this experiment is admirably calculated to display the manner in
which the imagination acts, the degrees by which it is exalted, and
the different exterior succours it requires in order to its displaying
itself in its greatest energy." Though clearly undercutting Mesmer's
hypothesis of an actual physical fluid or agent, this experiment
sheds light on the peculiar efficacy of the imagination in producing
exalted states of perception and, as importantly, points toward the
potential for crafting particular strategies or methods in inducing
more powerful effects. Significantly, the force of the woman's response can be linked to the magnetist's craft, that is, to the artful
practice of the procedure.[19]

Just as discussion of the imagination became common in texts on
animal magnetism, so too did the practical consideration of "how to"
magnetize a patient. In other words, given that magnetic states could
be of a lower or higher degree, the "art" of the method demanded
study. Thus, texts on mesmerism strive to define and standardize
the practice or procedures for directing the will, enhancing mutual
receptivity, and affecting the imagination. Receiving his information from a woman correspondent who attended a magnetist named
Holloway's lectures on magnetism, John Martin offers in *Animal*

19. Franklin et al., *Animal Magnetism*, 23, 29, 32. See "Imagination" in Rees,
The Cyclopaedia, n.p. Within the subsection entitled "IMAGINATION, *Influence of,
on the corporeal Frame*," the text includes a lengthy description of the experiments conducted by the French commission.

Magnetism Examined: In a Letter to a Country Gentleman (1790) an early firsthand account detailing the "how to" of magnetizing that warrants quoting at length:

> When the Magnetist attempts to take the sensations of a person, or to perform a cure, or to produce a crisis, he puts himself in the situation of sitting, kneeling, or standing, which ever is the most convenient: but for taking sensations, sitting in an easy posture, at a small distance from the person, is the usual method. Then the marvellous work begins. He must divest his mind of every care and anxiety, of every thought and thing, except the person before him. His mind must be calm and placid as a summer's evening, and his body in an attitude of ease. In this state of self abstraction, his attention must be wholly fixed upon the person before him, and upon the effects he desires to accomplish: this must be accomplished with as fixed an intention. Added to this intense attention and intention, there must be in the fourth place, affection, or desire; a strong, fervent, benevolent wish to perform this same wonder or cure. Fifthly, there must be sympathy, or a sympathetic concern for the person to be relieved. Sixthly, volition, or a determined resolution of the will to perform it: and seventhly, a perfect confidence of success. You will observe, Sir, there must be I. *Self Abstraction.* 2. *Attention.* 3. *Intention.* 4. *Affection or Desire.* 5. *Sympathy.* 6. *Volition.* 7. *Confidence,* or *faith* in the SUCCESS.

While both Martin and his correspondent find such a *"grand secret of Magnetism"* worthy of ridicule, they capture fairly accurately the typical schema of the time. In *A Practical Display of the Philosophical System Called Animal Magnetism* (1790), an anonymous pamphlet of sixteen pages that Martin mentions disparagingly in the final pages of his book, the author offers a more condensed version: "In order to treat a Patient with Success, the following Qualifications are essentially Necessary. I. Abstraction. II. Affection. III. Intention. IV[.] Volition." While Martin's text distinguishes two different dimensions of the "method" in separating affection (or desire) from sympathy, *A Practical Display* conflates these comparable concepts into the idea of affection. In his explanation of "affection" that soon follows, however, the author highlights a term that would recur in ensuing works: benevolence. "Let your affection and Benevolence," the text asserts, "go forth towards the Object you are about to treat, let the whole energy of your Mind be fixed on the Patient's Relief, and almost certain Success will ensue." In this emphasis on benevolence, we hear how the practice tried to integrate both the originating (and healing) presence of divine love and the psychological necessity for mutual trust in relation to a common purpose.[20]

In his chapter "Principles of the Science as Delivered by Dr. De Mainauduc," George Winter further reveals the progress toward a more standardized mesmeric process and a narrowing of key principles. (Winter's text represents a summary of ideas first acquired by Mainauduc when he was a student of D'Eslon's.) According to the text, animal magnetism "has for its particular principles, attention, intention and volition." In his explication of these main beliefs, however, Winter captures views that resonate with others of the period. For instance, in considering the role of "attention" in the process, he speaks of the need to "abstract the thoughts from every other idea whatever," and, with intention and volition, he means those "earnest desires to remove the disease, by a constant intention" of doing good. Winter reminds his readers that "by a vigorous exertion and the amazing powers of sympathy, great operations may be effected."[21]

Within the United States, early lectures and publications, during the 1820s and 1830s, continued to reflect the emphasis upon attention and intention. Given the findings that elevated the importance of the imagination and the will, such a preoccupation with the kind of focus necessary between patient and mesmerist is not surprising. In lectures first presented in New York on July 26, August 2, and August 9 of 1829 and published later in the year, Joseph Du Commun echoes Martin, the anonymous author of *A Practical Display*, and Winter in naming three "qualifications necessary to magnetise well": belief, will or volition, and benevolence. As described in his second lecture, it is the presence of a "vital fluid" that explains the ability of the will to cause movement or other effects in the world. Providing what might be seen as one of the definitive texts on the practice of animal magnetism, Joseph Philippe François Deleuze

20. John Martin, *Animal Magnetism Examined: In a Letter to a Country Gentleman*, 61–62, 63; *A Practical Display of the Philosophical System Called Animal Magnetism*, 6, 7.
21. George Winter, *Animal Magnetism: History of; Its Origin, Progress, and Present State; Its Principles and Secrets Displayed*, 32.

imbeds these same beliefs within a series of thirty-four "general views and principles" in the first chapter of *Practical Instruction in Animal Magnetism.* First published in 1825 and translated by Thomas C. Hartshorn in 1837, Deleuze's book argues that "the first condition of magnetizing is the will; the second is the confidence which the magnetizer has in his own powers; the third is benevolence, or the desire of doing good." To move from general principles or preconditions to the actual process of magnetizing, however, the guide introduces a critical addition. That is, the actual action of magnetism "springs from three things: first, the will to act; second, a sign, the expression of that will; third, confidence in the means employed." Like the members of Franklin's French commission, then, Deleuze too recognized the role of "signs" in the relationship between intent and effect.[22]

As with the focus on attention and intention, these triune components invite a link between the mesmeric and literary arts, for they locate factors that directly address ways in which to understand the power of signs. If, to return to Poe, the starting place is the desire for and consideration of an effect, then the next step involves an understanding of how literary choices might best aid the evocation of an impression or sensation within the heart, intellect, or soul. As the ensuing chapters will attest, writers of the period were especially intrigued by this consideration of how to elicit particular effects or impressions, that is, by the connection between theories of psychological states and the practice of inducing them. Clearly, given the inability to prove the existence of an actual fluid and the acceptance of the critical role of the imagination in the rapport between doctor and patient, writers could not help but see similarities between the emphasis on attention and intention in the healing arts and in the artful production of specific effects in a "sympathetic" readership.

Drawing from studies of exalted or somnambulant states, magnetic medical practices, and notions of the central role of the imagination and will in the healing sciences, nineteenth-century writers integrated the terms and concepts of animal magnetism into their artistic practices and products. In doing so, they demonstrated their

22. Joseph Du Commun, *Three Lectures on Animal Magnetism,* 26, 25; Deleuze, *Practical Instruction in Animal Magnetism,* 22, 23.

assimilation of an increasingly psychological orientation toward the world. For individuals such as Poe and Fuller, an understanding of the capacities of the mind and the imagination shaped their conception of particular creative forms as well as best critical practices—and thus important features of artistic endeavors and the critical "mind." Fuller's notion of apprehensive genius can be understood in terms of an individual's susceptibility to magnetic forces or access to the electrical reservoirs of the mind. The "word" is the manifestation of mind and useful primarily in its power to set in motion the divine electricity (or the evocative Beauty and Truth of the single effect) in the reader. If, as Fuller would write in "A Short Essay on Critics," the first essay in the fledgling *Dial*, "Nature is the literature and art of the divine mind,"[23] then poetry and criticism are but the unveiling of the inward life of the human mind. In such a framework, it is Nature that forms the imprint of the mind; it is the manifestation of thought. As magnetists induce healing and/or higher states through their ritual practices, so too do writers seek to evoke a transition state, a receptive state that fosters an ability to comprehend spiritual and material relations. Distinguishing itself from Pope's ideal poetry, true art arises from an original rather than a derivative relationship to the world. True artists seek to cultivate this original relationship through their attention to practices that best create sympathies between writer/text and reader. In the context of this new orientation toward literary craft, that is, this belief that the writer is one who seeks to elicit powerful impressions through psychological means, literary choices and their evocative force demand a new kind of knowledge. Though still drawing from past traditions, writers must first learn, as Townshend asserted, to follow "sensation inward." Insight into how he understood this assertion emerges in his belief that we "draw our sensations from the signs of things, and not from things themselves." In these reflections on the character of mesmeric sensation, Townshend further speculates on the nature of seeing and, in doing so, offers writers ways to posit the connection between their craft and its effects: "But when we come to consider the eye, it is hard to apprehend that all its beautiful representations of that external world with which it holds such distant communion are but signs and characters, consisting in nervous motions, which

23. Fuller, "A Short Essay on Critics," 7.

the soul, by an intellectual operation, translates into its own glorious and native language."[24] Such ideas position the locus of meaning in the manipulation of signs and characters, the resulting effect on the nerves, and the ultimate translation by an inward and apparently immaterial faculty. In the context of this new science and philosophy, the imagination is no longer what it used to be; the writer is a student of states of mind, of language and sensation.

In the shifting emphasis toward inner states that evolved between the sixteenth and twentieth centuries, Foucault traces the dissolution of the "profound kinship of language with the world." Considering the shift in the conception of language, he writes that the "eye was thenceforth destined to see and only to see, the ear to hear and only to hear" and that "[d]iscourse was still to have the task of speaking that which is, but it was no longer to be anything more than what it said."[25] However, while discerning the modern orientation toward language as signification and thus away from a classical notion of language as representation, Foucault's reading of the epistemological shift fails to account fully for the cultural work of antebellum writing. Rather than seeing the external and internal laws of motion as severing words and things, it is possible to interpret scientific and literary texts as theorizing the nature of harmonizing forces that facilitate connection, not dissolution. In other words, the gravitational, electric, and magnetic laws of attraction and repulsion consistently offer evidence that the mechanism of the mind is but a microcosm of macrocosmic principles. To remain true to the principles of the mind is to discover the language (and harmony) of the world. The student of higher forms of literary production, then, becomes the student of higher states of consciousness. In this "curriculum," Townshend's book, not Homer's epic, gains more prominence, for it provides the theoretical basis for literary choices.

That literature could still be seen as essential to social reform perhaps betrays this underlying and steady connection between physical and metaphysical truths. The findings concerning the nervous mechanisms of body and mind, the magnetic forces evidenced in mesmeric sensation, and the powers of the imagination suggest some stable process in the workings of the world. The challenge facing

24. Townshend, *Facts in Mesmerism*, 233, 235–36.
25. Foucault, *The Order of Things*, 42–43.

antebellum writers was the need to find a creative and critical practice that could embody the complex web of physical and psychological motion (that is, the unseen forces that affect bodies at a distance) and the dynamic nature of perceptual processes that seemed to suggest the malleability of the material world to imaginative/intuitive faculties. Thus, we can see the work of Fuller and Poe, and many writers of the period, as striving to articulate in form and theory the nature of this binding or unifying force.

The science of animal magnetism and its relationship to and evolution from an understanding of magnetic or electrical forces in the world, then, provided "scientific" principles for the Romantic sensibility. It offered a theory grounded in the empirical evidence of the physics of movement. Perhaps, for modern critics, it is hard not to read the era with a condescending eye. Perhaps, in fact, the shifting sensibility of the period is not so much a separation of words and things as a revelation into the harmonizing nature of the mind and the faculty of the imagination itself.

From a distance of more than one hundred and fifty years and in proximity to the alienating and disillusioning events of the twentieth century, we might be inclined to judge the reforming impulses of the antebellum period as naïve and to see the science of animal magnetism as more "pseudo" than "real." It is the vanity of the living to privilege the meanings of their more immediate histories. In striving to understand the brutal events of the French Revolution, the destructive forces of democracy, the unsettling implications of immigration and industrialism, the inhumane practices of slavery, and the urban violence surrounding immigration and abolitionist reform, however, Poe, Fuller, Emerson, and their contemporaries were not distant from the public and private chaos that we tend to claim as the intellectual property of the current century. It is more productive to see the discourse on animal magnetism as manifesting, in ways peculiar to their particular time and place, an effort to study the harmonizing or unifying forces of the imagination. If humankind shares a common configuration of the mind and if this mind mirrors the divine, then in interior spaces resides a common "vocabulary" of a common soul. For any antebellum writer attentive to medical advances and new insights into human psychology, the literary journey inevitably took an inward and mesmeric turn.

2 . . . .

The Psychology of the Single Effect

Poe and the Short-Story Genre

When we take the approach by genre, it appears that, despite its folk origins and the above- or below-ground survival of these roots, the art story is a special phenomenon, as different from novels and epics as it is from telephone gossip. For critical purposes, we have a new art form.

Susan Lohafer, *Coming to Terms with the Short Story*

That which we have learned, or, at least, that which has been proved to us, in a clear and satisfactory manner, by our inquiry into the phenomena of mesmerism, is, that *man can act upon man,* at all times and almost at will, by striking the imagination; that signs and gestures the most simple may produce the most powerful effects; that the action of man upon the imagination may be reduced to an art, and conducted after a certain method, when exercised upon patients who have faith in the proceedings.

Commission of the Academy of Science, France, quoted in Chauncy Hare Townshend, *Facts in Mesmerism*

IN RENDERINGS OF the history and form of short fiction, it is not infrequent to hear the modern tale described in terms that originate within the writings of Edgar Allan Poe. To a large degree, the origin and shape of the short story becomes synonymous with Poe's criticism and practice. In early editions of one of the most widely purchased anthologies for introductory short-fiction courses, Ann Charters asserts that "[m]ost historians of this genre agree that the short story did not appear until the nineteenth century" and that, within this unique literary form, "every word chosen in the structure of the plot, and every detail of description and characterization, contributed to a unified impression."[1] In this description of the form, we hear a summary of Poe's own reflections concerning "unity of impression" and how best to achieve a single effect within the "short prose tale." In part arising from his statements concerning the short story, it has also become commonplace for critics, writers, and students alike to see "effects" as progressing from a kind of geometric sequence involving exposition, rising action, climax, falling action, and a final conclusion or denouement. This typology of the "traditional" tale pervades conceptions of the genre, so much so that generations of writers have implicitly and explicitly written within and/or against the "closed" nature of the form, at times welcoming the conflict-generated plots and/or preferring the "open-endedness" of more lyrical strategies. Arguably, then, to understand the short story is to examine Edgar Allan Poe's criticism and craft.

But upon what foundation did Poe build his own understanding of the short prose tale? What principles guided his aesthetic? If he can be seen as introducing the vocabulary and techniques that reveal insights into the genre, then upon what did he establish his own principles? In the end, Poe's fascination with the subject matter of animal magnetism,[2] displayed in his "Mesmeric Revelation," and his ongoing speculation on the nature of the writing process illuminate the ideas that influenced his conceptions of the short story. In the mesmeric canon, including Chauncy Hare Townshend's *Facts in Mesmerism* (1841), we discover the thinking that shaped both Poe's theorizing and his writing. The notion of the single effect, for instance, resonates with Townshend's study of uniquely receptive states of con-

---

1. Ann Charters, "A Brief History of the Short Story," 1675–76.

2. In a January 7, 1846, letter to Sarah Helen Whitman, Mary E. Hewitt (?) notes, "People seem to think there is something uncanny about [Poe], and the strangest stories are told, what is more, *believed*, about his mesmeric experiences, at the mention of which he always smiles" (*Collected Works of Edgar Allan Poe*, ed. Thomas Ollive Mabbott, 3:1028). Hewitt's comments arise from observations of Poe made during his visits to Anne Charlotte Lynch's literary salons. For a discussion of Poe's part in Lynch's salons, see Kenneth Silverman, *Edgar A. Poe: Mournful and Never-ending Remembrance*, 278–93. Because of Poe's work and life, Joseph Jackson attributed an anonymous text on animal magnetism to Poe. See the 1928 reprint of *The Philosophy of Animal Magnetism Together with the System of Manipulating Adopted to Produce Ecstasy and Somnambulism—The Effects and Rationale. By a Gentleman of Philadelphia* (1837) with Jackson's introduction.

sciousness. If the body of Poe's work of the 1840s underscores a central tendency or direction, it may be the effort to understand the consonance of his artistic choices with psychological truths and to develop a critical theory and creative practice consistent with the motions of the mind. Investigating the mesmeric underpinnings to Poe's ideas, then, not only sheds light on definitive dimensions of his aesthetic but also suggests the foundation for modern fictional preferences.

Just as some of his most memorable narrators seem obsessively driven to order their interior world, so too does Poe appear preoccupied with understanding the nature of inward perception and its impact on how writers write and readers read. Inevitably, when contemplating the imaginative process, Poe finds himself considering the borderland between the physical and metaphysical, for, as he asserts in his "Marginalia," he sometimes experiences a "class of fancies" that seem to exist just beyond the reach of form and language. In describing his efforts to retrieve these "psychal" fancies, Poe applies an understanding of psychological states that helps explain his literary choices.

Poe's interest in this psychological interplay within writers' minds and between writers and readers mirrors his era's tendency to conceive of the imagination as connected to the soul and, as a result, to construct poetic principles that address the immaterial as well as material dimensions of the creative process. As late as June of 1849 in his "Marginalia," Poe describes art in a way that calls to mind definitions quite popular during the formative period of his early writings (and student days) in the late 1820s and early part of the 1830s. "Were I called on to define, *very* briefly, the term 'Art,'" he writes, "I should call it 'the reproduction of what the Senses perceive in Nature through the veil of the soul.'"[3] In *The Cyclopaedia* (1810–1824), *imagination* is defined in terms that also strive to encompass the material effects of physical sensation and the unifying or synthesizing force of an immaterial faculty: "Imagination, as it has been often defined, is a power or faculty of the soul, whereby it conceives and forms ideas of things, by means of impressions made on the fibres of the brain, by sensation."[4] Poe's musings on art, imagination, and

---

3. Edgar Allan Poe, "Marginalia," in *Edgar Allan Poe: Essays and Reviews*, 1458.
4. See "Imagination," in Rees, *The Cyclopaedia*, n.p.

fancy in his criticism reflect an interesting merging of the literary and the psychic. Mirroring Jerome Bruner's notions of the creative act as a "combinatorial activity," Poe asserted in August 1845 that "Imagination, Fancy, Fantasy, and Humor" all reflect "the elements, Combination, and Novelty." It is the imagination, however, that "is the artist of the four." In his "Marginalia" (May 1849), he explains:

> The *pure Imagination* chooses, from *either Beauty or Deformity,* only the most combinable things hitherto uncombined; the compound, as a general rule, partaking, in character, of beauty, or sublimity, in the ratio of the respective beauty or sublimity of the things combined—which are themselves still to be considered as atomic—that is to say, as previous combinations. But, as often analogously happens in physical chemistry, so not unfrequently does it occur in this chemistry of the intellect, that the admixture of two elements results in a something that has nothing of the qualities of one of them, or even nothing of the qualities of either. . . . Thus, the range of Imagination is unlimited.

In discerning this elevated capacity to form new qualities by combining seemingly unrelated elements, Poe reflects the era's distinction between the passive imagination ("retaining the simple impression of objects") and the active imagination (which "arranges the images that are received, and combines them in a thousand ways").[5]

Such a configuration echoes Samuel Taylor Coleridge's explanation of the difference between the primary and secondary imagination, as well as distinctions between imagination and fancy, asserted in *Biographia Literaria.* For Coleridge, the primary imagination is the "living Power and prime Agent of all human Perception, and as

5. For Poe's ideas on "Combination" and "Novelty," see "Thomas Hood," in *Essays and Reviews,* 278; for Poe's notions of *"pure Imagination,"* see "Marginalia," in *Essays and Reviews,* 1451. In considering "the conditions of creativity," Jerome Bruner discusses "effective surprise" in relation to the process of the imagination. The third and most difficult form of effective surprise is "metaphoric effectiveness." Referring to what Melville "celebrated as the shock of recognition" and a metaphoric connectedness that Jung termed "visionary," Bruner sees this form of surprise as "the connecting of diverse experiences by the mediation of symbol and metaphor and image." In the end, Bruner proposes, "all the forms of effective surprise grow out of combinational activity—a placing of things in new perspectives" (Bruner, *On Knowing: Essays for the Left Hand,* 19–20).

a repetition in the finite mind of the eternal act of creation in the in-finite I AM," and the secondary imagination is "an echo of the for-mer, co-existing with the conscious will, yet still as identical with the primary in the *kind* of its agency, and differing only in *degree,* and in the *mode* of its operation." In other words, between the im-material agency of the primary imagination and the material com-positions of the artist exists a continuum. Along this continuum, poets come into contact with this divine agency or force as well as engage the "conscious will" in the manipulation of material signs and forms. Writers, then, face the difficult task of employing their own will *without* closing off the wellspring of divine states of per-ception. To the lesser poets unable to sustain higher forms of their art, critics applied the term *fanciful;* that is, the less artful writers were seen as manifesting "Fancy" rather than truly engaging the imagination and thus coming into contact with divine creation. So, in defining fancy as "no other than a mode of Memory emancipated from the order of time and space; and blended with, and modified by that empirical phenomenon of the will, which we express by the word CHOICE," Coleridge names a significant faculty of the mind *yet* seems to suggest that more of the human will and less of the divine enters into such an artistic process. Thus, for the true artist of the beautiful, the creative process and product demand a state less im-peded by or reliant upon the conscious (or self-conscious) will. The pure poet/artist is a venturer of sorts into unconscious or spiritual states.[6]

Interestingly, Poe's effort to characterize features of the "pure Imagination" lead him to describe an active rather than passive agency as well as to consider how to induce such a state of consciousness as

6. Coleridge, *Biographia Literaria,* pt. 1, 304, 305. In his June 1836 review of *Letters, Conversations, and Recollections of S. T. Coleridge* in the *Southern Literary Messenger,* Poe concluded with these thoughts on Coleridge's text: "It has always been a matter of wonder to us that the *Biographia Literaria* here mentioned in the foot note has never been republished in America. It is, perhaps, the most deeply interesting of the prose writings of Coleridge, and affords a clearer view into his mental constitution than any other of his works. . . . They would be rendering an important service to the cause of psychological science in America, by introducing a work of great scope and power in itself, and well cal-culated to do away with the generally received impression here entertained of the *mysticism* of the writer" (*Essays and Reviews,* 188).

part of the creative act. In short, he seeks a "pureness" in the imaginative process, a place along the continuum that affectively engages the primary and secondary imagination. Within the realm of this purer imagination, a writer harnesses an ability to recover words and images that promise a greater degree of novelty. Just as the "effect" for readers arises from conditions (fostered through artful narrative choices) that evoke a greater receptivity, so too does novelty of material for writers emerge from moments of induced lucidity. Responding in his "Marginalia" (March 1846) to the assertion, attributed to Montaigne, that "[p]eople talk about thinking, but for my part I never think, except when I sit down to write," Poe works toward these notions by first asserting that "the mere act of inditing, tends, in a great degree, to the logicalization of thought." For Poe, then, most any thought is not outside the reach of language or the act of conscious will, and he suspects that commonplace remarks asserting so reflect an individual's "want either of deliberateness or of method." "For my own part," he adds, "I have never had a thought which I could not set down in words, with even more distinctness than that with which I conceived it." Such views are not surprising, for, after all, Poe left a legacy of criticism that seems to reduce the poetic process to a scientific or numerical enterprise. In "The Philosophy of Composition," to cite one well-known example, he expresses his desire to trace the blueprint for the creation of "The Raven": "It is my design to render it manifest that no one point in its composition is referrible either to accident or intuition—that the work proceeded, step by step, to its completion with the precision and rigid consequence of a mathematical problem."[7]

On one hand, then, Poe seems quite comfortable characterizing the artistic process in terms that privilege the rational over the intuitive, consciousness over the unconscious. And yet, quite important to understanding the totality of his theory of composition, readers must not overlook Poe's effort to discern states of mind—and the artistic forms that result from them—as inevitably involving speculation on psychical or psychological dimensions of the creative process. Thus, while admitting that most any thought can find expression if one attends deliberately to method, Poe still confesses

7. Poe, "Marginalia," in *Essays and Reviews,* 1382, 1383; Poe, "The Philosophy of Composition," in *Essays and Reviews,* 14–15.

that he has encountered a "class of fancies, of exquisite delicacy, which are *not* thoughts, and to which, *as yet,* [he has] found it absolutely impossible to adapt language." Such fancies are to be understood as "rather psychal than intellectual" and as "aris[ing] in the soul . . . only at its epochs of most intense tranquility—when the bodily and mental health are in perfection—and at those mere points of time where the confines of the waking world blend with those of the world of dreams." As Poe begins to discern the nature of this world between wakefulness and sleep, a state of awareness that seems to draw from both the conscious and unconscious mind and that can result in what he terms pleasurable ecstasies, he employs a language that resonates with descriptions of somnambulant or magnetic sleep and the truths that arise from such a condition:

> I regard the visions, even as they arise, with an awe which, in some measure, moderates or tranquilizes the ecstasy—I so regard them, through a conviction (which seems a portion of the ecstasy itself) that this ecstasy, in itself, is of a character supernal to the Human Nature—is a glimpse of the spirit's outer world; and I arrive at this conclusion—if this term is at all applicable to instantaneous intuition—by a perception that the delight experienced has, as its element, but *the absoluteness of novelty.*

Significantly, such thoughts suggest that achieving the pinnacle of artistic creation (that is, creating works that reflect a degree of novelty indicative of a higher imagination and thus offering the possibility of higher forms of art) engages writers in a rational and nonrational enterprise. This tension between what might be termed a "material" enterprise that involves "measurements" and a "spiritual" endeavor that transcends time and space and recovers divine truths or visions "supernal to the Human Nature" distinguishes the totality of Poe's artistic practice. And, as we will see, it is a tension that leads him to mesmeric philosophy and its investigation concerning this relationship between sensation and spirit.[8]

Given the dynamic nature of this striving toward the holy grail of novelty, it is to be expected that Poe—a writer whose canon reflects an effort to achieve a seamlessness between form and content or theory and practice—articulates his faith in the possibility

---

8. Poe, "Marginalia," in *Essays and Reviews,* 1383.

of maintaining a precarious balance between the rational and nonrational. Poe argues that, during favorable (though admittedly rare) circumstances, he can be sure of "the supervention of the [ecstatic] condition, and feel even the capacity of inducing or compelling it." After bringing about this state and arriving at the threshold between wakefulness and sleep, he indicates that he can startle himself back into wakefulness and *"thus transfer the point itself into the realm of Memory,"* when, for a brief period, he can "survey [the fancies or psychal impressions] with the eye of analysis." In essence, Poe translates findings articulated in mesmeric texts into terms appropriate to the art of writing and reading. Given this intersection between his understanding of purer forms of the imagination and higher states of consciousness, it becomes clear why Poe's notions of the short story rely not upon past narrative models but upon the era's findings concerning human physiology and psychology. If the short story represents a new art form, it is because it emerges within new conceptions of how perception informs the writing and reading process.[9]

In "Mesmeric Revelation," the second of his series of narratives published in 1844 and 1845 dealing with the subject of mesmerism, Poe anticipates the reflections expressed in fragmented form throughout his criticism and his "Marginalia" and provides further insight into the relationship between higher states of consciousness and an evolving narrative form. In addition to revealing his close familiarity with the popular interest in and scholarly writing on animal magnetism, the story explores the important interaction between the ratio-· nal and nonrational in recovering and communicating truths veiled to consciousness in the ordinary condition of the wakeful state. The tale opens with the matter-of-fact statement "Whatever doubt may still envelop the *rationale* of mesmerism, its startling *facts* are now almost universally admitted." (In fact, such was not the case, for, by the early 1840s, the initial receptivity of many prominent physicians and scientists began to be replaced with a growing skepticism, even cynicism.) The narrator continues:

> There can be no more absolute waste of time than the attempt to *prove,* at the present day, that man, by mere exercise of his will,

9. Ibid., 1384.

can so impress his fellow, as to cast him into an abnormal condition, of which the phenomena resemble very closely those of *death,* or at least resemble them more nearly than they do the phenomena of any other normal condition within our cognizance; that, while in this state, the person so impressed employs only with effort, and then feebly, the external organs of sense, yet perceives, with keenly refined perception, and through channels supposed unknown, matters beyond the scope of the physical organs; . . . and, finally, that his susceptibility to the impression increases with its frequency, while, in the same proportion, the peculiar phenomena elicited are more extended and more *pronounced.*[10]

In echoing Chauncy Hare Townshend's assertions that "all [sleep-waking's] phases and phenomena are only intense degrees of known and even ordinary conditions of man," Poe arguably demonstrates more than a passing knowledge of critical aspects of *Facts in Mesmerism.*[11] Interestingly, in this preface to a fictional dialogue between P (the narrator and mesmerist) and V (the patient, Mr. Vankirk), Poe describes differing states of consciousness in ways that echo the era's conceptions of the active and passive imagination. In essence, V seeks a higher state of mind, one that achieves a more

10. Poe, "Mesmeric Revelation," in *Collected Works of Edgar Allan Poe,* 3:1029–30. For a representative sampling of responses to animal magnetism from the medical profession between 1834 and 1841, see the following articles from the *Boston Medical and Surgical Journal:* Lemuel W. Belden, M.D., "An Account of Jane C. Rider, The Springfield Somnambulist," 53–84; "Progress of Animal Magnetism," 303–5; John Clough, M.D., "The Influence of the Mind on Physical Organization," 410–15; "The Mesmeric Epidemic," 428–29; and "The Philosophy of Mesmerism," 237–42. In the mid-1830s, articles had seriously considered—cautiously, but not with derision—medical phenomena associated with animal magnetism. By the early 1840s, the trend in medical journals was to discount the science. It is worth noting, however, that the imagination was still seen as producing significant effects. As John Clough, M.D., argued, "The influence of imagination, in aiding the happy effects of medicine in curing disease, should not, however, receive our unqualified censure. Too many facts are before us, and many others might be adduced, to show what I hope has already been proved. The influence of the imagination has indeed wrought many wonderful and important changes in the nervous and vascular systems, independent of those medicines which are considered specifics" ("The Influence of the Mind on Physical Organization," 412–13).

11. Townshend, *Facts in Mesmerism,* 201. See Sidney E. Lind, "Poe and Mesmerism." In his article, Lind notes that Poe's use of the term *sleepwaking* demonstrates his familiarity with distinctions that Townshend draws in his book.

"keenly refined perception" less constrained by information provided by the physical senses. He does so, we soon learn, because, having suffered from skepticism concerning the subject of the immortality of the soul, he now wishes to enter a state that promises to bridge the gap between feeling and ratiocination—unlike wakeful consciousness, where the intellect and the soul seem unable to assent to a feeling of immortality. In the normal waking state, V says, he "only half felt, and never intellectually believed."[12] In short, V wants to enter into a condition that will resolve doubt by dissolving the boundaries between emotion and intellect; he desires an in-between or transition state where truths can be understood and, potentially, articulated in language. Such a transition state bears striking resemblance to the ecstatic condition that Poe would later describe in his "Marginalia." The story is a fictional representation of the supervention, through the mesmeric process, of the ecstatic state.

"Mesmeric Revelation" includes musings to which Poe seemed to attach great significance. In a letter to the Reverend George Bush, professor of Hebrew at New York University, dated July 2, 1844, Poe confesses that "the article is purely a fiction; but I have embodied in it some thoughts which are original with myself and I am exceedingly anxious to learn if they have claim to absolute originality, and also how far they will strike you as well based." In *Mesmer and Swedenborg; or, The Relation of the Developments of Mesmerism to the Doctrines and Disclosures of Swedenborg* (1847), Bush demonstrated his own interest in how the study of mesmerism offered insight into questions regarding the material and immaterial worlds, maintaining that "we are continually approximating the true philosophy which underlies the enlarged and enlarging experience of the current age." He quickly added: "That this philosophy, when reached, will conduct us into the sphere of the *spiritual,* as the true region of *causes,* and disclose new and unthought of relations between the worlds of matter and of mind, is doubtless a very reasonable anticipation, and one which is even now widely though vaguely entertained." Clearly, then, Poe must have seen Bush as a sympathetic and informed reader, as one who would not dismiss "psychal rather than intellectual" disclosures. While Bush's response, if he offered one, is not extant, it might have echoed the sentiments that he expressed in his book, that is, that "the phenomena of Mesmerism have unfolded a

12. Poe, *Collected Works of Edgar Allan Poe,* 3:1031.

new phasis of our nature, replete with novel, striking, and momentous bearings upon the philosophy of mind."[13]

Certainly, as Thomas Mabbott relates in his preface to his edition of the tale, Poe's use of the term *essay* to describe "Mesmeric Revelation" in a February 24, 1845, letter to Rufus W. Griswold suggests that he saw the work's "principal significance not in the fictitious account of mesmerism but in the discussion of ideas" concerning the materiality or immateriality of God that concludes it. Interestingly, then, the form provides the venue to work out ideas concerning the nature of the universe. Here, Poe anticipates broader notions of the universe later voiced in *Eureka,* a work that he describes as both a "prose poem" and an "essay on the Material and Spiritual Universe." It should not be surprising that Poe's artistic beliefs closely mirror his notion of the grand scheme of things. Speaking of divine adaptation or the "complete *mutuality* of adaptation" that makes it impossible to discern cause and effect in "Divine constructions," Poe goes on to connect the art of storytelling with the way in which divine creations might also reflect this "absolute *reciprocity of adaptation*" manifested in the fluidity of cause and effect:

> The pleasure which we derive from any display of human ingenuity is in the ratio of *the approach* to this species of reciprocity. In the construction of *plot,* for example, in fictitious literature, we should aim at so arranging the incidents that we shall not be able to determine, of any one of them, whether it depends from any one other or upholds it. In this sense, of course, perfection of plot is really, or practically, unattainable—but only because it is a finite intelligence that constructs. The plots of God are perfect. The Universe is a plot of God.

While the terms are different, the notion of plot construction here remains consistent with the importance of the single effect in storytelling. Moreover, in the urge to achieve a state of seamlessness

---

13. Ibid., 1025; George Bush, *Mesmer and Swedenborg,* 13, 16. In his August 1845 "Marginalia," printed in *Godey's Lady's Book,* Poe may have had Bush in mind when he wrote: "The Swedenborgians inform me that they have discovered all that I said in a magazine article, entitled 'Mesmeric Revelation,' to be absolutely true, although at first they were very strongly inclined to doubt my veracity—a thing which, in that particular instance, I never dreamed of not doubting myself. The story is a pure fiction from beginning to end" (Poe, *Collected Works of Edgar Allan Poe,* 3:1367).

between cause and effect or to seek a state wherein such divisions cease to exist (or certainly cease to prevent a more expansive understanding of the universe), Poe also echoes the "mesmeric revelations" outlined in his short prose tale.[14]

Poe's "Marginalia" and "Mesmeric Revelation" offer the philosophic speculation that informs his influential ideas concerning the short story (and, more specifically, the notion of the "single effect") articulated in his "Review of Nathaniel Hawthorne's *Twice-Told Tales* and *Mosses from an Old Manse.*" Describing the necessary concentration that characterizes the short prose tale, Poe argues that the selection of each narrative element must contribute to a single effect:

> He has not fashioned his thoughts to accommodate his incidents, but having deliberately conceived a certain *single effect* to be wrought, he then invents such incidents, he then combines such events, and discusses them in such tone as may best serve him in establishing this preconceived effect. . . . In the whole composition there should be no word written of which the tendency, direct or indirect, is not to the one pre-established design. And by such means, with such care and skill, a picture is at length painted which leaves in the mind of him who contemplates it with a kindred art, a sense of the fullest satisfaction.

This hypersensitivity to each narrative choice reflects one who not only values the detail of craft but also links this detail to his own conception of the mind of the reader engaged in the act of reading. Writer and reader experience the tale with a "kindred art." While arguing that the tale should not be considered above the rhymed poem of a length not exceeding "what might be perused in an hour," he still considers short fiction to be a preferable form for those of genius. Moreover, in his characterization of the relationship between the writer and reader of the prose tale, Poe employs a language that resonates with depictions of the power relationships between his fictional mesmerists and their patients and that mirrors in interesting ways the era's scientific studies of animal magnetism: "Worldly interests, intervening during the pauses of perusal, modify, coun-

14. Poe, *Collected Works of Edgar Allan Poe,* 3:1025; Poe, *Eureka: A Prose Poem,* in *The Science Fiction of Edgar Allan Poe,* ed. Harold Beaver, 292.

teract and annul the impressions intended. But simple cessation in reading would, of itself, be sufficient to destroy the true unity. In the brief tale, however, the author is enabled to carry out his full design without interruption. During the hour of perusal, the soul of the reader is at the writer's control." Of particular interest is how the fundamental principle of the single effect arises from what lies beyond the text, that is, the eye or "I" of the reader. More specifically, it is the soul of the reader that succumbs to the will or control of the writer. The starting place is a consideration of reader receptivity to effects initiated through narrative gestures. Significantly, Poe constructs aesthetic principles that reflect aspirations beyond mere Fancy and toward the powers of the Imagination in their purer form. Or, in the language of the mesmeric sciences, he seeks to evoke that higher state of perception through a conscious (artistic) will. Poe traces, in effect, the psychology of the single effect; he builds his short-story aesthetic on the foundation of human psychology.[15]

Poe's emphasis on the importance of concentrated effort in relation to short fiction seems consistent with V's expressed desire to achieve a kind of harmony between the rational and nonrational in "Mesmeric Revelation." "I cannot better explain my meaning," states V, "than by the hypothesis that the mesmeric exaltation enables me to perceive a train of ratiocination which, in my abnormal existence, convinces, but which, in full accordance with the mesmeric phenomena, does not extend, except through its *effect,* into my normal condition. In sleep-waking, the reasoning and its conclusion— the cause and its effect—are present together. In my natural state, the cause vanishing, the effect only, and perhaps only partially, remains."[16] At first reading, it seems as if *effect* in this context refers to something quite distinct from the notion of the "single effect" that

15. Poe, *Essays and Reviews,* 586, 584, 586. Poe's views on the short prose tale found expression in three reviews of Hawthorne's work: a six-paragraph article on *Twice-Told Tales* (*Graham's Magazine,* April 1842), "*Twice-Told Tales*" (*Graham's Magazine,* May 1842), and "*Twice-Told Tales* and *Mosses from an Old Manse*" (*Godey's Lady's Book,* November 1847). While much of the piece in *Godey's* draws from his articles of 1842, I cite the 1847 review because it represents the latest and thus most definitive statement of Poe's ideas. For a complete study of Hawthorne's assimilation of mesmeric themes and theories, see Samuel Chase Coale, *Mesmerism and Hawthorne: Mediums of American Romance.*

16. Poe, *Collected Works of Edgar Allan Poe,* 3:1031–32.

Poe describes in his review of Hawthorne's fiction. V, after all, reflects upon "cause and effect" rather than a single "effect" evoked by narrative choices. In other words, the contexts are quite distinct: one dealing with the power of the mesmeric state to cause a more conclusive belief and the other dealing with the power of coherent narrative choices to cause the most forceful impact upon the reader. While such distinctions must be kept in mind, however, they do not entirely foreclose the suggestive correspondence between the "effect" caused by the methods that lead to the mesmeric state and those that create the most forceful prose tale. The signs and symbols of the two arts—the mesmeric and the narrative—have similar ends: a greater receptivity to and recovery of certain truths. For both, there is a greater possibility that the conflict caused by something that is "only half felt, and never intellectually believed" (to use V's words) may diminish. The realm of the intuitive and the ratiocinative meet in the borderland between wakeful and ecstatic states, and, in this in-between space, the intellect and the soul assent to the will. Such ideas clearly resonate with speculation on the nature of the imaginative faculty and suggest a way to conceptualize the relationship between intellect, will, and soul in actual artistic practice. In effect, the relationship between mesmerist and patient provides a model for the practice of romantic artistic creation, for, though seemingly metaphysical in its emphasis on immaterial forces (soul and the divine agency of the imagination), it points to the importance of certain techniques (for example, repetition or continuity of linguistic and physical signs and gestures) in generating desired effects.

In his fiction, "Marginalia," and reviews, Poe directly and indirectly demonstrates a conceptual debt to the era's publications on mesmerism. Turning more directly to these sources will even further demonstrate the indebtedness of the short-story form to the magnetic arts and their insights into human psychology. One of the most direct pieces of evidence that Poe was familiar with texts in the mesmeric canon emerges in an article first published in the April 5, 1845, issue of the *Broadway Journal* (and later excerpted in his November 1846 "Marginalia," printed in *Graham's Magazine*). Reviewing William Newnham's *Human Magnetism; Its Claims to Dispassionate Inquiry* (1845), Poe compares the work unfavorably to Townshend's *Facts in Mesmerism*: "In some important points—his ideas of prevision, for example, and the *curative* effects of magnetism—we radically disagree—and most especially do we disagree with him in his (implied) disparagement of the work of Chauncy Hare Townshend, which we regard as one of the most truly profound and philosophical works of the day—a work to be valued properly only in a day to come." In suggesting that Newnham's book should still be read by those who "pretend to keep pace with modern philosophy," however, Poe appears to validate the role of such studies in illuminating the nature of magnetic states and thus the relationship between body and mind. Moreover, he seems to imply that, as a writer, he would have found discourse on the connection between material signs and interior processes quite relevant to artistic productions. Thus, while criticized for certain illogical conclusions, Newnham's speculation regarding the nature of magnetic phenomena offered another textbook to guide literary figures like Poe. In one section that would have been interesting to writers, Newnham explains, "For instance, writing—a look—the sound of the voice—a gesture,—the expression of the countenance, are so many means by which the mind expresses, and renders manifest, the affections, and passions, and sentiments which animate and occupy its interior recesses." Speaking of somnambulism and clairvoyance, he offers thoughts that suggest the kind of ideal relationship that might arise between author and text:

> So also, the mind, intimately united to the body, and especially to the nervous system, impresses upon that system, by a powerful but inexplicable process, all the thoughts which are produced. These thoughts, it is true, may originate in the mind itself, yet the more deeply they spring, the more intimately are they attached to the individual man; but they are impressed upon the *brain,* as the *medium* of communication, to the entire nervous system, and to the organs dependent on it,—*or which may, from some incomprehensible modification of vitality, be placed in a certain relationship with it:* and *this too, although these organs may belong to another individual possessing also a rational mind,* and *by means of which incomprehensible modification* the two minds are thus placed in a state of *extraordinary inter-communication.*

Newnham conceptualizes the human body as constructed in such a way as to allow the potential for exalted states of communication. Clearly, thoughts that spring more deeply from the mind offer the promise of being communicated outward; thus, it is the mesmerist (or artist) who might be seen as having the capacity to generate powerful effects. Given such thoughts, then, it is not surprising that Poe considers the book of "vast importance and high merit," regardless of its momentary lapses.[17]

For Poe and many writers of the period, however, Chauncy Hare Townshend's work provided the more suggestive and most definitive principles, especially his section "On the Mesmeric Consciousness." Attempting to show that such consciousness—that is, a higher perceptiveness that occurs in the elevated state of "sleepwaking"—actually harmonizes with normal states of awareness, Townshend turns to a third "law of our being":

> Consciousness, whether it relate to sensation or to intellectual exertion, acts more forcibly the more it is brought to bear upon a single point.
>
> Who has not felt that the senses, by their simultaneous action, are restrictions the one upon the other? How seldom can we be wholly absorbed in the pleasures of the eye! How seldom, when listening to sweet sounds, can we become "all ear!" There is almost always a something to be deducted from our feelings by the interference of some other sense than that we desire to exercise. Were all our capacities of sensation concentrated upon any one property of matter, we may judge how much stronger would be the force of our perceptions by observing that, where one sense is actually wanting (as in the blind or deaf, for instance), the vivacity of impressions received through the other organs is greatly increased.

Of particular importance here is the fact that Townshend finds in this new area of study even further evidence for seemingly self-evident or common-sense "truths" of perception. In language that anticipates fundamental assertions in Poe's review of Hawthorne's *Twice-Told Tales,* Townshend goes on to assert that, "as regards the exercise of our mental capacities, experience inculcates, as one of the precepts of wisdom, that if we wish to do a thing perfectly, we must do it singly."[18]

Popular publications depicting the art of inducing the mesmeric state further employ the language evoked in Townshend's descrip-

17. Poe, *The Complete Works of Edgar Allan Poe,* vol. 12, ed. James A. Harrison, 123, 121; William Newnham, *Human Magnetism; Its Claims to Dispassionate Inquiry,* 221–22.

18. Townshend, *Facts in Mesmerism,* 211–12.

tion of this "law of our being." In the widely respected *Instruction pratique sur le magnètisme animal* (1825), or *Practical Instruction in Animal Magnetism* (translated in an American edition by Thomas Hartshorn in 1837 and later published in a revised edition in 1843), Joseph Philippe François Deleuze's views concerning the importance of limiting the time of the mesmeric sitting in order to maximize the experience coincide with Poe's stance concerning the ideal length of time to peruse a short story: "The first sittings ought to be about an hour in duration, when there is no reason to prolong or abridge them." Admittedly, this suggestive coincidence of views is not as important with regard to Poe's ideas as the text's ongoing emphasis upon the importance of concentration and singleness of focus in inducing and sustaining the mesmeric state. In a description reminiscent of Townshend's views, Deleuze underscores how the faculties of the somnambulist demonstrate a higher receptivity due to an exalted concentration: "Their surprising penetration may be regarded as the effect of a concentration upon one single class of sensations, upon one order of ideas; the more their attention is distracted by various objects, the less of it will they give to the essential object." In a later section entitled "Of the Means of Developing in Ourselves the Magnetic Faculties, and of Deriving Advantage from this Development," the book further elaborates upon the significance of the relationship between patient and physician/mesmerist: "When a man magnetizes, he puts himself, by the exertion of his will, in a state different from his habitual one; he concentrates his attention upon a single object; he throws off and directs beyond himself the nervous or vital fluid; and this new manner of being renders him susceptible of new impressions." The mutually reinforcing acts of will, concentration, and sympathy between the mesmerist and the mesmerized would have been suggestive to any writer who would receive it—whether these psychological insights come from directly reading Deleuze or indirectly registering the dissemination of his ideas in the era's pervasive discussions of mesmerism. Such views deepen an understanding of Poe's contention that the most vivid and enduring impressions derive from concentration and compression: "Without a certain continuity, without a certain duration or repetition of the cause, the soul is seldom moved to the effect."[19]

19. Joseph Philippe François Deleuze, *Practical Instruction in Animal Magnetism,* trans. Thomas C. Hartshorn, 36, 75, 193; Poe, *Essays and Reviews,* 585.

Certainly, the language of theorists such as Townshend and mesmeric practitioners like Deleuze offered rich ideas for any artist who thought seriously about how to engage an audience most forcefully. Yet, their emphasis on the necessity of concentrating upon some single object is just one way in which the literature on mesmerism provided a theoretical foundation for the art of the brief prose tale. An even more suggestive link occurs in Townshend's section entitled "On Mesmeric Sensation." Townshend briefly laid the foundation for this part of his work in his early translation of the report by the commission of the French Academy of Science. While dismissing the presence of a material fluid in animal magnetism, the investigators did concede the ultimate power of the imagination. "[T]he careful French Academy [commission], and their subsequent followers," Townshend points out, "have gone farther than the magnetizers themselves in attributing power to mind, and in relating wonders to prove that power." Again, according to the commission's report, Mesmer's practice suggested that *man can act upon man,* at all times and almost at will, by striking the imagination; that signs and gestures the most simple may produce the most powerful effects; that the action of man upon the imagination may be reduced to an art, and conducted after a certain method, when exercised upon patients who have faith in the proceedings."[20] In *The Cyclopaedia* (1810–1824), in fact, the "Imagination" entry includes an extensive description of experiments conducted by the French commission, for, clearly, these experiments underscored not only that the imagination produced significant physical effects but also that such effects or sensations were enhanced by the particular manner in which the doctor employed words, tone, and gestures.

Townshend's translation and later musings tell us much about how the period began to acquire and articulate an understanding of the workings of imagination and, importantly, how the "science" of animal magnetism offered the forum for such speculation. One could ask, then, how Townshend himself imagined the impact of "signs and gestures" upon sensation and thus upon the mind. Again, in "On Mesmeric Sensation," he offers a glimpse:

20. Townshend, *Facts in Mesmerism,* 20, 18. More than Townshend acknowledged this reference to the power of the imagination. In *Animal Magnetism; or, Psychodunamy,* Theodore Leger also cites this passage. See Leger, 15.

> Sensation, then, is personal to ourselves, and man is strictly con-
> fined to his individual sphere; yet, at the same time, our con-
> sciousness assures us that we are in sensible communication with
> objects which are not ourselves, and which are more or less re-
> mote from us. Consequently, between us and them there must be
> media; and thus, in considering sensation, we have three things to
> take into the account, namely, the external object or the exciting
> cause; the medium whereby we are, as it were, linked to that ob-
> ject; and the change in our own corporeal frame, which stands as
> the representative of the object.
>
> Hereafter I shall have the occasion to speak of the media where-
> by we are brought into communication with the visible universe.
> At present I restrict myself to considering the signs of things, of
> which our own persons are, as it were, the living alphabet and re-
> cording volume.

Given that the mesmerist and writer share an attentiveness to mas-
tering the most powerful use of signs and gestures, it is possible to
see the "exciting cause," the "medium," and the "change in . . . corporeal frame" as aligning with the author, the text, and the effect
upon the reader. In fact, when V explains that, "in full accordance
with the mesmeric phenomena," he can only bear witness to the increased perception of mesmeric exaltation through "its *effect*," he
voices a belief strikingly similar to Townshend's own admission that
only in an observable effect do we note evidence of the exciting
cause. Such a view clearly underscores the author's (and text's) critical role in inducing a higher state of receptivity. Moreover, it envisions such a dynamic between agent and medium in psychological
and physiological terms. In the end, Townshend concludes that we
"draw our sensations from the signs of things, and not from things
themselves." Later in the section, he goes on to suggest that, rather
than influencing an imponderable fluid, the signs and gestures of
the mesmerist affect the nervous system of the mesmerized patient. The eyes, for instance, need not actually see an object to con-
jure up the image in the mind. Or, in Townshend's terms, "we may,
by giving motion to a nerve of sense, convince ourselves that a sensation is the result." Quite obviously, words and verbal images initiate such "motion." He soon asserts that "it is hard to apprehend that
all [the eye's] beautiful representations of that external world with
which it holds such distant communion are but signs and charac-

ters, consisting in nervous motions, which the soul, by an intellectual operation, translates into its own glorious and native language."
Such a declaration underscores the fact that attending to formal literary devices within a compressed form evokes striking sensations
and thus can have a compelling impact upon body and soul.[21]

When readers today read short fiction, they participate in a form
that has been conceptualized with them in mind. More precisely,
they embrace a genre that has emerged from an understanding of
the nature of the mind itself. It would not be wrong to say that the
formal dimensions of short fiction are designed to foster a kind of
rapport with the reader. Turning to Poe's assertions regarding the
short story, Mary Rohrberger captures this fundamental aspect of
the form: "If I interpret correctly, Poe is saying we need a sense of
duration, repetition, and tension in short stories, and as he states in
the most famous of all his paragraphs, we need design. For the emphasis is on the artifact, on a product made by an artist. The artist,
however, needs a kind of cocreator, a reader, who participates in the
story with an art kindred to that of the author to accomplish the desired sense of 'the fullest satisfaction.'" This satisfaction or rapport
ensues from the pattern of an initial, intensive engagement, rising
and falling action, and denouement and points toward the special
significance of the "end" upon artistic choices. Poe's assertion of the
importance of the unity of impression and single effect in the design of the short story implies what critics have termed an "end orientation." Addressing the issue of closure in *Coming to Terms with
the Short Story,* Susan Lohafer comments, "Periodicity, in biology,
history, and aesthetics, is engendered by the notion of closure—not
the other way around. Short fiction, it has been said, is the most
'end-conscious' of forms. Readers of short fiction are the most end-
conscious of readers." The reasoning behind such an end-conscious-
ness is articulated repeatedly in the mesmeric literature of the
nineteenth century. In first asserting that the magnetist must im-
pose "constant will" through "continued attention," Deleuze offers a
revealing analogy: "A man who makes towards a designated goal, is
always attentive to avoid obstacles, to move his feet in a proper direction; but this sort of attention is so natural to him as to be easy,

21. Townshend, *Facts in Mesmerism,* 233, 234, 235–36.

because he has first determined his movement, and feels in himself the force necessary to continue it." Joining wills through an understanding of or predisposition toward a common goal, the mesmerist and patient achieve what might be termed "fullest satisfaction" through contemplation of a kindred art.[22]

Desire for this kind of satisfaction draws attention to why the "art form" of the short story has gained currency since its development in the nineteenth century. Something in its form promotes the possibility of a more elevated reading experience. That Poe saw the genre as best "serving the purposes of ambitious genius" implies, in conjunction with his other assertions concerning powerful effects upon the reader's soul, this potential for a qualitatively different response. The evidence for such higher states of perception occurs in more than the anecdotal descriptions of mesmerizing texts; it arises in the descriptions of effects resulting from magnetists' evocation of the imagination through artful methods. The mesmeric turn of the era, then, followed the larger paradigmatic reorientation toward inward states and inevitably fostered a reformulation of aesthetic principles and forms.

Ultimately, in developing his notions of the short story through the lens of mesmeric sensation and consciousness, Poe delineates the means with which to give shape to the intuitive dimensions of the writing and reading process. In his own way, he captures the same experience and impulse that led Coleridge to preface *Kubla Khan* with the circumstances that gave rise to the "Vision in a Dream" and for Hawthorne to offer numerous prefatory reflections on the distinction between the romance and the novel. Speaking of himself in the third person when describing an opium-induced trance, Coleridge confesses that he literally composed his poem in a state between sleep and wakefulness or in that realm of consciousness hovering between reality and dream: "The author continued for about three hours in a profound sleep, at least of the external senses, during which time he has the most vivid confidence, that he could not have composed less than from two to three hundred lines; if that indeed can be called composition in which all the images

22. Mary Rohrberger, "Between Shadow and Act: Where Do We Go from Here?" in *Short Story Theory at a Crossroads,* ed. Susan Lohafer and Jo Ellyn Clarey, 35–36; Susan Lohafer, *Coming to Terms with the Short Story,* 94; Deleuze, *Practical Instruction in Animal Magnetism,* 22–23.

rose up before him as *things*, with a parallel production of the correspondent expressions, without any sensation or consciousness of effort." For Hawthorne, the romance did not constrain him by demanding strict attention to "the probable and ordinary course of man's experience." Rather, one could argue, the form allowed him the freedom to follow the psychological realities of his characters as well as to capture the interior landscapes of his own mind. In many respects, Poe's "Mesmeric Revelation" marks another text representative of the era's endeavor to enter such transition states for artistic purposes.[23]

That Poe held Coleridge in high regard should not be surprising in light of his poetic and critical writings. In a review of Thomas Moore's poem "Alciphron" (January 1840), Poe clearly distinguishes Coleridge as one whose creations embodied the imaginative and mystic (as opposed to the merely fanciful). In addition to works such as Dante's *Inferno*, Cervantes' *Destruction of Numantia*, and Milton's *Comus*, Poe lists Coleridge's "*Auncient Mariner*, the *Christabel*, and the *Kubla Khan*" as poems "which mankind have been accustomed to designate as *imaginative*." In the preceding paragraph, Poe linked the term *mystic* to his notion of the imaginative, writing that the word is "here employed in the sense of Augustus William Schlegel, and of most other German critics" and is "applied by them to that class of composition in which there lies beneath the transparent upper current of meaning, an under or *suggestive* one. What we vaguely term the *moral* of any sentiment is its mystic or secondary expression. It has the vast force of an accompaniment in music. This vivifies the air; that spiritualizes the *fanciful* conception, and lifts it into the *ideal*."[24] In light of Coleridge's introduction to *Kubla Khan* and these mystic associations with what Poe later termed "pure Imagination," it is worth returning one more time to Poe's own consideration of the blending between wakefulness and sleep in his March 1846 "Marginalia." We again see Poe's articulation of an artistic belief that manifests a Romantic sensibility and draws from the era's scientific speculation on the nature of finer perceptive states:

23. Coleridge, "Of the Fragment of Kubla Khan," in *Poetical Works*, ed. J. C. C. Mays, pt. 1, 511; Nathaniel Hawthorne, *The House of the Seven Gables*, 1.

24. Poe, "Review of Alciphron, A Poem. By Thomas Moore," in *Essays and Reviews*, 337.

> Now, so entire is my faith in the *power of words,* that, at times, I
> have believed it possible to embody even the evanescence of fan-
> cies such as I have attempted to describe. In experiments with this
> end in view, I have proceeded so far as, first, to control (when the
> bodily and mental health are good) the existence of the condition:
> that is to say, I can now (unless when ill) be sure that the condi-
> tion will supervene, if I so wish it, at the point of time already de-
> scribed:—of its supervention, until lately, I could never be certain,
> even under the most favorable circumstances. I mean to say,
> merely, that now I can be sure, when all circumstances are favor-
> able, of the supervention of the condition, and feel even the ca-
> pacity of inducing or compelling it:—the favorable circumstances,
> however, are not the less rare—else had I compelled, already, the
> Heaven into the Earth.[25]

It is possible, of course, to see "Mesmeric Revelation" as Poe's effort
to narrate this ecstatic condition—and it is tempting to speculate, as
evidenced in his writing to Bush, that he sees the philosophical discourse on God as conveying the essence of his own "fancies." In the
context of his review of Hawthorne's *Twice-Told Tales,* "The Philosophy of Composition," and the concentration of effect revealed in
the practice of his fiction, however, a more important assertion
might be that, as we will see with Margaret Fuller, he connects his
conception of the literary—the use and impact of words—to his understanding of a science that traces the relationship between language,
sensation, and elevated perception. What differentiates Poe from
many others is that, in striving to find a method to induce the seemingly random moments of intuition or ecstasy, he directly and indirectly acknowledges the mesmeric arts and imprints their legacy
upon the short-story genre.

In the continuum between the hyperrational poetics of "The Philosophy of Composition" and the metaphysical speculations in
"Mesmeric Revelation," we see the puzzle pieces that Poe strives to put
together in *Eureka.* Still, even in seemingly incomplete ventures into
that borderland between the rational and the intuitive dimensions of
the creative process, Poe manages to illuminate the psychology of the

25. Poe, *Essays and Reviews,* 1384. See F. O. Matthiessen, *The American Renaissance: Art and Expression in the Age of Emerson and Whitman,* 232–34. In his
discussion of Hawthorne, Matthiessen reflects on this section from Poe's "Marginalia."

single effect and thus profoundly influence the evolution of a form that arguably best maps out the motions of the mind. The epic poem and novel, after all, simply did not provide the formal structure most conducive to invoking a particular state of consciousness. The tradition of the short story traceable to Poe would not have emerged without the psychological (and mesmeric) truths that legitimized the form's brevity, its concentration of narrative choices, and its peculiar repetition of sensation.

3 . . . .

Laws of the Heart Divine

Eureka and the Poetics of the Mind

> We must trust the perfection of the creation so far as to believe that whatever curiosity the order of things has awakened in our minds, the order of things can satisfy. Every man's condition is a solution in hieroglyphic to those inquiries he would put. He acts it as life, before he apprehends it as truth. In like manner, nature is already, in its forms and tendencies, describing its own design.
>
> Ralph Waldo Emerson, *Nature*

> Guiding our imaginations by that omniprevalent law of laws, the law of periodicity, are we not, indeed, more than justified in entertaining a belief—let us say, rather, in indulging a hope—that the processes we have here ventured to contemplate will be renewed forever, and forever, and forever; a novel Universe swelling into existence, and then subsiding into nothingness, at every throb of the Heart Divine? And now—this Heart Divine—what is it? *It is our own.*
>
> Edgar Allan Poe, *Eureka: A Prose Poem*

GIVEN THE TRAGIC ARC of Edgar Allan Poe's life, it is tempting to see *Eureka: A Prose Poem* as an autobiographical cosmology that has as much relevance in understanding the denouement of his career as the trajectory of his art. First presented as a lecture on February 3, 1848, and published in revised form in July, the "prose poem" offers an exploration of the *"Physical, Metaphysical and Mathematical—of the Material and Spiritual Universe;—of its Essence, its Origin, its Creation, its Present Condition and its Destiny"*[1] and, in

---

1. Edgar Allan Poe, *Eureka: A Prose Poem,* in *The Science Fiction of Edgar Allan Poe,* ed. Harold Beaver, 211. All subsequent references to *Eureka* will be from this edition and cited parenthetically in the text.

doing so, presents a text that leaves modern readers with interpretive dilemmas as perplexing as Poe's final days. Starting with the proposition that the cause, diffusion, and ultimate annihilation of all things lies in an initial unity born of divine volition, the work endeavors to intuit the principles of this original unity that manifest themselves in the forces of attraction and repulsion governing matter. In tracing an original oneness through expansion and ultimate collapse, then, *Eureka* seems an artistic rendering (and portending) of Poe's ultimate self-destruction or "subsiding into nothingness." To let the myth of Poe affect a reading of the text, however, would be to succumb to the more romantic configurations of Poe as the tormented artist and to explain away the seemingly incomprehensible exploration of the material and spiritual universe as the rantings of a tired or troubled mind. Moreover, it would overlook how the work includes a striking synthesis of scientific, psychological, and philosophical insights in arriving at principles behind the "superficial symmetry of forms and motions" (300). Rather than classify the text as an "elaborate anticosmological joke screed"[2] or parody, it is illuminating to orient a critical reading in the era's understanding of the invisible forces shaping celestial and psychological motion.

While it is tempting to question and even dismiss Poe's assertion that, since *Eureka*, he had "no desire to live" and that he "could accomplish nothing more," we might arrive at a richer sense of his aesthetic principles if we take him at his word.[3] In his preface to *Eureka*, Poe gives some sense of his intentions. "To the few who love me and whom I love—to those who feel rather than to those who

2. Versluis, *Esoteric Origins,* 79. In the various critical studies of the period, it is not unusual for *Eureka* to be addressed briefly, dismissed, or classed as another of Poe's parodies or satirical pieces. In *The Continuity of American Poetry*, Roy Harvey Pearce reflects on the tendency of Poe's poetry to "project disembodied creativity, so to speak—the force of an imagination driven to be true to itself at all costs." In parenthesis, Pearce then comments that, in *Eureka*, "Poe tried to construct a rationale for such disembodied creativity; the net effect of the work is at the least one of helpless megalomania, at the most one of wilful demonism" (152). For an introduction to the text, see Roland W. Nelson, "Apparatus to Poe's *Eureka.*" Nelson offers a definitive history of the text, summarizes its critical reception, and documents Poe's changes to the original 1848 Putnam publication of the lecture.

3. See Poe to Maria Clemm, July 7, [1849], in *The Letters of Edgar Allan Poe,* ed. John W. Ostrom, 2:452.

think—to the dreamers and those who put faith in dreams as in the only realities," he asserts, echoing views of the mystic aspects of the poetic voiced in his "Marginalia," "I offer this Book of Truths, not in its character of Truth-Teller, but for the Beauty that abounds in its Truth; constituting it true." Though the content of his work would have positioned it alongside such scientific studies as the "Bridgewater Treatises" and other cosmogonies evolving from mesmeric findings, he writes that, to his envisioned readers, "I present the composition as an Art-Product alone: let us say a Romance; or, if I be not urging too lofty a claim, as a Poem" (209).[4] In this sense, Poe gestures toward two central beliefs of the Romantic era: first, that the Poet can be understood as unifier, as one who discerns larger patterns in the seemingly discrete and disconnected laws of the material world, and second, that the highest art conforms to the intent and design of divine creation.

Through a look at central ideas from *Eureka* and their relationship to the mesmeric discourse on celestial motion, this chapter discerns the scientific and psychological underpinnings to how Poe understood the conceptual affinity between the creative forces of God and of man. Charting these affinities unveils the particular importance of the intuitive faculty to an artist's ability to unify seemingly disparate forces in the world. Rather than an anomalous document that distinguishes Poe's literary cosmology from other configurations of artistic powers, *Eureka* manifests "poetic" principles that reflect broader Renaissance conceptions of the imagination and the unifying power of the true artist. Thus, it will be instructive to position Emerson alongside Poe—to see both, in fact, as responding to a cultural dialogue regarding motion and thus to comparable notions of thought, mind, and the centrality of higher perceptive (or intuitive) states to American literary acts.

To what extent do narrative and poetic acts partake of divine creation? In what ways do human beings engage in divine acts? In what ways are our hearts and minds godlike, and to what laws do

4. In *Nature,* Emerson's reflections in his section "Idealism" offer a context within which to understand this tendency to align poetry with Beauty and Truth: "The true philosopher and the true poet are one, and a beauty, which is truth, and a truth, which is beauty, is the aim of both" (*Selections from Ralph Waldo Emerson,* 46).

(and should) our writing and thinking conform? To writers of the period, such questions did not exist solely within the realm of theological or philosophical discourse. If human beings were created in God's image and if the laws of creation were imprinted in the macrocosm of the universe as well as the microcosm of the human mind, then Poe and others would have rightly concluded that an understanding of celestial motion provided essential aesthetic principles. Knowing the mechanism of the body and mind, then, was a precursor to establishing best practices for the manipulation of words and forms. Moreover, literary theories and artistic genres that only superficially captured essential symmetries between God and man inevitably remained incomplete and offered the promise of less powerful effects. Sensation would be but half felt and the soul but half moved.

Poe's assertion in "Marginalia" that a class of "fancies" exist that seem "rather psychal than intellectual" and that such fancies can be retrieved from the space between the conscious and unconscious indicates a link between ideas or impressions in "nature" and those within the self. In reflections on "motion" in "Mesmeric Revelation" and "The Power of Words," we see Poe's ongoing attempt to articulate this connection between imprinting motions of the external world and their psychal impressions on individual consciousness. In "Mesmeric Revelation," when striving to describe the paradoxical truth of God's materiality and immateriality, V argues that as particles of matter increase in "rarity or fineness," they become "matter *unparticled*—without particle—indivisible—*one.*" God is this "ultimate, or unparticled matter" that permeates and impels all things. Moreover, "[w]hat men attempt to embody in the word 'thought,' is this matter in motion." "Motion," he continues after a brief observation from P, the narrator/mesmerist, is "the action of *mind.*"[5] In other words, thought is but the imprint of the divine on a receptive mind.

Similar to the exchange between V and the narrator of "Mesmeric Revelation," "The Power of Words" employs a dialogue between the heavenly spirits Oinos and Agathos as a means to explore the nature of divine knowledge, the infinity of matter, and, ultimately, the relationship between thought, motion, and the power of language.

5. Poe, "Mesmeric Revelation," in *Collected Works of Edgar Allan Poe,* 3:1033.

According to Agathos, just as "no thought can perish, so no act is without infinite result." In explaining himself, the spirit draws from ideas common to philosophical and mesmeric treatises relating thought and motion:

> *Agathos.* —In speaking of the air, I referred only to the earth: but the general proposition has reference to impulses upon the ether—which, since it pervades, and alone pervades all space, is thus the great medium of *creation.*
>
> *Oinos.* —Then all motion, of whatever nature, creates?
>
> *Agathos.* —It must: but a true philosophy has long taught that the source of all motion is thought—and the source of all thought is—
>
> *Oinos.* —God.

In the end, Agathos invites Oinos (and readers) to accept the "physical power of words," for, in giving impulse to an infinity of vibrations to the atmosphere, the act of speaking literally partakes of the infinite. Earlier, in reference to vibrations set in motion by the movement of a hand, Agathos argues that such pulsations were "indefinitely extended, till it gave impulse to every particle in the earth's air," a fact that "mathematicians of our globe well knew."[6] In both this story and "Mesmeric Revelation," Poe invites readers to envision themselves within a world of constant motion. Though unseen, the thoughts of God permeate and impel all things, and, similarly, human thoughts and words pulse outward from the self. To be moved, in a very real sense, is to be receptive to the presence and force of the reciprocal impulses of the divine mind and the human heart.

Tracing at length the grand designs of the universe, *Eureka* exhaustively studies this pulse and impulse and thus the laws of divine creation and human imagination. For Poe, the delineation of the poetical essence of the universe and human consciousness and their fundamental unity and simplicity emerges through a systematic exposition of the following truth: "*In the Original Unity of the First Thing lies the Secondary Cause of All Things, with the Germ of their Inevitable Annihilation*" (211). In his extended explication of this principle, Poe explores the nature of Infinity by affirming that God is the First Cause or First Mover. In short, God created the universe

---

6. Poe, "The Power of Words," in *Collected Works of Edgar Allan Poe*, 3:1213, 1215, 1213.

or matter out of nothing by divine will and thought. Given this assertion, Poe intuitively arrives at a conclusion "that what God originally created—that that Matter which, by dint of his Volition, he first
made from his Spirit, or from Nihility, *could* have been nothing but
Matter in its utmost conceivable state of—what? of Simplicity?" (227).
Thus, a fundamental assumption in *Eureka* is this belief in an initial
"absolute extreme of *Simplicity*" (227).

And what might one conclude from such a fact of Divine Volition?
Clearly, at least to Poe, we must see that matter in its first state existed as a single, undivided particle—or, in other words, a Oneness.
Importantly, however, "the assumption of absolute Unity of the pri-
mordial Particle includes that of infinite divisibility" (228). In the
Oneness conceived by the First Cause exists both the reality of an
expansive though not unlimited diffusion of atoms and their inevitable tendency to return into Unity. As Poe soon admits, this tendency—that is, this principle of attraction—can be seen as the laws
of Newtonian gravity. He adds, "[W]hat I have spoken of as a repul-
sive influence prescribing limits to the (immediate) satisfaction of
the tendency, will be understood as *that* which we have been in the
practice of designating now as heat, now as magnetism, now as *electricity;* displaying our ignorance of its awful character in the vacilla-
tion of the phraseology with which we endeavor to circumscribe it"
(231).

Interestingly, Poe assigns to electricity the cause of difference or
the principle of heterogeneity and thus seems to offer a view that
contrasts with other literature on animal magnetism. "*Only* where
things differ," he contends, "is electricity apparent" (232). However,
while Poe was clearly mistaken in attributing the principle of heterogeneity to electricity on scientific grounds,[7] he does not necessarily
delineate a position that contrasts markedly with the harmonizing
dimensions of mesmeric principles: "To electricity—so, for the present, continuing to call it—we *may* not be wrong in referring to various physical appearances of light, heat, and magnetism; but far less
shall we be liable to err in attributing to this strictly spiritual principle the more important phaenomena of vitality, consciousness and
Thought" (232). Regardless, as Poe himself hints in his connection of

7. See Harold Beaver's footnote to *Eureka* in *The Science Fiction of Edgar Allan
Poe,* 405.

electricity to thought, he chooses to discard what he terms the two "equivocal terms, 'gravitation' and 'electricity' " in favor of " '*Attraction*' and '*Repulsion*' " (232–33). In doing so, he asserts a dynamic process woven into the nature of human creation. The art product, in effect, manifests these aspects of outward and inward forces in its ultimate unity.[8]

Ultimately, such reflections lead to discussion of a third necessary principle, that of radiation, and finally to speculation on the nature of the centrifugal and centripetal forces that characterize an initial dispersion and then the eventual collapse back to unity. Important to Poe is the notion that the First Cause, that is, the Divine Volition or "Thought of God" that led to material creation, is "to be understood as originating the Diffusion—as proceeding with it—as regulating it—and, finally, as being withdrawn from it on its completion" (251). In other words, the principles of attraction and repulsion were a part of the movement of creation at the point of conception; at no time did God intervene to shape the planets or their orbits or to initiate the return to Unity. That is, in concluding that "*each law of Nature is dependent at all points upon all other laws*" (264), he anticipates his reflections on the mutuality or reciprocity of adaptation that is the "idiosyncracy of the Divine Art" (304). He thus describes the qualities of the finite creations of the mortal artist: they are most beautiful in their ability to capture the dynamic fluidity of cause and effect and most truthful in the way each element contributes to a single, controlling effect. The "sense of the symmetrical," he posits,

> is an instinct which may be depended on with an almost blindfold reliance. It is the poetical essence of the Universe—*of the Universe* which, in the supremeness of its symmetry, is but the most sublime of poems. Now symmetry and consistency are convertible

8. In *Six Lectures on the Philosophy of Mesmerism, Delivered in the Marlboro' Chapel, January 23–28, 1843,* John Bovee Dods describes a law of the universe that forms an interesting precursor to Poe's formulations: "In the first place, then, I contend that there is but one common LAW [that] pervades the whole universe of God, which is the law of EQUILIBRIUM. In perfect accordance with this law there is kept up a constant *action* and *reaction* throughout every department of nature" (8). In 1852, Fowler and Wells published an expanded edition of the book, entitled *The Philosophy of Electrical Psychology: In a Course of Twelve Lectures.*

terms:—thus poetry and Truth are one. . . . We may take it for
granted, then, that Man cannot long or widely err, if he suffer himself to be guided by his poetical, which I have maintained to be his
truthful, in being his symmetrical, instinct. He must have a care,
however, lest, in pursuing too heedlessly the superficial symmetry
of forms and motions, he leave out of sight the really essential symmetry of the principles which determine and control them. (300)

According to Poe, then, acting within the structure of creation seems
both instinctual and intentional. In effect, God's creative act initiated motions that should inform and shape the symmetries of
human creation.

For the artist, Poe's conclusions further underscore the importance of a receptivity to the creation of the most sublime works. The
most truthful and beautiful art forms arise not from the workings of
the rational mind (and deductive and inductive reasoning), but
from a way of knowing that goes beyond reason and seems inherent
in human existence. Significantly, he arrives at these notions through
an intuitive "reflection" on material laws. Or, perhaps more accurately, he discerns these principles in the space between the material and the spiritual and finds support for such ideas within texts
that address the physical and psychological aspects of motion. Unlike Emerson, for instance, he enters through the door of science,
not philosophy. As Poe articulates in his "Marginalia" and hints at in
"Mesmeric Revelation," important insights might be induced through
and elicited from higher states of consciousness.

Considering Poe's poetic translation of universal forces of attraction and repulsion alongside texts that form both the center and periphery of the mesmeric canon brings to light the scientific and
psychological dialogue that influenced the era's literary theory. His
emphasis upon motion and centripetal and centrifugal forces resonates with discourse on the physics of planetary motion and the
mind. To learn the fundamental rules of the creative process requires an intuitive gaze upon celestial motion.

The imprint of this doctrine of celestial ebb and flow emerged in
the organized training and publications of Franz Anton Mesmer's
students and fellow doctors. In the Society of Harmony, formed in
Paris in 1783 to teach paying students Mesmer's principles, Nicholas Bergasse opened his lectures with a consideration of "motion."

Not surprisingly, Dr. John Bell's *General and Particular Principles of Animal Electricity and Magnetism* (1792)—a text "authorized" by first acknowledging Bell's attendance at the "LECTURES upon the Science of ANIMAL ELECTRICITY and MAGNETISM, &c. as read by Messrs. DUVAL DESPREMINIL and BERGASSE" in the summer of 1785—begins with a section entitled "General Ideas on Motion." Bell asserts, "Motion exists in all parts of the universe: all bodies are endowed with a certain degree of it, in proportion to their different organizations." Since no things are in a "perfect state of rest," he goes on to say, it is "impossible to imagine how motion destroys itself." Given this principle of motion and the belief that things tend toward the center of the earth, Bell soon wrestles with the problem of eventual annihilation. In other words, if things tend toward a center point and will not rest once set in motion, what is to become of this force that displaces bodies? "Where is it to be annihilated?"—or, is it ever annihilated?

> It therefore must absolutely follow, that those motions must be reflected with new directions from the centre of the earth, or they must be destroyed. But, if it be true, that in the art of reasoning, the analogy or method of simplifying the principle as much as possible, is to be considered as the surest way of proceeding, we shall be authorised to think that nature modifies, alters, and distributes, rather than destroys. Thus, as we acknowledge in all organized bodies, a faculty which divides, distributes, and returns all those motions, whose impressions they receive, or rather which are communicated to them; since we see that those motions are never annihilated; why should we imagine that there is an incomprehensible proceeding in nature, a secret quality which we are not in want of? Why cannot we suppose, that it operates upon spheres as well as upon individuals?[9]

9. John Bell, *General and Particular Principles,* 7, 8, 9, 11. A prefatory "COPY of the CERTIFICATE" confirms Bell's membership in what he calls the "Philosophical Harmonic Society of Paris." In *A Key to Physic and the Occult Sciences,* Ebenezer Sibly underscores the success of Dr. Bell's practice in England and includes a lengthy excerpt from the physician's book: "Every body is endowed with a certain quantity of electric fluid. There exists an attraction and repulsion, or sympathy and antipathy, between animated bodies. . . . As there exists a general and reciprocal gravitation of all celestial bodies towards each other, so there exists a particular and reciprocal gravitation of the constitutive parts of the earth towards the whole, and of that whole towards each of its parts" (Bell, quoted in Sibly, 258).

While Bell's answer to the dilemma of this tendency toward a center and potential annihilation of this force differs from Poe's, it still indicates that both men were striving to settle one of the central issues in understanding the principles of animal electricity and thus the implications of motion initiated by divine volition. Moreover, Bell's reasoning is consistent with the first and second of Mesmer's twenty-six propositions first published in 1779: "A universally distributed and continuous fluid, which is quite without vacuum and of an incomparably rarefied nature, and which by its nature is capable of receiving, propagating and communicating all the impressions of movement, is the means of this influence" (between "Heavenly bodies, the Earth and Animate Bodies"). (In *Physical-Medical Treatise on the Influence of the Planets* [1766], Mesmer opens with a clear articulation of the importance of motion to the human body: "My purpose is solely to demonstrate that the celestial bodies act on our earth. Furthermore, that all things which are here act upon these celestial bodies in turn; that these move, act, and that all parts are changing, and that our bodies are equally submitted to the same dynamic motion.") For Bell, nothing should hinder us from accepting both "Electricity and Magnetism" as the product of "that interior elaboration." In short, electric or magnetic forces form the powerful medium in this grand scheme of internal movement.[10]

Significantly, Bell saw humankind as able to affect or harness these invisible forces of nature. He believed that "art can imitate nature, and even surpass it" in many cases. In a statement that found ongoing expression in magnetists' emphasis upon attention and intention in inducing a magnetic state, he presumed that it "is natural to conclude from hence, that nature has an uniform manner of acting, but directed by the knowledge of man, she is capable of encreasing that power, and of concentrating, by her strength, in a determined point." This belief in the ability of individuals to control such forces formed the cornerstone of magnetic medical practice. It also suggestively affirmed the potential of the artistic enterprise

10. Mesmer, *Dissertation on the Discovery of Animal Magnetism,* in *Mesmerism: A Translation of the Original Scientific and Medical Writings of F. A. Mesmer,* trans. and ed. George Bloch, 67; Mesmer, *Physical-Medical Treatise on the Influence of the Planets,* in *Mesmerism: A Translation,* 3–4; Bell, *General and Particular Principles,* 11.

to achieve powerful effects through a formal focus and concentration.[11]

From the late eighteenth century through the 1840s, speculation on the nature of movement and the effects of this universal and continuous motion on the body and mind became pervasive in philosophical and psychological discourse. In the mesmeric journals of the 1840s, this belief in the direct relationship between celestial and terrestrial bodies appears in striking ways. In La Roy Sunderland's *Magnet*—a magazine "devoted to the investigation of HUMAN PHYSIOLOGY, embracing VITALITY, PATHETISM, PSYCHOLOGY, PHRENOPATHY, PHRENOLOGY, NEUROLOGY, PHYSIOGNOMY and MAGNETISM"—we see the emblematic representation of what we might call, to borrow Bell's language, the interior elaboration of natural forces. In the "Preliminary" of the initial issue, Sunderland captures just how far succeeding generations "interiorized" forces first witnessed in celestial motion. Through both phrenology and magnetism, the article asserts, changes in "Mental Philosophy" will undergo greater modifications than ever "wrought in the science of Astronomy, or Medicine." "And what can be more interesting," Sunderland asks, "than to see the human mind itself, as it were, dissected? To be able to look into its hidden recesses, and explore the sources of *thought*? To understand how it is, that the *immaterial, conscious, self-determining* PRINCIPLE controls matter, and gives expression through the physical organ to its own desires and emotions?"[12] In the context of the era's mesmeric literature, this principle can be understood as the progressive influence of divine motion on human consciousness.

The June 1842 opening issue of the *Magnet* visualizes dynamic laws of the "philosophy of mind" through an etching on the title page that calls to mind the principles of attraction and repulsion described by Poe, Bell, and others. Suggestive of the outward and

11. Bell, *General and Particular Principles,* 16. In *On the Sentient Faculty, and Principles of Human Magnetism* (1819), a translation of the writings of Swedish nobleman Sigismund Ehrenreich graf von Redern, we hear a similar connection between the motion of the spheres and the unique receptivity of the nervous system. "All [the senses] convey perceptions to us," Redern explains, "and become cause of sensation, from some movement, some sort of modification in a part of our nervous system" (27). For another discussion of motion in relation to animate and inanimate bodies, see Sibly, *Key to Physic and the Occult Sciences,* 14–16.

12. La Roy Sunderland, "Preliminary," *Magnet,* 2.

inward movement that Poe characterized both as a kind of pulsing and, at another point, as embodying centripetal and centrifugal forces, the image simultaneously draws the eye to the periphery as well as to the originating center (see fig. 1). Additional sketches of these forces appear in Dr. Henry Hall Sherwood's "The Magnetic Forces," an article that opens with the telling assertion that the "action of the forces on which motion depends, is illustrated, in the most simple manner, by the magnet" (see fig. 2).[13] In fact, readers of the opening issue did not need to look far to see the overwhelming emphasis upon magnetic or electrical forces in understanding the larger principles of motion and their connection to the human mind, for, in the second issue of the *Magnet,* the editor conspicuously merges the movement of external bodies with the interior workings of the mind. The spherical image on the title page now takes the shape of a cross section of the human brain; such an evolution of the image affirms that little distinction existed between what Poe termed the "universe of the stars" and what Sunderland might have called the universe of the mind (see fig. 3).

In the Reverend Gibson Smith's *Lectures on Clairmativeness; or, Human Magnetism* (1845), we hear reflections that suggest the implications of the cosmological truths of attraction and repulsion to an artistic sensibility. In language that calls to mind Poe's discussion of motion in "The Power of Words" and of reciprocal forces in *Eureka,* Smith argues that "[m]otion is the result of certain fixed laws, established by the Deity" and that "[i]n seeking for those laws we are only approaching one step nearer to him who is the Author and Creator of all things." For Smith, the laws initiated by this "Author" and "Creator" are the same laws that embody Poe's "poetical essence of the Universe" (*Eureka,* 300). That is, for both, the workings of magnetism and electricity provide evidence of counterbalancing forces, of a kind of harmonizing between centripetal and centrifugal movements.[14]

13. Henry Hall Sherwood, M.D., "The Magnetic Forces," *Magnet,* 3. Having published *The Motive Power of Organic Life, and Magnetic Phenomena of Terrestrial and Planetary Motions, with the Application of the Ever-Active and All-Pervading Agency of Magnetism, to the Nature, Symptoms, and Treatment of Chronic Diseases* (1841), Sherwood contributed to Sunderland's magazine as one well versed in neurology.

14. Gibson Smith, *Lectures on Clairmativeness; or, Human Magnetism,* 28.

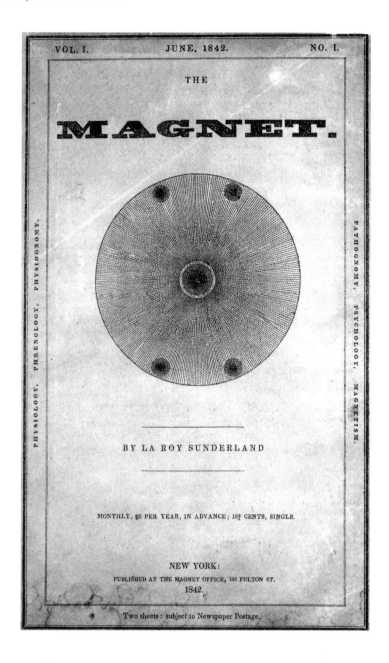

Fig. 1. Title page of the first issue of the *Magnet* (June 1842).

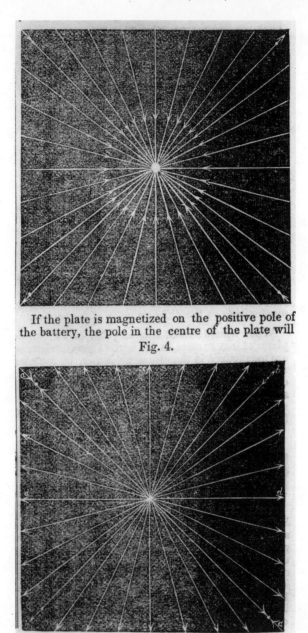

Fig. 2. Images showing the inward and outward direction of magnetic forces (June 1842).

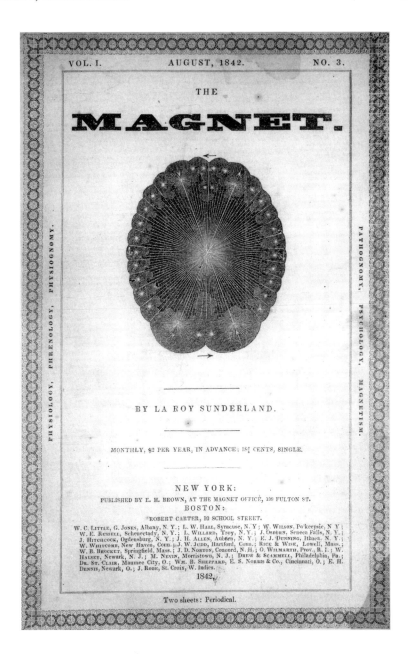

Fig. 3. Title page from the second issue of the *Magnet* (July 1842).

It is telling to follow Smith's path from the cosmological implications of motion to the closer sphere of individual consciousness and
to the creative powers within intuitive faculties. Smith unveils the
nature of bodily response to immaterial forces through the help of
the clairvoyant Jackson Davis. "Animal Magnetism," Davis asserts
at the beginning of Smith's fourth lecture, "is a modification of
caloric or atmospheric magnetism." The body in effect processes
the perpetual movement of the magnetic fluid, which enters the
system by the lungs, the pores, and the glands, "so that it is fitted for
its office in the sympathetic nerves," which then produce bodily
sensations that can be transmitted to the brain. For Smith, "[m]ind is
magnetism. It is produced, or rather formed in the brain, by means
of the five senses. . . . It is then life—pure intelligence—that breath
of God which he breathed into man when he became a living soul."
In short, it is a motion that embodies the principles of the First
Cause. In further citing Davis, the text asserts a similar conclusion:

> Most men require ocular demonstration of a thing before they will
> consent to believe it; but this is a subject, among many others,
> which will not admit of such demonstration. I, however, have this
> ocular demonstration whilst I am in the clairvoyant state, for I can
> see this fluid, as it is discharged by the will into the cerebellum,
> passing from thence along the muscular nerves, contracting them,
> and thus producing voluntary motion. I can also see the magnetic
> fluid which exists in the sympathetic nerves,—it is very brilliant,
> and lights up to my view the whole system, so that I can see every
> part of the animal frame. I can also see the mind itself, which is
> still more refined and luminous;—I can see every motion of the
> mind, and this is the reason why I am able to tell you all your
> thoughts,—*thought is simply the motion of the mind.*

Again, Smith's text is one more expression of the period's pervasive
belief concerning thought. The ensuing implications are clear: created in the image of God, man manifests this motion, this presence
of Divine Consciousness.[15]

15. *Lectures on Clairmativeness,* 32–33. In *A Lecture on the Magnetism of the
Human Body* (1843), Dr. Robert W. Gibbes echoes these conclusions: "The
human body is magnetic, and possesses polarity. May I be allowed here to al-
lude to the beautiful analogy, which the innate principle of our being, pointing
to the Great First Cause, has to the mysterious tendency of the needle to the

• • • •

Seeing that the motion of the world is imprinted within individual consciousness or thought, then, the artist discovers the ultimate truth of creation. Therefore, the laws of attraction and repulsion and other principles woven into the order of things must guide the artistic act. Poe captures this understanding of the heart divine in his consideration of the link between divine and artistic plots. Speaking of divine adaptation, or the "complete *mutuality* of adaptation" that makes it impossible to discern cause and effect in "Divine constructions," Poe associates the art of storytelling with the way in which divine creations reflect an "absolute reciprocity of adaptation" manifested in the fluidity of cause and effect: "The pleasure which we derive from any display of human ingenuity is in the ratio of *the approach* to this species of reciprocity. In the construction of *plot,* for example, in fictitious literature, we should aim at so arranging the incidents that we shall not be able to determine, of any one of them, whether it depends from any one other or upholds it. In this sense, of course, perfection of plot is really, or practically, unattainable—but only because it is a finite intelligence that constructs. The plots of God are perfect. The Universe is a plot of God" (*Eureka,* 292). Quite simply, Poe transfers his understanding of electrical and magnetic principles to his own theories of short fiction, one of which being that every narrative element of the short prose tale must contribute to its overall effect. Truth and Beauty emerge in the seamlessness between cause and effect. We hear Poe's idea of the single effect grounded more firmly in notions of the symmetrical or cyclic motions of the world: "Moons have been seen *revolving* about planets; planets about stars; and the poetical instinct of humanity— its instinct of the symmetrical, even if the symmetry be but a symmetry of surface:—this *instinct,* which the Soul, not only of Man but of all created beings, took up, in the beginning, from the *geometrical* basis of the Universal radiation—impels us to the fancy of an endless extension of this system of *cycles*" (293). Such a statement offers

---

pole? Our benevolent and wise Creator may have intended the same power, with which he regulates the terrestrial movements of our planet, to be the instrument of communication between matter and mind, and mind and his Divine influence" (35).

a material translation of spiritual laws. In the end, Poe discerns the rules of the universe from the material effects of planetary motion and the outward effects of inward sensations.

But, as we have seen, the term *instinct* suggests the central place of an inward faculty in comprehending the meanings of outward forces. So, while Poe's text demonstrates that the true poet analyzes Nature as a way to understand central aspects of creation and the poetic instinct and indicates that comprehension of divine laws requires a disciplined study of and reflection on the natural or material world, it also directs attention toward the use of an inward faculty in the journey toward higher laws.

Though often interpreted as a sign of the larger satirical design of *Eureka,* the opening pages of the "prose poem" reveal Poe's effort to underscore the centrality of intuition in synthesizing deductive and inductive truths. Through the insertion of extracts from a fictitious letter "found corked in a bottle and floating on the *Mare Tenebrarum*" (213), Poe lampoons figures who remain caught in the simplistic truths derived either from *a priori* maxims or from the general laws arising from the endless observing, analyzing, and classifying of facts. Rather than give ultimate authority to such methods, the voice from the unbottled manuscript confirms that the most important advances occur "by seemingly intuitive *leaps*" (214). As evidence of this fact, the mock letter emphasizes how the fact of gravitation emerged from the guesswork of Kepler:

> Newton deduced it from the laws of Kepler. Kepler admitted that these laws he *guessed*—these laws whose investigation disclosed to the greatest of British astronomers that principle, the basis of all (existing) physical principle, in going behind which we enter at once the nebulous kingdom of Metaphysics. Yes!—these vital laws Kepler *guessed*—that it is to say, he *imagined* them. Had he been asked to point out either the *de*ductive or *in*ductive route by which he attained them, his reply might have been—"I know nothing about *routes*—but I *do* know the machinery of the Universe. Here it is. I grasped it with *my soul*—I reached it through mere dint of *intuition.*" (220)

Not unlike the "dint of [divine] Volition" (226) that Poe soon names as leading to creation, this dint of mortal intuition transforms the universe. It is another kind of creation, for, through its embrace of far-reaching principles, such an act of will can change the nature of human understanding and action.

Just as students of animal magnetism came to see the imagination as an essential faculty in the mesmeric arts, so too did they understand intuition as an important power in receptivity to divine "movement." In his chapter "The Mesmeric Medium," Chauncy Hare Townshend offers some compelling reflections on the centrality of "intuition." Starting with the premise that the human mind can conceive of no effect without a cause, Townshend suggests that we accept the possibility of invisible forces because we witness certain effects, for example, the movement of a needle by a magnet: "We infer that the effect is produced by means of a magnetic current or medium, a something which propagates motion from the magnet to the needle." He continues: "This something we cannot indeed behold, yet do we believe in it, and with justice; for that which reason perceives to be necessary is *not* an invention, and can never be superfluous: on the contrary, the *only* immutable and essential truths come out of the mould of the intuitive reason, which, as Coleridge observes, stops not at 'this *will* be so,' but at once decides, 'This *must* be so.' "[16] Inevitably, then, the highest truths demand this willingness to go beyond a strictly materialist view of things. While much of what we conclude from the operation of the five senses is rooted in a rational assessment of sensation, we must inevitably move beyond reason to come to "know" those invisible causes to visible effects.

In contemplating the nature of the somnambulant state, Townshend also considers one of the most striking demonstrations of mesmeric motion: clairvoyant insights that appear to transcend the limitations of time and space and that suggest the presence of a higher mental (that is, intuitive) faculty. For instance, he wonders to what we can attribute the ability of a person to read the thoughts of another. In order to arrive at some understanding of actions that seem

16. Townshend, *Facts in Mesmerism,* 278. Townshend goes on to offer a familiar rendering of the idea of the motion of atoms: "Now, in all cases where motion is communicated from one body to another, the line of communication must be maintained unbroken. The first impulse gives motion to certain atoms, which in their turn propel others, and so on, till the whole series between the active body and the body which is to receive the original impulse is set in motion, and then, at length, the sequence of events is complete, and the body toward which motion tended, is set vibrating" (278–79).

to defy natural laws of creation (and thus signal the intervention of supernatural forces), Townshend reminds readers, "There is sensation, and there is also the language of sensation; in other words, nervous motions, which are equivalent to a language." Thus, we can only conclude that "every thought moves the brain in its own appropriate manner" and that "[o]ur personal ignorance of these specific changes . . . is no proof whatever that they do not take place." Such assertions, of course, would have been persuasive to an era newly awakened to the implications of gravitational laws, that is, to the empirical evidence that immaterial forces affect bodies at a distance. In other words, rather than representing supernatural forces, clairvoyance simply embodies the highest manifestation of laws of motion already woven into God's creation. Is it not possible that the clairvoyant simply has the capacity to receive and read the signs of a more subtle mental movement? Given the nature of the body electric, it seems only natural that those of a more apprehensive disposition—or capable of entering the special sensitivity of a magnetic state—should embody a power so consistent with the nature of creation:

> If it should be asked in what manner the sleepwaker has come to be so well acquainted with the signs of characters of thought, I might think it, perhaps, a sufficient answer to reply, "The soul is wise: yes, wiser than we know." There are more intuitions, or (as Kant calls them) "cognitions *à priori*," than we suppose. What if motions of the ethereal medium were the native and universal language of the mind? Or, to answer one question by another, How, in sensation, have certain motions come to be representative of certain external objects? I may be told, By experience; but, again, experience itself must have a basis. What first taught the mind the connexion between the sign and the object? Plainly an intuition; for it is self-evident that we cannot advance to new knowledge but by the aid of previous knowledge.

The nature of Townshend's speculations is reminiscent of Poe's fictional conversations in "Mesmeric Revelation" and "The Power of Words." Both Townshend's and Poe's texts strive to understand the affinities between motions in the universe and those that occur within the mind.[17]

17. Ibid., 313, 314. See pp. 327–31 on the relationship between the mesmeric medium and electricity.

. . . .

Though he arrives at the centrality of intuition by a path different from those of prominent American Renaissance figures, most notably Ralph Waldo Emerson, Poe expresses views that echo Transcendentalist perspectives and thus provide a broader sense of the shared principles between seemingly distinct writers and discourses. Drawing from Kantian philosophy, many Transcendentalists of the period equated intuition with the faculty of pure Reason. In the second series of her popular essay collection *Letters from New York* (1845), Lydia Maria Child defines this "inward revealing faculty" that transcends "mere intellectual perception" in ways that illuminate the fundamental affinities between figures like Poe and Emerson. First noting that the philosophy of John Locke asserted that "*all* knowledge is received into the soul through the medium of the senses; and thence passes to be judged of and analyzed by the understanding," Child goes on to characterize a faculty that clearly parallels the philosophy of mind articulated by Sunderland:

> The German school of metaphysics, with the celebrated Kant at its head, rejects this proposition as false; it denies that all knowledge is received through the senses, and maintains that the highest, and therefore most universal truths, are revealed within the soul, to a faculty *transcending* the understanding. This faculty they call pure Reason; it being peculiar to them to use that word in contradistinction to the Understanding. To this pure Reason, which some of their writers call "The God within," they believe that all perceptions of the Good, the True, and the Beautiful, are revealed, in its unconscious quietude; and that the province of Understanding, with its five handmaids, the Senses, is confined merely to external things, such as facts, scientific laws, &c.[18]

Later, after asserting that the Transcendentalist style has an "oracular and mystical sound" and announces rather than argues a truth (thus echoing Townshend's views concerning Coleridge), she describes the style of this "doctrine of intuitive perception" in a manner that seems remarkably consistent with Poe's synopsis of a "class of composition in which there lies beneath the transparent upper current of meaning, an under or *suggestive* one": "Therefore, there is

18. Lydia Maria Child, *Letters from New York. Second Series*, 125–26.

about their writings 'a tone and colour *sui generis;* something of the clear and the mysterious, like the sea in a beautiful day in summer. A light, cold and colourless, pierces the liquid mass, giving it a certain transparency that captivates the eye, but which imports that there is always, at the bottom, a mystery unexplained.' "[19] While Poe should not be classed as a Transcendentalist, he did express views that mirror this privileging of a higher intuitive faculty, and he attributed a kind of mystic quality to the most imaginative writings, such as Coleridge's *Kubla Khan.*

What Poe termed the "poetical instinct of humanity" has long been examined through the lens of Transcendentalist terms and concepts, which is to say that Nature took on a more spiritual shading than a material one. If we consider "thought" in the context of "motion" and "intuition" within the discourse of mesmeric psychology, we allow our understanding of the period to open to a larger view. In this conceptual space, Poe and Emerson share a common vista. Significantly, this new vantage point introduces a different but complementary vocabulary, that is, another way to conceptualize and name the dominant belief that the soul contains the imprint of divinity.

The fundamental truth for Emerson and for Poe was that the universe of the mind contains the ultimate expression of Beauty and Truth. Drawing from key ideas in *Nature,* Emerson's "American Scholar" further articulates the relationship between Nature and the human mind. Defining the young mind as one that first sees things in the world as distinct or individual, he goes on to note the growing maturity of a mind recognizing its "unifying instinct." Not unlike Poe's "poetical instinct," this aspect of "Man Thinking" recognizes the coherence between what is within and what is without, that is, that "geometry, a pure abstraction of the human mind, is the measure of planetary motion" and that "science is nothing but the finding of analogy, identity, in the most remote parts." The true scholar comes to understand that the laws of the material world and those of the individual soul are the same:

> . . . when he has learned to worship the soul, and to see that the natural philosophy that now is, is only the first gropings of its gigantic hand, he shall look forward to an ever expanding knowl-

19. Child, *Letters from New York. Second Series,* 127–28; Poe, *Essays and Reviews,* 337. Child does not include the source of her quotation.

> edge as to a becoming creator. He shall see that nature is the op-
> posite of the soul, answering to it part for part. One is seal and one
> is print. Its beauty is the beauty of his own mind. Its laws are the
> laws of his own mind.

It is possible, though certainly overstating the point, to see most of
Emerson's writings as an exploration of this central assertion and its
implications to how one acts (and creates) in the world. In *Nature,*
Emerson's earlier "eureka"-like explication of this and other ideas,
the implications of this relationship between the mind and the material world find expression in the perception of art: "A work of art is
an abstract or epitome of the world."[20]

In his briefer essay "Nature," one of eight pieces in *Essays: Second
Series* (1844), Emerson turned directly to the language and conceptions concerning motion in his ongoing exegesis of the affinity
between nature and mind. Interestingly, he did so not long after
suggesting that mesmerism marks a reductive display of more profound truths. ("Astronomy to the selfish becomes astrology; psychology, mesmerism [with intent to show where our spoons are
gone]; and anatomy and physiology become phrenology and palm-
istry.") Not unlike Poe, Emerson wished to distinguish between
superficial and essential principles and, in the end, to assert the
underlying simplicity amid complex processes and forms. "Motion
or change, and identity or rest," Emerson declares, "are the first and
second secrets of nature: Motion and Rest. The whole code of her
laws may be written on the thumbnail, or the signet of a ring." To
his imagination, the ultimate truth of such principles manifests itself in the correspondence between human and natural forms: "This
guiding identity runs through all the surprises and contrasts of the
piece, and characterizes every law. Man carries the world in his
head, the whole astronomy and chemistry suspended in a thought.
Because the history of nature is characterized in his brain, therefore
is he the prophet and discoverer of her secrets." With such a resonance between Poe's explication of the material and spiritual worlds
and Emerson's exegesis on external forms and an internal, "guiding
identity," one can almost predict the trajectory of Emerson's reflections. Like Poe, he found himself speculating on the dynamic motions behind the inner mechanism of the human mind:

20. Emerson, *Selections from Ralph Waldo Emerson,* 66, 30.

> If the identity expresses organized rest, the counter action runs
> also into organization. The astronomers said, "Give us matter, and
> a little motion, and we will construct the universe. It is not enough
> that we should have matter, we must also have a single impulse,
> one shove to launch the mass, and generate the harmony of the
> centrifugal and centripetal forces. . . ."

That "the craft with which the world is made, runs also into the
mind and character of men" implies profound and wide-reaching
implications for the artist. The poet-maker must create out of the
dynamic aesthetic of his own mind.[21]

"The Poet" marks one of Emerson's most direct and thorough expressions of this principle in relation to literary practice. And, while
Emerson does not speak directly to how mesmeric sensation un-
veiled the psychological underpinnings of his aesthetic, he clearly
associates his poetic principles with the motions of the mind. So, it
is revealing to consider one of his most famous assertions in this
context of divine thought and motion:

> For it is not metres, but a metre-making argument that makes a
> poem,—a thought so passionate and alive that like the spirit of a
> plant or an animal, it has an architecture of its own, and adorns
> nature with a new thing. The thought and form are equal in the
> order of time, but in the order of genesis the thought is prior to the
> form.

For the poet, then, it is thought that precedes form; its architecture
is the blueprint behind artistic products. To paraphrase a scriptural
interpretation of divine creation, form is thought (or word) made
flesh. (Hence, for Emerson and eventually Whitman, the idea of
America must precede its poetic expression.) If the "Universe is the
externalization of the soul," then divine and human creations should
betray common symmetries and must emerge from similar impulses. As Emerson explains, "Our science is sensual, and therefore
superficial. The earth and the heavenly bodies, physics, and chemistry, we sensually treat, as if they were self-existent; but these are
the retinue of that Being we have." Perception, then, becomes pre-
eminent in the poetic process. And, importantly, the true poet (or

21. Emerson, *The Essays of Ralph Waldo Emerson,* 322, 323, 324, 325, 326.

sayer) ultimately demonstrates a higher comprehension or a perceptive state that facilitates the unfolding of outward forms from inward visions. For Emerson, this correlation between the things that impress themselves upon the senses and the potential forms of expression in their suggestive symmetries embodies an insight that communicates "itself by what is called Imagination" and "is a very high sort of seeing."[22]

Without question, the mesmeric literature most directly addressed the particular physical, physiological, and psychological dimensions of this perceptive power, this unifying vision. If one could get beyond the spectacle and chicanery of the mesmeric demonstrations that, to use Emerson's terms, seemed most interested in showing where our spoons are gone, and get to the authoritative treatises that, to use Poe's words, trace essential motions of the heart divine, then the poet-unifier would discover the most basic principles of the creative process. This lesson informs the content and form of countless antebellum narratives—from Poe's "The Fall of the House of Usher" to Nathaniel Hawthorne's "The Artist of the Beautiful" to Margaret Fuller's *Summer on the Lakes*.

In the year following the publication of *Eureka* and in the months prior to his death, Poe delivered a lecture on poetry that was eventually published posthumously. Along with "The Philosophy of Composition" and "The Rationale of Verse," "The Poetic Principle" introduces key concepts in Poe's poetic theory, including a final elaboration on the inconsistency of the peculiar beauties of poetry and the epic poem. Given *Eureka*'s extensive efforts to delineate principles of symmetry and its prefatory endeavor to encourage the audience to see the text as poem, readers might expect "The Poetic Principle" to draw quite *directly* from the earlier lecture. However, in first asserting that he has "no design to be either thorough or profound" and that he intends to focus solely on considering "some few of those minor English or American poems" which best suit his own taste and have left the "most definite impression" on his fancy, Poe seems to announce that it is not his intent to draw from his literary cosmology.[23]

---

22. Emerson, *Selections from Ralph Waldo Emerson*, 224–25, 227, 233.
23. Poe, *Essays and Reviews*, 71.

Not surprisingly, however, as Poe employs those terms that he consistently aligns with the poetic (Beauty and Truth), he offers reflections that would form an appropriate postscript to *Eureka:*

> An immortal instinct, deep within the spirit of man, is thus, plainly, a sense of the Beautiful. This it is which administers to his delight in the manifold forms, and sounds, and odours, and sentiments amid which he exists. And just as the lily is repeated in the lake, or the eyes of Amaryllis in the mirror, so is the mere oral or written repetition of these forms, and sounds, and colours, and odours, and sentiments, a duplicate source of delight. But this mere repetition is not poetry. He who shall simply sing, with however glowing enthusiasm, or with however vivid a truth of description, of the sights, and sounds, and odours, and colours, and sentiments, which greet *him* in common with all mankind—he, I say, has yet failed to prove his divine title. There is still a something in the distance which he has been unable to attain. We have still a thirst unquenchable, to allay which he has not shown us the crystal springs. This thirst belongs to the immortality of Man. It is at once a consequence and an indication of his perennial existence.[24]

In light of his cosmology, it is not inconsistent to read "immortal instinct" as synonymous with *intuition* or to see the repetition of forms, sensations, and sentiments as a literary echo of the "law of periodicity." Even near the end of Poe's life, the persistent pulse of his criticism captures the sense that, just beyond the border of the poem, of consciousness, or of an artist's striving, exists the wellspring of inspiration from which forms of Truth and Beauty emerge. It is suggestive to see his criticism and art as endeavoring to discover and then embody these invisible laws of the divine. *Eureka* signals a serious enterprise, then, though certainly laced with enough irony to continue to lead readers to question the author's intent.

That Poe more directly integrated the discourse on the mind that was pervasive in the mesmeric, medical, and philosophical texts suggests that, rather than lampooning what now seems pseudo-scientific findings, he sought to offer his own unifying vision. In Poe's poetic, however, the self or originating oneness or consciousness does not disperse beneath the boot soles; instead, it seems to

24. Ibid., 76–77.

become part of the Universe of the Stars. As early as 1841, Poe anticipated such thoughts in "The Island of the Fay": "As we find cycle within cycle without end—yet all revolving around one far-distant centre which is the Godhead, may we not analogically suppose, in the same manner, life within life, the less within the greater, and all within the Spirit Divine."[25] Triumphantly, in a final acknowledgment of the heart divine in *Eureka,* Poe's verbal repetition seems an unconscious enactment of the larger laws delineated in the work: "In the meantime bear in mind that all is Life—Life—Life within Life—the less within the greater, and all within the *Spirit Divine*" (309).

In turning to Margaret Fuller, we will see another writer of the period striving to articulate the nature of this Spirit Divine through an exploration of an apprehensive consciousness. While assimilating the findings associated with magnetic states in different terms and forms, Fuller shares Poe's incessant endeavor to delineate the broader implication of the interior elaboration of natural forces.

25. In his annotation for the ending of *Eureka,* Harold Beaver notes this source (414n61).

4 . . . .

Reading the Self

Fuller's Magnetic Juvenilia

If [Amariah] Brigham's theory were correct it would be curious to trace the singular traits of mind I exhibited up to my twenty first year to this ugly and very painful flush in the forehead. The summer of that year [1831] my forehead and indeed my whole system was pretty fairly exhausted of the vital fluid under the care of Dr. Robbins. Thanks to his medicines, my nerves became calmed, flushes and headaches gradually disappeared. I craved sleep, so long almost impossible to me. My wakefulness had always been troublesome to myself and others. I would now lie down in the middle of the day and sleep for hours. Since that time I have certainly grown wondrous calm but had flattered myself, O, Amariah, that this was attributable to the maturity of character I had attained, to a command over my passions and thoughts, an acquired reliance upon the God of Truth. Can it be that I am doomed in accordance with thy fiat to be driven down the stream of time ere my summer is well begun or leaf too early dried from its natal tree. Forbid it ye *im*material philosophers. Forbid it—my own energies—Amariah! I defy thee—though I secretly confess with a quaking heart.

Margaret Fuller, private journal (ca. March 1834)

COMING OF AGE IN THE 1830S, Margaret Fuller acquired a notion of mental health that shaped her understanding of the unique physiological attributes of genius and thus the critical vocabulary surrounding a vital life and art. Reading herself as a "somnambulist" in childhood, she confesses that she was "subject to attacks of delirium" and "spectral illusions." In reminiscences concerning her fear of going to bed, she notes that her mother "seemed ashamed of my sleepwalking" and that her father attributed her "dreadful dreams" and the occasional convulsions that ensued to "my overheating myself." Perusing Amariah Brigham's *Remarks on the Influence of Mental Cultivation upon Health* (first published in 1832), Fuller came across a more material explanation for her state of mind: "1st That the brain is the organ of thought. 2^{d} That all mental derangement is the result of organick disease in the brain." Her journal musings on her own health, in fact, follow an admission that she cannot "pretend to decide on [Brigham's] premises" and thus that a "positive decision of these two questions requires an examination of evidence." Addressing "Amariah" in the context of her own self-diagnosis, she challenges his premises for their deterministic implications even while she appeals to "*im*material philosophers" and admits to a "quaking heart." That Fuller would see a reflection of her own precocity in the life of Scottish philosopher Sir James Mackintosh and seek to understand his lack of production in terms of a limited storage of vital powers indicates the degree to which physiological and psychological findings on the mind informed her self-examination and her notions of talent and genius. In raising the question of Mackintosh's great promise but limited achievements, she echoes an observation concerning Anna Letitia Barbauld that prefaced the journal ruminations on her sleepwalking: "But her mind was *never* active in *production.*"[1]

The intersecting concerns in Fuller's private self-examination and public criticism raise important questions. How did findings regarding magnetism and mental health affect her self-understanding, that is, the reading of her self? How did notions of electricity and mesmeric states provide a critical language and conceptual framework for her understanding of the genius of writers and their texts? Not surprisingly, given the history of her own physical health and mental struggles, Margaret Fuller's early criticism demonstrates a special interest in "reading" how figures such as Mackintosh—and, later, the German Romantics and British poets—manifest or fail to manifest a kind of energizing vitality. Within her early work, we can discern a link between conceptions of mental health that envision

1. Margaret Fuller, Fuller Manuscripts and Works, 3:85, 77, 79, bMS Am 1080, Houghton Library, Harvard University. The journal entry in the epigraph is cited from 3:87.

some vital fluid being developed and stored and notions of creativity that assert the centrality of "thoughts or mind-emotions" to a utilitarian culture. In a period that witnessed significant advances in an understanding of the physiology and psychology of "mind," Fuller becomes an emblematic figure, one whose self-conception and critical perception signal a common foundation in the era's notions of psychological states. Understanding in deeper ways the evolving terms of Fuller's critical lens, then, invites a closer look at the era's reporting on (and her application of) the conceptual implications of vital fluid and the somnambulant state.

In Margaret Fuller's private and public writings of the 1830s and early 1840s, we can discern illuminating though fragmentary efforts to understand the nature of the "true laws" of the human soul. In part, a distinctive aspect of her precociousness was this intensive questioning into the soul and its harmonies. Writing in 1840 of a mystical experience she had had in 1831, when she was twenty-one, Fuller articulates the questions and inward probing that would lead to an intensive examination of her own life and the life of others called by the divine:

> I remembered how, a little child, I had stopped myself one day on the stairs, and asked, how came I here? How is it that I seem to be this Margaret Fuller? What does it mean? What shall I do about it? I remembered all the times and ways in which the same thought had returned. I saw how long it must be before the soul can learn to act under these limitations of time and space, and human nature; but I say, also, that it MUST do it,—that it must make all this false true,—and sow new and immortal plants in the garden of God, before it could return again. I saw there was no self; that selfishness was all folly, and the result of circumstance; that it was only because I thought self real that I suffered; that I had only to live in the idea of the ALL, and all was mine.[2]

It is suggestive and perhaps not inaccurate to see Fuller's writing of the 1830s as a manifestation of her apprenticeship to the soul, as evidence of her effort to understand and apply the laws of the soul to

2. Margaret Fuller, "[Mystical Experience at Age 21]," *The Essential Margaret Fuller,* ed. Jeffrey Steele, 11.

her life and criticism. Not surprisingly, given the juxtaposition of Amariah Brigham's warnings of overstimulating the intellect along-side the mesmeric literature on the capacity of the mind to achieve higher states of consciousness, her investigations reveal the language of the era's "soul sciences." In the notion of vital fluid, in speculation on the affinity between laws of electricity and the nervous system, and in the study of the somnambulant state, she found a merging of the material and the immaterial.

Fuller's understanding of the mind as a reservoir of vital fluid resonates with literature of the period that articulates a belief in the magnetic and electrical nature of mental activity. During his lectures on animal magnetism in 1829, Joseph Du Commun speculates on the relationship between sleep, fluid, and vital energy: "During sleep, atmospheric air is inhaled into the lungs, caloric (which, in the Mesmerian language, may as well be called universal fluid) is disengaged, animalised, and from thence carried to and accumulated in the brain, where it receives from us the name of vital fluid. The anatomy of the brain, according to Dr. Gall's system, shows that, being a series of lamina folded on each other, it is very proper for this accumulation, as if in an electrical reservoir."[3] For Du Commun, inducing a magnetic or healing state depended upon the doctor's ability to direct his or her vital fluid to another person. It is logical to conclude that the quantity of and ability to store such fluid—coupled with a strong will to direct it—could lead to the most significant effects.

With the widespread coverage of somnambulist Jane C. Rider starting in the latter months of 1833 and continuing through 1834, we see a case study in the "electric" potential of the human mind. In *An Account of Jane C. Rider, the Springfield Somnambulist,*[4] Dr. Lemuel W. Belden offers one of the first books on the phenomenon published in the United States. Revised and reprinted in the September 10, 1834, *Boston Medical and Surgical Journal,* the work offers an extensive description of Rider's unusual ability, while in the somnambulistic state, to perform complex domestic tasks in the dark, recall

3. Joseph Du Commun, *Three Lectures on Animal Magnetism,* 24–25.

4. The full title of Belden's text indicates the initial forum within which he presented his account: *An Account of Jane C. Rider, the Springfield Somnambulist: The Substance of Which Was Delivered as a Lecture before the Springfield Lyceum, Jan. 22, 1834.*

and recite long-forgotten poetry, and, seemingly, read without light. Belden's initial description of the eighteen-year-old Rider sounds strikingly like Fuller's own private reflections: "She, however, has always been subject to frequent headaches, and other symptoms arising from an undue determination of blood to the head," and, in her childhood, "occasionally arose and walked about in her sleep."[5] The family with whom Rider resided as a domestic witnessed her agitated states, including a time when she imagined that she was in her father's house in Brattleborough, Vermont, rather than in Springfield, Massachusetts. During a second "paroxysm," Belden observed his patient making preparations for breakfast, preparations that required Rider to negotiate numerous obstacles in the dark, skim milk in a dimly lit pantry without spilling a drop, and slice bread as delicately as if she were awake. To the best judgment of Belden and others, she performed all the tasks with her eyes closed. By the winter of 1833–1834, word of Rider's inexplicable powers spread from regional newspapers to Boston medical journals.

Interestingly, Rider's especial gift seemed to be her enhanced sensitivity and quickness of perception. "Were I to select a single trait which more than any other distinguished these paroxysms, and which in fact unlocks the mystery of the whole," notes Belden, "it would be the astonishing quickness, vividness and distinctness of her perceptions." On the basis of his observations, he asserts that Rider's remarks displayed a higher "degree of brilliancy and wit." Moreover, while reading poetry, her "tones and inflexions" were "more just and better adapted to express the sentiments of the author."[6] In the end, however, Belden was unwilling to attribute these qualities or her apparent clairvoyance (that is, her seeming ability to read without the use of her eyes) to the phenomenon of animal magnetism.

The report of Rider's case in the reputable forum of the *Boston Medical and Surgical Journal* marked the start of extensive public speculation concerning somnambulism, animal magnetism, electromagnetism, and more.[7] Moreover, the question not fully articulated by Belden finds expression in ensuing reports. In "Case of

5. Belden, "An Account of Jane C. Rider, the Springfield Somnambulist," *Boston Medical and Surgical Journal,* 54.

6. Ibid., 60.

7. The *Boston Medical and Surgical Journal* provides an excellent example of the proliferation of speculation on animal magnetism initiated by Rider's case.

Somnambulism" (November 1834), Dr. Joseph H. Barnard asks, "How far is the pathological state of these somnambulists analogous to the state of the system said to be produced by animal magnetism?" He continues, "The magnetists pretend to produce the same state of clairvoyance, in which their subjects see with their eyes closed, through opaque bodies and even behind the head."[8] The transition from a consideration of clairvoyance to one of magnetic or electric states, then, seems the logical next step in a time when the motion of fluid or electric charges offered an explanation for the movement of thought between distant bodies.

In "Medical Philosophisings: Remarks on the Senses, Somnambulism, and Phrenology" (March 1835), the unnamed author begins with the kind of claims that often marked the early fascination with the somnambulistic state: "The mind, soul, or immaterial essence of man, is sometimes endowed with powers which ordinarily it does not possess, that seem to be deviations from the common course of things, and unsusceptible of a satisfactory explanation." Moving beyond the purely empirical evidence that Belden took great care to delineate, the writer characterizes somnambulists such as Rider in ways that call to mind descriptions of the imaginative faculty and the peculiar qualities of genius often attributed to writers and thinkers of the period:

> . . . there *may* be persons so circumstanced as to possess other inlets to the soul, other faculties, or other senses, besides those generally assigned us, without this envelope being removed or taken away, as was the case with the person before referred to. Whether they are endowed with this new faculty by the connection between the body and soul being in part dissolved, or from something being in reality bestowed upon them, which others do not possess, matters not in regard to the principle of the thing.

Later, alluding to phrenologists' assertions that certain regions of the brain (evidenced by the shape of the cranium) reflect specific

---

For a full listing of articles within the *Boston Medical and Surgical Journal*—as well as work in other medical and literary journals—that directly or indirectly address animal magnetism, see the bibliography under Journal Sources on Mesmerism/Animal Magnetism.

8. Joseph H. Barnard, M.D., "Case of Somnambulism," *Boston Medical and Surgical Journal,* 204.

faculties, the author concludes that men "endowed with superior endowments in any art or science, have that particular compartment of the brain assigned to such art or science a little larger than others. Those vestiges, or embryo rudiments of new faculties, are more perfectly developed, and furnished with a more abundant supply of the nervous secretion than is common in ordinary cases."[9]

We can further understand the era's urge to spiritualize the material in a gloss of one of the published documents that, for a time, centered the national dialogue on animal magnetism: William L. Stone's *Letter to Doctor A[mariah]. Brigham, on Animal Magnetism: Being an Account of a Remarkable Interview between the Author and Miss Loraina Brackett While in a State of Somnambulism* (1837). Given the apparent position of Dr. Brigham as a "materialist" in his sensibilities and medical practice, the book offers another representation of the period's effort to understand the implications of magnetic forces for a resisting "practical" world, or materialist vision. In this instance, Stone's record of Brackett's ability to see objects at a distance provides evidence of individuals who, when embodying a nervous susceptibility, seem capable of harnessing magnetic forces. Stone frames his own reflections as a response to an actual letter from the renowned physician. In fact, Brigham's epistle to Stone forms the "preface" to Stone's account of his interaction with Loraina Brackett. In a letter dated September 1, 1837, Brigham writes that he has heard of Stone's experiments and is eager to find out what changed his reader from a skeptic to a believer. Expressing views that echo Fuller's private characterization of his beliefs, Brigham notes that the "remarkable effects [of animal magnetism] may result from extreme sensibility, or disease of the nervous system." He continues:

> In every age great moral commotions, by affecting the organization of some very sensitive persons, have produced very singular physical and intellectual phenomena. The *Trembleurs des Cevennes,* and the *Convulsionnaires de Saint Médard,* are memorable instances. Many of the results attributed to Animal Magnetism may be accounted for, by supposing an unusual augmentation of sensibility,—but other phenomena ascribed to it cannot be thus explained, and an *immensity of proof* appears to me to be necessary,

9. "Medical Philosophisings: Remarks on the Senses, Somnambulism, and Phrenology," *Boston Medical and Surgical Journal,* 58, 59, 62.

in order to establish things so extraordinary, and so contrary to the common sense and to the testimony of all times.[10]

The reflections here recall observations on animal magnetism that Fuller had read more than three years earlier in Brigham's *Remarks on the Influence of Mental Cultivation upon Health*. Speaking of unusual cases of enhanced memory, Brigham briefly considers how somnambulant patients have been able to recall events and things long forgotten. "During the state of 'extase,' caused by *magnetism*," he observes, "the memory has been often surprisingly perfected." Significantly, a physical change often marks such a state: "This state was always accompanied by symptoms that showed an increased determination of blood to the head. All had slight convulsions, the face became red, the eyes bright, and after a while humid." In his footnote to these observations, Brigham lists a number of "interesting accounts," including those of Cevennes and Saint Médard. "Like effects," he adds in the next paragraph, "are produced by disease."[11] That Fuller had considered herself a somnambulist and confessed in her journal that especially disturbing dreams were "succeeded by a determination of blood to the head" again underscores important resonances between increased mental cultivation or activity, a natural precocity or genius, and magnetic forces.

Interestingly, the friendly invitation of a skeptic to provide evidence that defies "common sense" and the "testimony of all times" establishes a distance that Stone himself maintains even as he narrates phenomena that defy the laws of time and space. This in-between stance—what Stone describes as no longer a "position of a positive skeptic" but a "dead pause" of not knowing what to believe—constitutes a common response. It is in this state of wonder, however, that Stone, Fuller, and many other readers or witnesses of magnetic incidents offered the speculation that shaped conceptions of how special individuals harness and transfer to others a higher level of perception and/or a kind of knowing that defies the limits of time and space.

10. William L. Stone, *Letter to Doctor A. Brigham, on Animal Magnetism*, 3–4.

11. Amariah Brigham, *Remarks on the Influence of Mental Cultivation upon Health*, 35–36. Interestingly, the second edition of Brigham's book added "and Mental Excitement" after "Mental Cultivation" in the title to call attention to the culture's concern with overtaxing children.

In the particular case of Brackett, her special sensitivity to unseen magnetic forces induced a state that allowed her to view things from a distance. Once magnetized by Dr. George Capron and having established a one-to-one rapport with Stone, she transferred herself from Providence to Stone's home in New York. Especially striking was her ability to "see" pictures within Stone's home, paintings of which she and others had no prior knowledge. (After a head injury, Brackett had impaired vision.) While unwilling to describe the subject of the paintings to Stone himself (as was apparently typical during her trances), she later told Capron what she saw:

> "Did you notice particularly any other pictures? Mr. Stone told me he had several in his library, upon which he set a high value. Did you see them?"
> "Yes."
> "What were they?"
> Here she again became affected, as she replied—"One of them was Christ in his agony, with a Crown of Thorns!"
> This reply was astounding. The picture is an admirable copy of the *Ecce Homo* by Guido. It had only been sent home a week before, and I had cautiously avoided mentioning it to my most intimate friends present at this extraordinary interview, until she thus proclaimed it.

Though Brackett was not always accurate in her replies, her inexplicable ability to describe what could not have been known through the five senses led Stone to a range of questions. Quoting Henry Cogswell Knight's *Sybilline Leaves and Wayward Criticisms* (1825), Stone invites readers to reconsider their skepticism: "How common . . . when we have just spoken and thought of a person, to see him immediately afterward. If it be even more than casualty [*sic*], is it unphilosophical to suppose that there may be a certain attractive, although invisible emanation, not unlike that of the magnetic, electric, gravid, or cohesive influence; each emanation being peculiar to, and characteristic of, each individual, coming from the body into the air, which prompts the forethought?" Given his experience with Brackett, Stone himself asks, "Why deny to the soul the faculty of recognizing external objects through unusual ways, without the help of the senses, and of annihilating time and space in its movements?" Again, while he refuses to call himself a believer, he admits to a greater openness to the truths of immaterial philosophers.[12]

In both private and public discourse, Fuller and her contemporaries endeavored to assimilate findings associated with the scientific and philosophical investigation that the peculiar state of somnambulism initiated. Given her own health history as well as her literary aspirations, it is not surprising that the cultural dialogue engaged Fuller intellectually and that some of her first published criticism attempted to discern between lives and works that manifest a transforming vitality and those that may show promise but fail to electrify. With "The Life of Sir James Mackintosh" in the *American Monthly Magazine*, she offers a narrative of squandered treasures and broken threads—or, from a medical-literary perspective, a biography of diminished vitality and halting will. In tracing definitive features of an individual always poised for greater things, the scrutinizing but sympathetic eye of Fuller detects the outlines of the true poet/artist through a life representative in its ill health.

And what does Fuller most critique in one whose "natural vocation" is "for literature and philosophy"? Particularly lamentable to her is his inability to give direction or force to his inward power, his proclivity to leave buried that which breathes of the divine. At one point, after observing Mackintosh's decision to go to India rather than enter Parliament, Fuller suggests that he was to act from that point onward with a "divided soul" and that "his life could be nothing better than a fragment." This sense of division may reflect a self-critique as well, since Fuller confessed in her journal that "my faculties have always been rather intensely in action and produced no harmonious result."[13] Praising that class of men "who suggest thoughts and plans" over "those who develop and fit for use those already suggested," Fuller concludes that Sir James Mackintosh did not belong to either class: "Much he learned—thought much—collected much treasure; but the greater part of it was buried with him." Echoing later criticism by those she read and/or befriended (including Coleridge and Emerson), her reflections on the life of Mackintosh indirectly lead to telling glimpses of representative

12. Stone, *Letter to Doctor A. Brigham*, 43, 59–60.
13. Fuller, Fuller Manuscripts and Works, 3:81, bMS Am 1080.

features of the true artist. Such a class of individuals includes "intellects of the higher order, gifted with a rapidity and fertility of conception too great to be wholly brought out in the compass of a short human life." In their genius, Fuller reminds us, we mine an ore of greater value; to them, we assign the designation "visionaries" or "Demigods of literature and science." While tempered with a deeper gloom, the men of genius also experience a richer happiness: "For theirs are hours of 'deep and uncommunicable joy,' hours when the oracle within boldly predicts the time when that which is divine in them, and which they now to all appearance are breathing out in vain, shall become needful as vital air to myriads of immortal spirits." It would appear, then, that the true genius offers a kind of cleansing and replenishing breath. From within exudes a vital and transformative air.[14]

Later, when considering the peculiar power of conversation, the article describes "eloquent talkers" in terms of a special sensitivity and receptivity that often characterized the unique powers of a somnambulist as well as the rapport between medium and magnetist:

> The ready tact to apprehend the mood of your companions and their capacity for receiving what you can bestow, the skill to touch upon a variety of subjects with that lightness, grace, and rapidity, which constantly excite and never exhaust the attention, the love for sparkling sallies, the playfulness and variety which make a man brilliant and attractive in conversation, are the reverse of the love of method, the earnestness of concentration, and the onward march of thought, which are required by the higher kinds of writing.

Moreover, Fuller sees in the method of certain kinds of writing a dryness, "a languid way of transmitting thought to one accustomed to the electric excitement of personal intercourse." The point, of course, is not to dismiss the force of writing in favor of the dynamic quality of conversation, for the article notes that "[e]very kind of power is admirable, and indefinitely useful." Rather, the lesson is in the recognition and embracing of one's special gifts; the power is manifest in the action that ensues. And, of course, Fuller's use of the term *electric* gestures toward studies on the nervous system and

14. Margaret Fuller, "The Life of Sir James Mackintosh," 574.

texts on animal magnetism that, since Mesmer, had spoken of the vital fluid as having electric properties.[15]

Within this first published critical essay, however, Fuller still seems to be searching for the terms within which to understand Mackintosh's failings—which, while the article underscores his youthful precocity, critical astuteness, and fairness of mind, so preoccupies her. It is revealing that she finds such terms in medicine and psychology. Asserting that much "has been well-written and much ill-spoken to prove that minds of great native energy will help themselves, that the best attainments are made from inward impulse, and that outward discipline is likely to impair both grace and strength," she still acknowledges that, allowed to take its own course, the mind "is apt to fix too exclusively on a pursuit or set of pursuits to which it will devote itself till there is not strength for others." In effect, a key concern is that of the interplay between the physiological limitations of the brain, the formative nature of the inward impulse, and the constructive effects of outward discipline. At least in the case of Mackintosh, Fuller argues, his innate genius did not generate sufficient structure or discipline to foster a sustained productivity. And yet, intriguingly, Fuller's description of Mackintosh as one who "never had power to electrify at will a large body of men" because "he had not stored up within the dangerous materials for the 'lightning of the mind'" also implies a failure that points to something other than a "want of systemic training in early life." That is, it calls to mind Fuller's and the era's efforts to discern the material and immaterial explanations of electric or magnetic forces.[16]

It would appear, then, that medical findings of the period led to debate over the nature of intellectual precocity and the best way to

15. Ibid., 578. In the July 5, 1831, issue of the *Boston Medical and Surgical Journal,* the editors reprinted an extract from Dr. David's Inaugural Thesis entitled "Identity of the Nervous Fluid and Electric Fluids." Long struck by the "numerous analogies which had been detected between the phenomena of electricity and the nervous power," David had conducted a number of experiments on chickens and rabbits confirming that the nerves "transmitted an electric current" ("Identity of the Nervous Fluid and Electric Fluids," 336, 337). Mary Shelley's *Frankenstein; or, the Modern Prometheus,* first published in 1818, further reveals that the interest in galvanic forces and electricity had become well known to more than scientists and physicians by the first decades of the nineteenth century.

16. Fuller, "The Life of Sir James Mackintosh," 575, 573, 575.

nurture its qualities. In a section of his book entitled "Consequences which have resulted from inattention to the connexion between the mind and Body," Brigham offers his perspective on these issues: "The early history of the most distinguished men will I believe lead us to the conclusion, that early mental culture is not necessary, in order to produce the highest powers of the mind. . . . On the contrary, it often appears, that those who are kept from school by ill health or some other cause in early life, and left to follow their own inclination as respects study, manifest in after life powers of mind which make them the admiration of the world." For Brigham, the early period of life should allow for the predominance of the nervous system, for it is "the source of all vital movement, and presides over, and gives energy to those actions which tend to the growth of the organization"; in infancy and childhood, a disproportionate taxing of the nervous system may ultimately lead to derangement or death. According to him, a youthful precocity arising from the mental excitement and an "unnatural flow of blood to the head" and thus an enlargement of portions of the brain is the symptom of a disease, not the sign of especial powers.[17] To a woman who embraced the Transcendentalist belief that the soul cannot be checked and that the only sin is limitation, medical arguments of some organizational impediment to the divine would be problematic or would, at the very least, check an overly optimistic view of the expansive soul. Ultimately, while understanding on a personal level the ill effects of youthful mental excitement, Fuller seemed drawn to the argument presented within the mesmeric literature that the mind has the capacity to achieve seemingly limitless states of consciousness, states of perception that resist the organic limits of the brain and the material constraints imposed by time and space.

Clearly, as Charles Capper has underscored in *Margaret Fuller: An American Romantic Life,* Fuller found in Mackintosh "more than a little of herself." In assessing Mackintosh's exceptional promise early in the essay, she maintains: "For precocity some great price is always demanded sooner or later in life. Nature intended the year of childhood to be spent in perceiving and playing, not in reflecting and acting; and when her processes are hurried or disturbed, she is

17. Brigham, *Remarks on the Influence of Mental Cultivation upon Health,* 54–55, 30, 31.

sure to exact a penalty."[18] It is possible, however, to see Fuller's critical examination of his life as a more "objective" study into the nature of "mental cultivation" and the "effects of mental excitement upon health." Of course, to consider how better to marshal or cultivate people's mental culture is inevitably to explore how to construct more effectively the culture of one's own life. If these speculations led Fuller to reject "Amariah's" deterministic fiat against overtaxing the brain's limited capacities (or to question the materialist orientation of his views) and to embrace the liberating possibility of her own inward impulses and energies, then she might well have asked how she must attend to the inherent potential of this inward electricity. To what extent might personal and cultural reform be informed by theories concerning the nature of the mind and the effect of immaterial forces in the material world? Given the apparent determinism of hereditary endowments and the seeming receptivity to (and potential to store) magnetic fluid, it is no wonder that Fuller felt compelled to examine the nature of this electric or magnetic agent. More specifically, it is not surprising that peculiar properties of a *fluid* agent or a nonmaterial force caught Fuller's eye, for such a force indicated both receptivity and conductivity and thus suggested a framework within which to develop an understanding of literary genius.

Fuller's interest in the studies of Brigham, Stone, and others must have informed her thinking of and preparation for her role as a teacher as well as her conception of her particular effect on students. As a teacher, she would have been concerned with how best to cultivate the intellectual and moral life of her students. Texts exploring the effects of "mental excitement," then, would have been of special interest. In a letter to good friend James Freeman Clarke on April 28, 1835, she writes of her "magnetic power over young women." In fact, others also applied the term *magnetic* to Fuller's presence. In describing one of her characteristic physical traits, poet William Henry Channing provides an especially suggestive portrayal, one

18. Charles Capper, *Margaret Fuller: An American Romantic Life; The Private Years,* 176; Fuller, "The Life of Sir James Mackintosh," 572. Drawing attention to her own precocity in the same journal entry as her assessment of Brigham's book, Fuller confesses, "I am confident I should have been much superior to my present self had sense, intellect, affection, passion been brought out in the natural order" (Fuller Manuscripts and Works, 3:82–83, bMS Am 1080).

that seems to see Fuller as a medium: "The first [physical trait] was a contraction of the eyelids almost to a point,—a trick caught from near-sightedness,—and then a sudden dilation, till the iris seemed to emit flashes;—an effect, no doubt, dependent on her highly-magnetized condition."[19]

As Fuller turned from Mackintosh to the German and British Romantics in her ensuing series of *American Monthly Magazine* articles during the summer of 1836, we see efforts to integrate the discourse on mental health and magnetism within her criticism on the peculiar qualities of literary genius. Thus, the recurring motif of the magnetic or electric suggests that Fuller understood people of healthy mental culture in terms that underscore the important relationship between material and spiritual endowments. In the words of the anonymous author of "Medical Philosophisings," she seemed to gravitate toward writers "so circumstanced as to possess other inlets to the soul, other faculties, or other senses, besides those generally assigned us" and who appeared "endowed with this new faculty by the connection between the body and soul being in part dissolved, or from something being in reality bestowed upon them."[20] Those most capable of reforming "tired" ideas, Fuller seems to assert, have the capacity to store and draw from a reservoir of vital powers.

It is revealing to read the early part of Fuller's "Present State of German Literature" (July 1836) as a diagnosis of the ills that weaken the nation. To Fuller, her era's growing interest in German writers is both a symptom and a cure. It unveils and seeks to address the nation's utilitarian impulse, that is, "in its lowest sense—a vulgar, sordid, eating, and drinking utility." Of course, such a prognosis is not unusual for artists of the period, nor is the notion that "there are internal improvements of another sort very proper to immortal beings." Considering the cultural pressure to engage in *practical* enterprises, Fuller continues: "No word is so frequently used as this in our somewhat prosaic state of society, and yet, though so confidently, often mistakingly used. Not practical! Is nothing practical that has no immediate effect upon matter? Is no man practical who cannot with the quickness of a conjurer convert his thoughts into pounds, shillings, and pence? Whatever has its birth in the uncorrupted human

19. Fuller's self-description and Channing's characterization are quoted in Capper, *Margaret Fuller,* 190, 266. For a thorough examination of Fuller's teaching experiences, see Capper, 190–251.

20. "Medical Philosophisings," *Boston Medical and Surgical Journal,* 59.

soul, is and must ever be practical." In constructing her argument, Fuller moves from the mechanistic and material language of railroads and rust to the natural images of flowers and gardening:

> We are not merely springs and wheels, which, when put in certain places and kept oiled, will undoubtedly . . . do their work and fulfil their destination. No! In each one of us there is a separate principle of vitality, which must be fostered if we would be as trees in the public garden, rich in leaves, blossoms, and perfumed fruit, rather than as dry boards in the public ship-yard, fit only to be hewn, used, and when grown old left to return in rottenness to their native dust.

For Fuller, then, German literature offered a sufficient dosage of "idealism" to balance the utilitarianism of American life and thus provide remedies for a too-material diet. As demonstrated in her descriptions of Madame de Staël and Goethe, however, the most promising therapy is magnetic rather than homeopathic; the national and individual malaise calls for the magnetist, not the apothecary. Echoing Heine's image of Staël, Fuller too sees one whose work includes "meteoric flashes" that "illuminate the firmament of thought." Even more revealing in the context of Fuller's understanding of the body and magnetic states is her assessment that Staël's "lightnings have electrified many minds which would otherwise have remained for ever untouched by the divine fires from whose sources she drew." The predisposition for this kind of "magnetic" critical vocabulary emerges even more directly in a closing panegyric of Goethe:

> When we hear voices telling us to wit, that they think, as far as they can judge from slight acquaintance with his works, Goëthe has been absurdly over-rated and vainly adored, our first impulse is to say that those shrill disapproving notes must proceed from the depths of ignorance or the shallows of mediocrity, and to rank them with those whom the Germans call Philistines, made by nature non-conductors to the electricity of genius, and who do not recognize her unless she comes in some form they have been early drilled to respect.

That Fuller sees individuals as "by nature non-conductors to the electricity of genius"—or, as in the case of Goethe, as natural conductors

of this harmonizing force—encourages readers to consider both the
physical and metaphysical dimensions of creative powers. If the
terms *practical* and *property* demand a spiritualizing redefinition,
then so too might the literary abstractions of "genius" and "effect"
require a material understanding.[21]

If Fuller was inclined to entertain ideas that fell beyond the limited premises of Amariah Brigham, her acceptance of a teaching position at the Greene Street School in Providence, the home of Loraina
Brackett and a thriving center of mesmeric activity, ushered her
into an intellectual climate that offered a more complete education
in the immaterial philosophy of animal magnetism during her mat-
uration as a literary critic. Arriving in Providence in the same month
as Brigham's letter to Stone, September 1837, she soon visited the
well-known Brackett herself. As her good friend James Freeman
Clarke notes in his journal, Dr. Capron induced the magnetic state
and then, as with Stone, Brackett "was put in communication with
S. M. F." According to Clarke, the somnambulist "discovered the point
in [Fuller's] head where she suffered from violent pain, and after
some rubbing this pain was relieved."[22] Apparently responding to
Caroline Sturgis's desire to hear more about the new science from
her mentor, Fuller presents a brusque and less enthusiastic rendering of the experience:

>—I cannot tell you now the little I know about Magtism [*sic*], or
>any thing else that requires detail. I am tired and busy; besides I
>shall soon see you and be able to communicate in a less laborious
>manner—
>   The blind girl said my head would never be better while I read
>so much.—She has almost entirely lost the gift of clairvoyance (if
>she ever possessed it,) and is good for nothing.[23]

21. Margaret Fuller, "Present State of German Literature," 2, 3, 5, 11.
22. Clarke is quoted in Margaret Fuller, *The Letters of Margaret Fuller,* ed. Robert N. Hudspeth, 1:306.
23. Ibid., 313. It is likely that the context of the letter leads to the particular
way in which Fuller depicts the meeting with Brackett. The epistle to "My dear
Cary" addresses Sturgis's desire to visit Providence, but, according to Fuller, her
correspondent is "somewhat inconsistent." "In two of her letters," she continues, "she has said that she wished to come if only for a fortnight, in two others,
that she did not wish to come at all, if only for a fortnight." The terseness of the

Evidence from her Providence years, however, does not fully support this offhanded dismissal of Brackett's powers. It is likely, in fact, that Sturgis asked about animal magnetism because Fuller herself had invited the question. Writing her protégé in October 1837, Fuller ends her letter with the lament "I wish I had room to tell you about some of my late experiences[:] Deleuze's history of Prevision—six sermons from James Clarke—W. Simmons's recitation and what I thought. Russell's songs and what I thought, my visit to the blind somnambulist her pity for my head and what she said and what I thought but here is no room for any thing except ys afftly S.M.F."[24]

That Fuller's reading included Joseph Philippe François Deleuze's text suggests that she knew of the definitive books on the subject or, perhaps, that she received some guidance from members of an intellectual community leading the nation in the study of the mesmeric arts. In addition to his *Histoire critique du magnétisme animal* (*Critical History of Animal Magnetism,* first published in 1813), Fuller also read Deleuze's *Instruction pratique sur le magnétisme animal* (*Practical Instruction in Animal Magnetism,* first published in 1825 and translated by Providence's Thomas Hartshorn for an 1837 republication).[25] In their extensive examination of the theory and practice of animal magnetism and their emphasis on a doctor's benevolence toward a patient, both texts, and especially the Hartshorn translation of *Practical Instruction,* offered authoritative studies that widely influenced those learning of the science. Of particular interest to Fuller as well as a community inundated with the wonders of Rider and Brackett would have been the section "Of Somnambulism, and the use to be made of it," in *Practical Instruction.* For Deleuze, certain somnambulists manifested what he considered "very different phenomena; and the only distinctive and constant character of somnambulism is, the existence of a new mode of perception." Later, he would explain further:

---

closing comments on Brackett, then, resonates with the tone toward Sturgis's indecisiveness concerning her visit. For a discussion of the relationship between Sturgis and Fuller, see Capper, *Margaret Fuller,* 225–27.

24. Fuller, *Letters of Margaret Fuller,* 1:304–5.

25. One of Fuller's journal entries includes extracts from Deleuze's *Critical History of Animal Magnetism.* See Fuller, Fuller Manuscripts and Works, 4:669–89, bMS Am 1080.

> Sometimes the prodigious difference [the somnambulist] perceives
> between his new manner of viewing objects and that which he had
> in his ordinary state, the new lights which shine for him, the new
> faculties with which he finds himself endowed, the immensity of
> the horizon which is spread before his eyes, persuade him that he
> is inspired; what he says seems to him dictated by a voice from
> within. . . .[26]

That the language of Hartshorn's translation so closely echoes the Transcendentalist emphasis on the "God within" is telling. In her investigation of inspired lives and of special conditions that offered the possibility of "new modes of perception," Fuller again found compelling evidence for a kind of spiritual materialism. Through the employment of long-practiced methods in the art of inducing a somnambulistic state and through some understanding of the seemingly magnetic properties of the universal fluid, it appeared possible to defy the constraints of space and time and, in this lucid state, to communicate facts and transcendent truths attributed to visionaries or inspired poets.

Given the extent to which Providence became a center for discussion and demonstration of animal magnetism, it is possible that Fuller's thinking on the relationship of the new science to her earlier reflections on the "conductive" genius of Goethe and select British poets further developed as a result of conversation with fellow teachers. In fact, Hiram Fuller, the man who hired her to come from Boston to Providence to teach in the summer of 1837, had submitted his own rendering of an evening with well-known somnambulist Cynthia Gleason to the *Providence Journal* on November 24, 1836. In association with Charles Poyen, a Frenchman who wrote *Progress of Animal Magnetism in New England* (1837), Gleason gained a reputation as a clairvoyant.[27] In his description, Hiram Fuller raises compelling questions:

> Standing before that senseless body—that faintly-breathing, half-
> living corpse, I questioned more deeply within myself, than ever

26. Joseph Philippe François Deleuze, *Practical Instruction in Animal Magnetism,* trans. Thomas C. Hartshorn, 91, 93–94.

27. Poyen also participated in the national debate over the phenomena first reported in William L. Stone's *Letter to Doctor A. Brigham, on Animal Magnetism.* See Poyen, *A Letter to Col. Wm. L. Stone, of New York, on the Facts Related in His Letter to Dr. Brigham. . . .*

before, what is the human soul? And what are the true laws of its action and existence? Alas! there was no responsive philosophy, which, at such a moment, could satisfactorily explain the momentous problem. But I feel, and there was consolation in this feeling, for the aching want of true wisdom and soul-science, that God and eternity are the only answer to these mysterious phenomena—these apparitions of the Infinite and the Unknown.[28]

If Margaret Fuller did not herself read the letter (later published in Poyen's book within the chapter "Miss Cynthia Ann Gleason") or join her fellow teacher in dialogue over the "soul-science" of animal magnetism, she certainly would have been aware of his beliefs and engaged in her own way with a phenomenon that was absorbing the city.

That Fuller voices some skepticism in relation to Brackett and the study of animal magnetism docs not mean a wholesale rejection of what her experience and readings revealed to her. For, as she notes as a prelude to recorded excerpts from Deleuze's book on prevision in her private journal, "In the argument of this book there is not much force, but it is pleasing from the mildness of tone & real love of truth obvious in it."[29] Clearly, as her continued investigation in and involvement with animal magnetism in the 1840s demonstrates, she saw in mesmeric or magnetic "principles" a manifestation of laws of the soul that embodied the truths of her own experience. Significantly, however, these principles guided more than an understanding of her own genius; they informed and shaped concepts of special importance to a maturing literary theory and practice.

28. Quoted in Charles Poyen, *Progress of Animal Magnetism in New England,* 136–37.
29. Fuller, Fuller Manuscripts and Works, 5:669, bMS Am 1080.

5 . . . .

Transition States

All this conflict and apparently bootless fretting and wailing mark a transition state—a state of gradual revolution, in which men try all things, seeking what they hold fast, and feel that it is good. But there are some, the pilot-minds of the age, who cannot submit to pass all their lives in experimentalizing. They cannot consent to drift across the waves in the hope of finding *somewhere* a haven and a home; but, seeing the blue sky over them, and believing that God's love is every where, try to make the best of that spot on which they have been placed, and, not unfrequently, by the aid of spiritual assistance, more benign than that of Faust's Lemures, win from the raging billows large territories, whose sands they can convert into Eden bowers, tenanted by lovely and majestic shapes.

Margaret Fuller, "Modern British Poets"

IN HER SECOND AND LAST installment of "Modern British Poets" included in the *American Monthly Magazine,* Margaret Fuller begins an essay in praise of Southey, Coleridge, and Wordsworth by noting great poets of earlier days who "addressed themselves more to passions or heart-emotions of their fellow-men than to their thoughts or mind-emotions." But in the current era of Faust and Manfred, she exclaims, how different the sensibility, how different the poetic impulse and outcome. Desiring individuality within a complex society and thus amid the need for combined efforts to regulate the populace, the new self strives to reconcile the tension between a passion "to make its own world independent of trivial daily circumstances" and that "grand maxim of the day, *the greatest happiness of the greatest number.*" In such an era, Fuller argues, the "mind struggles long, before it can resolve on sacrificing any thing of its impulsive nature to the requisitions of the time." Of importance in her conception of this transitional period is the poet who can mediate the line between the temporal and eternal, represent "in letters of fire" that which lies beyond our earthly existence, and capture "the voice of Nature and God, humanized by being echoed back from the understanding hearts of Priests and Seers!" Of the three poets that form the subject of her essay, she identifies Coleridge as her ideal bard. Though less prolific, he is "far more suggestive, more filled with the divine magnetism of intuition, than [Southey and Wordsworth]." Later she asserts, "There is nothing of the spectator about Coleridge; he is all life; not impassioned, not vehement, but searching, intellectual life, which seems 'listening through the frame' to its own pulses."[1] Through the fires of such inner and outer struggle, then, pilot-minds like Coleridge create the poetry of the day, a poetry of mourning and lamentation that betrays the signs of a transition state.

Fuller admonishes the Emersonian Self-Poise in *Summer on the Lakes* (1843), characterizing "apprehensive genius" in terms that call to mind her praise of Coleridge. In the resonance between Coleridge's "divine magnetism of intuition," his apparent magnetic receptivity to the pulses of life, and this notion of an apprehensive state, we detect a reverberating chord in Fuller's literary and social melody. In fact, the chapter "Wisconsin" in *Summer on the Lakes* can be read as a response to a number of requests from friends, starting in her Providence years, to write of her knowledge of the new science of animal magnetism.[2] Though announcing that she will consider

1. Margaret Fuller, "Modern British Poets," *American Monthly Magazine* 8 (October 1836): 320, 321, 325. Fuller's analysis calls to mind Emerson's critique of poets and philosophers who speak "*from without,* as spectators merely, or perhaps as unacquainted with the fact, on the evidence of third persons" ("The Over-Soul," in *The Essays of Ralph Waldo Emerson,* 170).

2. In a November 1837 letter to Caroline Sturgis, Fuller had written, "I cannot tell you now the little I know about Magtism [*sic*], or any thing else that requires detail" (*Letters of Margaret Fuller,* 1:313). Urging Fuller to submit something for his *Western Messenger,* good friend James Freeman Clarke had also suggested she take up the topic of animal magnetism, but, as with her reply to Sturgis, she dismisses the possibility: "'Tis a subject in which I take no interest at present." For Clarke's letter, see *The Letters of James Freeman Clarke to Margaret Fuller,* ed. John Wesley Thomas, 126. Fuller is quoted in Capper, *Margaret Fuller,* 240. Both letters belie the fact that she had already read a good deal on the subject and demonstrated enough interest privately to elicit the requests from two intimate friends.

"one of the most remarkable cases of high nervous excitement" in an age with "all its phenomena of clairvoyance and susceptibility of magnetic influences," she delays her lengthy translation and review of Justinus Kerner's *Die Seherin von Prevorst (The Seeress of Prevorst)* (1829) in order to offer her views on wonders associated with animal magnetism: "As to my own mental position on these subjects it may be briefly expressed by a dialogue between several persons [*Old Church, Good Sense,* and *Self-Poise*] who honor me with a portion of friendly confidence and of criticism, and myself expressed as *Free Hope*."[3] Responding to Good Sense's advice to "be completely natural, before we trouble ourselves with the supernatural" (146), Old Church's call to avoid transgressing "certain boundaries" and thus "waste our powers" and unfit us to "obey positive precepts, and perform positive duties" (147), and Self-Poise's aphoristic summons to accept the truth that "[f]ar-sought is dearbought" (148), Free Hope concludes with her plea for a greater expansiveness of intellect and spirit:

> You, Self-Poise, fill a priestly office. Could but a larger intelligence of the vocations of others, and a tender sympathy with their individual natures be added, had you more of love, or more of apprehensive genius, (for either would give you the needed expansion and delicacy) you would command my entire reverence. As it is, I must at times deny and oppose you, and so must others, for you tend, by your influence, to exclude us from our full, free life. We must be content when you censure, and rejoiced when you approve; always admonished to good by your whole being, and sometimes by your judgment. And so I pass on to interest myself and others in the memoir of the Seherin von Prevorst. (149–50)

3. Fuller, *Summer on the Lakes,* in *The Essential Margaret Fuller,* ed. Jeffrey Steele, 145. All subsequent references to this work will be cited parenthetically in the text. In a review of Catherine Crowe's translation of Kerner's book in the July 23, 1847, *New-York Tribune,* Fuller acknowledges that she had been "familiar with the book in the original" (*Margaret Fuller, Critic: Writings from the New-York Tribune, 1844–1846,* CD-ROM, ed. Judith Mattson Bean and Joel Myerson, C163). In addition to reviewing *The Seeress of Prevorst, Being Revelations concerning the Inner-Life of Man, and the Inter-diffusion of a World of Spirits in the One We Inhabit* (1845), she also considered Gibson Smith's *Lectures on Clairmativeness; or, Human Magnetism* (1845). On her trip, Fuller would have read *Die Seherin von Prevorst. Eröffnungen über das innere Leben des Menschen und über das Hereinragen einer Geisterwelt in die Unsere.* It was first published in 1829; second and third editions appeared in 1832 and 1838.

In underscoring Self-Poise's need for a greater sympathy, Fuller calls for qualities that could better accommodate territories—exterior and interior—that were in fact expanding and in need of a more delicate sensibility. In the transition state of Wisconsin and within individuals in the throes of self-definition, much can be learned from the sensitive existence of the Seeress of Prevorst.

Margaret Fuller's conception of a "full, free life," then, reveals a maturing sense of the implications of animal magnetism to the life of the mind. First providing the vocabulary with which to assess and describe the peculiar genius of Sir James Mackintosh, Madame de Staël, Goethe, and Coleridge in her early critical essays, the descriptive and theoretical writings on the science soon offered a way to conceptualize the nature of a receptive consciousness. In this receptive, or apprehensive, state, individuals demonstrate a special capacity to negotiate both material existence and nonmaterial forces; they exist in the productive state of both/and, in the borderland of possibility. In effect, such mediums—whether they be poets, critics, or somnambulists—embody in artistic form and/or actions the fluid nature of the world, "this vital principle, principle of flux and influx, dynamic of our mental mechanics, human phase of electricity" (146). Within *Summer on the Lakes* and *Woman in the Nineteenth Century,* Fuller articulates a consistent vision of an apprehensive creative energy.

Evidence that Fuller had for some time envisioned individual and national reform in terms of "transition states" recurs prior to her travel narrative and feminist treatise. In a short piece on Meta, the wife of German poet Friedrich Gottlieb Klopstock (1724–1803), Fuller seems especially interested in envisioning Meta's insights in the space between life and death, between material and immaterial existence: "The delicious clearness of every feeling exalted my soul into an entire life. Some time elapsed thus. The whole of my earthly existence passed in review before me. My thought, my actions, were brought in full relief before the cleared eye of my spirit. . . . As I was striving to connect my present with my past state, and, as it were, poising myself on the brink of space and time, the breath of another presence came upon me, and gradually evolving from the bosom of light, rose a figure, in grace, in sweetness, how excelling!" In "Leila," Fuller considers an individual who seems more a "*fetiche*" and who appears to the "mere eye almost featureless." Hard to find and define in her night existence, she has a beauty on which "transitoriness has set its seal." Fuller adds: "Men watch these slender tapers which seem as if they would burn out next moment. They say that such purity is the seal of death. It is so; the condition of this ecstasy is, that it seems to die every moment, and even Leila has not force to die often; the electricity accumulates many days before the wild one comes, which leads to these sylph nights of tearful sweetness." Further imagining Leila in ways that resonate with Fuller's understanding of Goethe in terms of an electrical force and that anticipate her fascination with the Seeress of Prevorst, the sketch depicts this transitory figure as one who "beats with the universal heart, with no care except to circulate as the vital fluid." And, finally, in her review of various lectures available in the Boston area during the winter of 1842, Fuller applies her notion of transition states not to individuals on the border between life and death, material and spirit, but to the condition of New England:

> We must not then quarrel with the lecture, the only entertainment we have truly expressive of New England *as it is* in its transition state, cavilling, questioning, *beginning to seek,* all-knowing, if with little heart-knowledge, meaning to be just, and turning at last, though often with a sour face, to see all sides, for men of sense will see at last it is not of any use to nail the weathercock the pleasantest way; better to leave it free, and see the way the wind does blow, if it *will* be so foolish as to blow in an injudicious direction.[4]

In the chapter titled "Wisconsin" in *Summer on the Lakes,* however, Fuller presents a more extensive examination of the outer and inner landscapes that promise insights into the relationship between expansive energies and the magnetic life. After opening with a series of reflections on the new city of Milwaukee, Fuller goes on to devote two-thirds of the chapter to the life of somnambulist Frederica Hauffe, or the Seeress of Prevorst. Thus, while the book appears to announce itself as a travel narrative, it often digresses—as in this odd chapter—to matters that seem quite distant from experiences along the shores of the Great Lakes. For an audience well versed in

---

4. Fuller, "Meta," 295; "Leila," 462, 464; "Entertainments of the Past Winter," 50. In this last article, Fuller also offers a brief notice of Vincenzo Bellini's opera *La Somnambula* (*The Somnambulist*).

the popular form of the travel narrative, then, the "Wisconsin" chapter tests the limits of the genre, for it refuses to focus on the material journey from Niagara Falls to the outer points of Chicago and Milwaukee and back. Clearly, Fuller wishes to investigate more than her outward journey. As intent upon inquiring into inward landscapes, she travels to states of mind that take her far from the shores of Lake Michigan.

Fuller's preoccupation with exploring what might be termed a borderland, or transition state, first arises in the single fragmented line that forms the opening paragraph of the chapter: "A territory, not yet a state; still, nearer the acorn than we were" (135). The statement presents a kind of epigraph to the chapter and, in its suggestion that actual settlement is in process, evokes the sense that Fuller (and thus the reader) visits a landscape and a time that is new and fluid. After describing the bustle of activity that greets arriving boats, she offers an image of a place still trimming the outgrowth of the wilderness: "The town promises to be, some time, a fine one, as it is so well situated. . . . It seems to grow before you, and has indeed but just emerged from the thickets of oak and wild roses. A few steps will take you into the thickets, and certainly I never saw so many wild roses, or of so beautiful a red" (136). As she does throughout the book, Fuller allows these physical realities to suggest connections to the past; in this instance, the border of roses elicits an allusion to the legend of Venus and Adonis as well as a brief description of Titian's picture of the divinities, a portrait that, Fuller concludes, reveals the goddess of love's growing recognition of her inability to keep the fickle Adonis by her side. Interestingly, Fuller urges Venus to "[s]it there, by thyself, on that bank, and, instead of thinking how soon he will come back, think how thou may'st love him no better than he does thee, for the time has come" (137). While the lesson has partly emerged in the earlier question "Why must women always try to detain and restrain what they love?" (136), the "moral" also seems to reside in the fact that Venus appears to be portrayed as if on the verge of a new knowledge, a consciousness of a truth that may free her. If the goddess is to be in repose, she must hold within herself a kind of knowledge that prevents too much focus outward. Her stasis should not signal the debilitating immobility of self-deception.

In this borderland, then, Fuller seems cognizant of how temporal and spatial thresholds prefigure new things or provide the context within which to revitalize or reinterpret the old. Given this dynamic interpretive space, it is not surprising that her narrative next transports the reader beyond the frontier line. Turning to observations of the new settlers and to her brief time in an Indian tent during a sudden rainfall, she considers the uneasy amalgamation of diverse states or positions and discerns profoundly different perspectives. But, at least in this chapter, Fuller devotes relatively little space to descriptions of actual settlers and Indians and instead concludes with a homestead indicative of a "transition state." After alerting readers that "insuperable obstacles" prevent the expeditious procuring of "comforts, or a home," she more hopefully affirms: "But let him come sufficiently armed with patience to learn the new spells which the new dragons require, (and this can only be done on the spot,) he will not finally be disappointed of the promised treasure; the mob will resolve itself into men, yet crude, but of good dispositions, and capable of good character; the solitude will become sufficiently enlivened and home grow up from the rich sod" (142). According to Fuller, she found such a congenial home positioned on a fair knoll near Milwaukee, where a husband and wife whose struggles have turned their "gay smiles grave" live within a domestic space undergoing evolution. Seeing the signs of refinement in an album full of drawings and verses and imagining the young wife's need of a sister, she remarks that "both must often miss that electricity which sparkles from the chain of congenial minds" (144). For antebellum readers, these words would call to mind the practice of enhancing the curative effects of the magnetic fluid by joining hands. In the end, however, the description of Milwaukee, the delineation of her digression further inland, and the ongoing commentary and critique form but a brief portion of the chapter.

Interestingly, the allusion to that missing "chain of congenial minds" seems to initiate both the narrative transition back to her hotel in Milwaukee and the ensuing discussion of magnetic forces manifested in the life of the Seeress of Prevorst, Frederica Hauffe. Once in her hotel room, Fuller tells us, she spent the next few days relaxing with Justinus Kerner's book, a text that offered a "strong contrast with the life around me" (144). While a contrast in circumstance, however, it was not one in kind. Clearly, in turning to the book at this moment in *Summer on the Lakes*, she suggestively continues rather than abandons her theme. In this instance, the passage to a life situated between a material and spiritual existence marks additional reflections on the unfamiliar territory of another kind of transition state. "Very strange was this vision of an exalted and sensitive existence," Fuller reflects, "which seemed to invade the next sphere, in contrast with the spontaneous, instinctive life, so healthy and so near the ground I had been surveying" (144–45).

Of all the material available to such a voracious reader, why would this particular text find its way into her hands and, more importantly, assert its place in a work that seems to offer few visual resonances with the European landscape of Hauffe's homeland? In a text so conscious of American realities and so self-conscious of the textual legacy of the "West"—so much so that Fuller often seems more comfortable reviewing published descriptions of the land and people than characterizing her own experiences—why turn to a "foreign" narrative? Indeed, in the Seeress's "exalted and sensitive existence," we seem to witness a life disconnected not only from American realities but also from her own time and place.

Of course, some simple answers to these questions exist beyond the thematic concerns of the text itself. In a letter to Emerson dated May 9, 1843, Fuller remarks, "I have a really good book Die Seherin von Prevorst."[5] Thus, it appears that, rather serendipitously, the book happened to be a part of her summer reading. Clearly, Fuller's ongoing interest in somnambulism and in the unique perceptive states associated with animal magnetism led her to seek out the book and carry it with her on the trip west. As she must have anticipated, Kerner's life of the Seeress offered an intriguing German counterpart to her own readings on magnetic states and experiences

5. Fuller, *Letters of Margaret Fuller,* 3:124. By the end of May 1843, Fuller was dating her letters from Niagara Falls. With the financial assistance of Sarah Black Sturgis Shaw and James Freeman Clarke, she accompanied Clarke and his sister Sarah on a nearly four-month excursion from Niagara Falls through the Great Lakes to Milwaukee and Chicago. In addition to Kerner's book, it is possible that Fuller may have been familiar with another German source on somnambulism and animal magnetism. In "Select List of Recent Publications," for the October 1840 issue of the *Dial,* Fuller includes notice of *Der Somnambulismus von Prof. Friedr. Fischer, in Basel:* vol. 1, *Das Schlafwandeln und die Vision;* vol. 2, *Der thierische Magnetismus;* vol. 3, *Das Hellsehen und die Besessenheit* (Basel: Schweighauser, 1839).

with American somnambulists such as Loraina Brackett and Cynthia Gleason.

It is possible to see her interest in Hauffe's apprehensiveness, however, as part of her ongoing reflection on the nature of the artistic or poetic sensibility and the qualities of the ideal critic. In "A Short Essay on Critics," her first contribution to the *Dial* during her two-year editorship, Fuller in fact describes the model critic in terms that recall the cultural discourse on animal magnetism and her own early criticism of German and British writers in the *American Monthly*. Rather than offering a "record of mere impressions" that betray the influences of the critic's "nation, his church, his family even," Fuller considers the best reviewers as being both "apprehensive" and "comprehensive." Unlike the "subjective class," the apprehensive critics

> can go out of themselves and enter fully into a foreign existence. They breathe its life; they live in its law; they tell what it meant, and why it so expressed its meaning. They reproduce the work of which they speak, and make it better known to us in so far as two statements are better than one. There are beautiful specimens in this kind. They are pleasing to us as bearing witness of the genial sympathies of nature. They have the ready grace of love with somewhat of the dignity of disinterested friendship. They sometimes give more pleasure than the original production of which they treat, as melodies will sometimes ring sweetlier in the echo.

In describing the features of the comprehensive critic, "who must also be apprehensive," Fuller further delineates qualities that resonate with the peculiar characteristics of the magnetic state. In addition to being able to "enter into the nature of another being and judge his work by its own law," this kind of critic knows how to establish the place of the writer and the work within some larger scheme. "And this the critic can only do," Fuller asserts, in a language reminiscent of Edgar Allan Poe's "essential symmetry" of forms and motions, "who perceives the analogies of the universe, and how they are regulated by an absolute, invariable principle."[6]

6. Fuller, "A Short Essay on Critics," 6–7. See Edgar Allan Poe, *Eureka*, in *The Science Fiction of Edgar Allan Poe*, 300. Interestingly, Fuller follows this lead article of the first number of the *Dial* with Christopher Cranch's poem "Aurora Borealis." Cranch wonders, "Who can name thy wondrous essence, / Thou elec-

Through an extended examination of Frederica Hauffe, Fuller travels beyond the spatial and temporal boundaries of Wisconsin territory to inquire into the life of one who lives on the threshold, that is, within a space that promises insight into the nature of this larger scheme. In light of her critique of Self-Poise, this "jumping off" into the biography arguably marks an exploration into representative features of an "apprehensive" or receptive state. Though sickly and of a nervous temperament, the Seeress revealed a "peculiar inner life" (150) from youth until her death at twenty-nine. According to Kerner, Hauffe was "in so deep a somnambulic life, that she was, in fact, never rightly awake, even when she seemed to be; or rather, let us say, she was at all times more awake than others are; for it is strange to term sleep this state which is just that of the clearest wakefulness. Better to say she was immersed in the inward state" (157). In this transition state that Chauncy Hare Townshend termed sleepwaking in *Facts in Mesmerism,* Hauffe revealed a susceptibility to spiritual influences to such a degree that her body seemed upon the threshold of death. "Should we compare her with anything human," Fuller notes, "we would say she was as one detained at the moment of dissolution, betwixt life and death; and who is better able to discern the affairs of the world that lies before, than that behind him" (158). Able to discriminate the "written words of men" simply by touch, to travel beyond her body, and to prescribe healing remedies for herself while in the magnetic sleep, Hauffe presents a figure who seems to reveal aspects of a higher state.[7]

To see such redeeming qualities in the emaciated form of Hauffe's body certainly goes against the grain of modern readers. We are more inclined to overlook her magnetic spirit-life, to lament her physical decline, and to seek some social or psychological cause for such a debilitating sensibility. That Fuller should script Kerner's work as a kind of antebellum hagiography, then, is suggestive. In

---

tric Phosphorescence?" During the period, the aurora borealis had come to signify, for many believers in the power associated with animal magnetism, the all-pervading, electrical energies.

7. Describing the somnambulant state as a condition wherein one seems to hover between life and death formed a recurrent motif in the literature on animal magnetism. For a real account, see Hiram Fuller's reflections in Poyen, *Progress of Animal Magnetism,* 136–37. For a fictional example, see Poe's "The Facts in the Case of M. Valdemar," in *Collected Works of Edgar Allan Poe,* 3:1228–44.

emphasizing the Seeress of Prevorst's receptiveness to the electric forces in nature and among the people surrounding her, the story appears to provide Fuller an example of one who is poised, yet "fluid" enough to remain connected to the spiritual. In fact, the perpetual crisis of living so continually on the threshold begins to suggest Fuller's feminist aesthetic. The possibility for reform, after all, depends to a large degree upon the peculiar power of the "feminine," a power linked not solely to biological womanhood, but to the capacity to exist in an apprehensive state. If women are in fact inclined by biology to live in a more sensitive condition, then they are much more receptive to forces conducive to insight and social transformation.[8]

Just prior to her trip to Wisconsin, Fuller addresses this power in "The Great Lawsuit. MAN *versus* MEN. WOMAN *versus* WOMEN." First written for the July 1843 issue of the *Dial* (and later revised and published in 1845 as *Woman in the Nineteenth Century*), the essay includes numerous references to women's susceptibility to magnetic states that eventually culminate in telling reflections on two articles entitled "Femality" that Fuller had read in the *New-York Pathfinder.* According to Fuller, the author "views the feminine nature as a harmonizer of the vehement elements, and this has often been hinted elsewhere; but what he expresses most forcibly is the lyrical, the inspiring and inspired apprehensiveness of her being." In the ensuing paragraph, Fuller elaborates:

> More native to her is it to be the living model of the artist, than to set apart from herself any one form in objective reality; more native to inspire and receive the poem than to create it. In so far as soul is in her completely developed, all soul is the same; but as far as it is modified in her as woman, it flows, it breathes, it sings, rather than deposits soil, or finishes work, and that which is especially feminine flushes in blossom the face of earth, and pervades like air and water all this seeming solid globe, daily renewing and purifying its life. Such may be the especially feminine element,

8. Most any medical text that spoke of women's distinctive "nature" underscored this sensitive state. For a representative study of cultural notions concerning women, see Amariah Brigham's *Remarks on the Influence of Mental Cultivation upon Health* (1832). See especially the fifth section, "Influence of mental cultivation and mental excitement, in producing insanity and nervous affections."

spoken of as Femality. But it is no more the order of nature that it should be incarnated pure in any form, than that the masculine energy should exist unmingled with it in any form.

   Male and female represent the two sides of the great radical dualism. But, in fact, they are perpetually passing into one another. Fluid hardens to solid, solid rushes to fluid. There is no wholly masculine man, no purely feminine woman.[9]

In her changes to "The Great Lawsuit," Fuller would extend these reflections on the nature of this higher state by revising an earlier section and placing it a few lines after this introduction of the "great radical dualism": "What I mean by the Muse is the unimpeded clearness of the intuitive powers which a perfectly truthful adherence to every admonition of the higher instincts would bring to a finely organized human being. It may appear as prophecy or as poesy. It enabled Cassandra to foresee the results of actions passing round her; the Seeress [of Prevorst] to behold the true character of the person through the mask of customary life. (Sometimes she saw a feminine form behind the man, sometimes the reverse.)"[10]

   Fuller's preface to *Woman* voices this need for re-vision and thus the preoccupation with a state that promises some wholeness or union. Referring to her earlier title "The Great Lawsuit. MAN *versus* MEN. WOMAN *versus* WOMEN," Fuller establishes the purpose of the text: "I meant, by that title, to intimate the fact that, while it is the destiny of Man, in the course of the Ages, to ascertain and fulfil the law of his being, so that his life shall be seen, as a whole, to be that of an angel or messenger, the action of prejudices and passions, which attend, in the day, the growth of the individual, is continually obstructing the holy work that is to make the earth a part of heaven. By Man I mean both man and woman: these are two halves of one thought."[11] Could we not see Fuller's earlier critique of Self-Poise as defining a state of mind that in part obstructs "the holy work"? Could we not see the long discussion of the Seeress of Prevorst as an evocative description of a feminine body that offers a literal and figurative medium illuminating some greater possibilities? Clearly,

   9. Fuller, "The Great Lawsuit. MAN *versus* MEN. WOMAN *versus* WOMEN," 42, 43.
   10. Fuller, *Woman in the Nineteenth Century,* in *The Essential Margaret Fuller,* ed. Jeffrey Steele, 310.
   11. Ibid., 245.

Fuller's ideal critic and artist is one who achieves a state of mind that opens avenues to the divine rather than introducing impediments to wholeness.

It is worth noting as well that Fuller may have been prompted to seek out Kerner's book after a reading of Chauncy Hare Townshend's *Facts in Mesmerism, with Reasons for a Dispassionate Inquiry into It* (1840), a text that she mentions in her review of *Die Seherin von Prevorst* in the chapter titled "Wisconsin."[12] In significant ways, *Facts in Mesmerism* reads like an extended study of the nature of transition states, for, in exhaustively analyzing the nature of "mesmeric sleepwaking," "mesmeric consciousness," "mesmeric sensation," and the "mesmeric medium," the book offers an informative description of and theorizing on a kind of "in-between" condition. Fundamental to Townshend's argument is the assertion that, rather than mesmeric phenomena being completely distinct from known forms of consciousness, they actually conform to general experience even while they reveal a higher state of awareness. After considering widely witnessed and accepted states of distinct consciousness (for example, sleepwalking or other activities conducted while asleep), he indicates that he will proceed to "assimilate the state of mesmeric sleepwaking itself to our intimate personal convictions, striving to demonstrate that all its phases and phenomena are only intense degrees of known and even ordinary conditions of man." Considering what constitutes or defines consciousness, he offers a classification that calls to mind Fuller's efforts to describe different kinds of critical perspectives:

> Simple consciousness, that is to say, the mind's action in those absent and dreamy moods when much thought is accompanied by no reflection, and is succeeded by no memory of the subjects of its meditation.

12. Speaking of the Seeress's interest in and impressions of precious stones, Fuller comments, "The ancients, in addition to their sense of the qualities that distinguish the diamond above all gems, venerated it as a talisman against wild beasts, poison, and evil spirits, thus expressing the natural influence of what is so enduring, bright, and pure. Townshend, speaking of the effect of gems on one of his sleepwakers, said, she loved the diamond so much that she would lean her forehead towards it, whenever it was brought near her" (*Summer on the Lakes*, 164).

> Retrospective consciousness, the mind's action when it passes
> through a series of former thoughts and sensations, without mak-
> ing them objects of scrutiny.
> Introspective consciousness, the mind's action when self-
> regardant. It is distinguished from mere memory in two marked
> particulars. It immediately succeeds the thoughts, on which it casts
> a reflective glance, and it has ourselves for its object. It is a state in
> which thought, and observation of thought, succeed each other so
> rapidly, and with such even alternation, as to seem identical.

According to Townshend, introspective consciousness is absent in
the mesmeric state. "Thus," he asserts, "the perfection of motion
and superior coherence of thought which mesmeric sleepwakers
display, in connexion with the absence of introspective consciousness, is but a higher grade of a known condition; the extension, and
not the alteration, of a principle." To a great degree, then, mesmeric
consciousness represents a realm of thinking—of registering, mediating, and reflecting upon sensory input—that is unimpeded by a
too self-conscious or self-reflective state of mind. Whether these
ideas concerning the removal of the introspective consciousness be
seen as a transitional period before a fourth or next state of abstraction, "in which pure intellectuality reigns alone," or as providing a
space within which the individual might experience "a higher state
of intellect and of corporeal activity," they nevertheless offer an
understanding of the greater capacities of the mind in assimilating
both material and spiritual realities or the external and internal
life.[13] For both Townshend and Fuller, mesmeric sleepwaking and
magnetic sleep offer evidence of individuals with especially refined
nervous systems and/or people more receptive to achieving higher
states. Intuition and reason exist simultaneously—for the ideal critic,
the somnambulist, and, as we have seen in Poe's fiction, for such
figures as V in "Mesmeric Revelation."

Still, it may at first seem that Townshend's notions of mesmeric
consciousness are in opposition to Fuller's conception of the ideal
critic, for they appear to diminish the importance of an analytical
perspective or synthesizing consciousness, that is, a kind of "self-
regardant" or self-reflexive mode of thinking that can discern "an
absolute, invariable principle." Reading Fuller's essay in light of

13. Townshend, *Facts in Mesmerism,* 201, 204, 208–9, 206–7.

Townshend's ideas, however, suggests parallels between her central attribute of "apprehensiveness" and his description of that higher state of receptivity or consciousness. In effect, the ideal critic must cross into a space of abstraction uninhibited by the constraints of personal views and community prejudices. Individual reflection or introspection must be refined to such a degree that the critic can "enter into the nature of another being and judge his work by its own law." In short, sympathies must be enlarged, not restricted.

By the time Fuller set forth on her travels to the West, she had been immersed in nearly a decade of speculation on animal magnetism. In the 1840s, Fuller would not have had to look far for texts examining animal magnetism or exploring the nature of the "electric." As documented in Adam Crabtree's authoritative bibliography of the period, texts dealing directly with animal magnetism more than doubled in number from the previous decade.[14] (In fact, in the same year as her trip, James Braid published *Neurypnology; or, The Rationale of Nervous Sleep, Considered in Relation with Animal Magnetism,* the text that first coined the term *hypnosis* and that initiated Freud's early fascination with the therapeutic use of what the period had previously termed magnetic sleep.) Summarizing and inevitably simplifying Townshend's analysis of mesmeric consciousness and mesmeric sensation, the anonymous author of *The History and Philosophy of Animal Magnetism, with Practical Instructions for the Exercise of This Power* (1843), a much more obscure volume published out of Boston, suggests another context within which to consider Fuller's thinking. According to the "Practical Magnetizer," as the author's name is given, the human system consists of four great divisions: "1. A material body. 2. A vital or animating principle. 3. A mental power. 4. A soul, or spirit." The author notes that "when the avenues of natural or external sensation are closed, by the action of the *vital or magnetic fluid* communicated by the magnetizer, the *in-*

---

14. See Adam Crabtree, *Animal Magnetism, Early Hypnotism, and Psychical Research, 1766–1925: An Annotated Bibliography.* Crabtree limits his bibliography to only those works "immediately connected with animal magnetism and the themes that arise directly from it" and that are "the most significant writings within the historical tradition arising from animal magnetism." Thus, he omits texts that deal "exclusively with occultism, possession, or witchcraft; theosophy, anthroposophy, Christian Science, or other spiritual philosophies; theology or religious thought; and conjuring or stage magic" (xvii). Between 1820 and 1829, 1830 and 1839, and 1840 and 1849, Crabtree lists 45, 76, and 166 texts, respectively.

ternal sense (or spirit) becomes, as it were, somewhat relieved from
the ordinary influences of the body, (as it will be after death,) and
consequently displays its spiritual power; that the spirit exists, in
fact, in a new atmosphere, (the magnetic) in a state of being governed by *new laws,* and presenting most wonderful phenomena."[15]
Not unlike the suggestive possibilities of Fuller's notions, these ideas
have both literary and social implications. That is, in a nation expe-
riencing increasing immigration, resettlement west, and profound
social experimentation and change, it is possible to see the psychological insights arising from the philosophy of animal magnetism as
providing the framework for mediating cultural flux. Distinguished
by an apprehensiveness and receptivity to that which resides outside the self yet anchored by the stabilizing force of an "internal
sense," mesmeric consciousness did certainly offer the foundation
for a full, free life.

The relationship between the era's speculations regarding animal
magnetism and Fuller's canon might be further suggested by images of the ouroboros that form the concluding emblem of *The
History and Philosophy of Animal Magnetism* and the frontispiece to
the first edition of *Woman in the Nineteenth Century.* Without any
preceding textual explanation, the author of the short work on animal magnetism included the ancient image of the snake swallowing
its tale (see fig. 4). The snake encircles another esoteric image of
the sun, suggestive of an eye, within a triangle. In sixteenth- and
seventeenth-century texts, the images often came together to capture both the wholeness and multiple dimensions of the universe.
According to Anastasius Kircher's *Obeliscus aegyptiacus* (1666), Egyp-
tians, when seeking to represent the universe, drew "a snake scat-
tered with bright scales, swallowing its own tail; the flakes indicate
the stars of the universe." The ouroboros, then, was "Eon, the entirety of time and space, and also Okeanos, the water-belt in the
gnostic cosmology, which separates the upper sphere of the Pneuma
from the lower, dark waters." Throughout history, the triangle has
come to offer many meanings: from the embodiment of the strength
and mystery of the pyramid to the triune nature of the divine (and,
of course, the Christian trinity). In some manifestations of the image,
the "inner circle represents the microcosmic One which, through

15. A Practical Magnetizer, *The History and Philosophy of Animal Magnetism,*
15–16.

Fig. 4. Closing image from *The History and Philosophy of Animal Magnetism* (1843).

the step of four, becomes the macrocosmic ten, which, in turn, as the quintessence of the alchemists, encompasses all other possibilities." In his consideration of Fuller's "very Hermetic understanding of nature," Arthur Versluis underscores the significance of the esoteric image, drawing attention to the way it stands as a symbol of unity between oppositions.[16]

The absence of any explanation for the concluding symbol is intriguing. However, in assigning "Faith," "Will," and "Power" to the sides of the triangle, the author skillfully integrates central aspects of the art of inducing a magnetic state: the need for the patient's faith in the proceedings, the exertion of the magnetist's will, and the ensuing power initiated through such efforts. In fact, earlier in the

16. Kircher, cited in Alexander Roob, *Alchemy and Mysticism,* 425, 424, 467; Versluis, *Esoteric Origins,* 147.

work, the writer had introduced aspects of this trilogy: "Then abstracting his mind from all other thoughts and objects, and fixing his eyes upon the eyes of the subject, with earnest, determined, penetrating, but somewhat mild expression, he exerts an unremitted, unchanging effort of *will,* increasing in intensity the longer it continues, until the subject yield before his superior power, and closes his eyes in the magnetic sleep."[17] Because preceding pages delineated the importance of a shared belief (or faith) in the healing attributes of magnetic forces and the centrality of the magnetist's will in inducing mesmeric sleep, it would appear that the "Practical Magnetizer" assumed that readers would see the appropriateness of combining the ancient symbol with the emerging science.

Given that Fuller included her own version of what she called the "Serpent, triangle, and rays" in a July 13, 1844, letter to Emerson, an image that she had drawn in her private journal in the first days of the month, it would be tempting to assert her familiarity with the Boston publication (see fig. 5). However, because no evidence exists confirming her knowledge of the work (and because of the possibility of coming across the image in other venues), it is of more significance that the figure appears to embody, for both the "Practical Magnetizer" and Fuller, an emblem of Nature's flux and influx and thus the dynamic wholeness of spiritual and material worlds. Fuller captured the symbol's sense of harmony and wholeness in a poem that accompanied her letter to Emerson:

> Patient serpent, circle round
> Till in death thy life is found,
> Double form of godly prime
> Holding the whole thought of time,
> When the perfect two embrace,
> Male and female, black and white
> Soul is justified in space,
> Dark made fruitful by the light,
> And centered in the diamond Sun
> Time, eternity, are one.[18]

---

17. A Practical Magnetizer, *The History and Philosophy of Animal Magnetism,* 11.

18. Fuller, *Letters of Margaret Fuller,* 3:209–10. For the sketch and poem, see Fuller, "'The Impulses of Human Nature': Margaret Fuller's Journal from June through October 1844," ed. Martha L. Berg and Alice de V. Perry, 73, 74.

The poem voices a conception of union—between male and female, black and white—that informs the whole of "The Great Lawsuit" (published in the same month as her letter to Emerson was written). In his explication of the poem, Versluis further suggests the ways in which the sketch and "Double Triangle" poem capture the complementary nature of seemingly opposing forces: "This union, condensed symbolically in the illustration, reflects what we have seen as central also to the views of nature in Alcott and Emerson's works: duality (man and nature) is resolved in the presence of a third (spirit). In this illustration and poem, there is duality (black and white, male and female), but this duality is not oppositional. Rather, it forms a greater whole, the union of time and eternity." A similar version of the sketch appears as the frontispiece to *Woman in the Nineteenth Century* (see fig. 6). While not accompanied by her poem or any direct explication, the image provides a visual epigraph to her preface's emphasis upon man and woman as representing "two halves of one thought" and "twin exponents of a divine thought."[19]

Clearly, Fuller's letters, private symbols, published travel narrative, and "feminist" treatise all strive to express a consistent vision, one that acknowledges temporal and spatial thresholds while also envisioning the all in one and timelessness of the inward life. In the context of this effort to define the apprehensive state in visual and verbal signs, Fuller integrates findings from the present as well as gesturing toward the power of ancient symbols. Perhaps Fuller had in mind this resonance between contemporary and historically distant emblems when composing Free Hope's remarks in the prefatory dialogue to the Seeress review: "Long before these slight attempts were made to establish as a science what is at present called animal magnetism, always, in fact men were occupied more or less with this vital principle, principle of flux and influx, dynamic of our mental mechanics, human phase of electricity" (*Summer on the Lakes*, 146). In recontextualizing this ancient emblem, Fuller enacts the revisionist interpretive strategy employed throughout her works and seems to be both describing and invoking unseen forces, forces that signal an apprehensive and comprehending consciousness.

19. Versluis, *Esoteric Origins*, 150; Fuller, *Woman in the Nineteenth Century*, 245.

Fig. 5. "Double Triangle, Serpent and Rays" sketch from Margaret Fuller's 1844 journal. Reproduced courtesy of the Massachusetts Historical Society.

• • • •

To understand the conceptual importance of mesmeric "theory" to Fuller's ideas invites a final return to her response to Good Sense in *Summer on the Lakes.* In the guise of Free Hope, Fuller presents a telling allusion to another dimension of the magnetic state and to notions of reform arising from the belief in such a condition:

Who sees the meaning of the flower uprooted in the ploughed field? The ploughman who does not look beyond its boundaries and does not raise his eyes from the ground? No—but the poet who sees that field in its relations with the universe, and looks oftener to the sky than on the ground. Only the dreamer shall understand

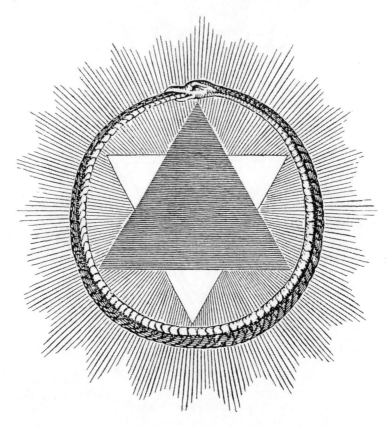

Fig. 6. Frontispiece to *Woman in the Nineteenth Century* (1845).

realities, though, in truth, his dreaming must not be out of proportion to his waking!

   The mind, roused powerfully by this existence, stretches of itself into what the French sage calls the "aromal state." From the
hope thus gleaned it forms the hypothesis, under whose banner it
collects its facts. (146)

For the "French sage" Charles Fourier, the philosophy of animal
magnetism provided a way to conceptualize social crisis. His theory
of the "aromal state" draws from Mesmer's belief in the purging
quality of mesmeric sleep and of physical crises that might precede
such a sleep. In mesmeric terms, the "crisis" was the moment that
marked the entrance into a magnetic state and thus precipitated a

healing. In fact, the prevalence of such crises in Mesmer's practice—and the resulting need to construct rooms to receive the entranced bodies of patients—unsettled the French Academy of Science.
What doctors like Mesmer and his adherent Charles Nicholas
D'Eslon saw as a necessary physical transition from illness to health
seemed like chaos or madness to outsiders. To be healed, Mesmer
argued, often demanded a passage through a crisis—especially if the
patient's animal fluid was out of harmony.

As Christina Zwarg underscores in *Feminist Conversations: Fuller,
Emerson, and the Play of Reading,* Fourier provided Fuller an especially suggestive way in which to imagine transition states. The
Frenchman, Zwarg observes, "applied the concept of a universal
fluid—which he called 'aroma'—to culture itself. In Fourier's vision,
the production of a crisis or an 'aromal state' could lead to social
harmony; death itself was such a crisis, a transition state 'hav[ing]
little to do with the orthodox Christian view of the afterlife.' Believing that our souls 'experience a series of rebirths and transmi-
grations' formed 'by the element we call Aroma,' Fourier theorized
that a productive cultural critique depended on such transitional
moments." Zwarg concludes that Fuller's "use of Kerner's narrative
makes it clear that she agreed with Fourier that unusual personali-
ties, like unusual states of mind, would become 'eminently favorable to the development of social virtues.' "[20]

Significantly, the introduction of the Seeress of Prevorst in *Summer on the Lakes* seems a continuation of Fuller's efforts to imagine
avenues for changing sensibilities in the territory of national reform. In a science that described states of higher perception, Fuller
found not only evidence of the kind of refined consciousness that
promises new things but also a language with which to communicate such possibilities to her readers. In the state of the territory of
Wisconsin, in the state of woman in the nineteenth century, and,
one could argue, in the state of domestic union (between the masculine and feminine or even the national body), Fuller draws attention to a shared knowledge of a new condition and thus the
potential for greater harmony. It is possible, then, to read *Summer on
the Lakes* as a description of the nature of the state (a travel narrative

20. Christina Zwarg, *Feminist Conversations: Fuller, Emerson, and the Play of
Reading,* 116–17.

"state of the union"). More importantly, it is revealing to see the conversation within this narrative as well as that within "The Great Lawsuit" and its sister version, *Woman in the Nineteenth Century*—a conversation resonating with Townshend, Fourier, and others—as imagining ways to reconstitute or revitalize both selfhood and statehood.

Shifting from her remarks on the Seeress to the conclusion of "Wisconsin," Fuller begs readers' sympathies: "Do not blame me that I have written so much about Germany and Hades, while you were looking for news of the West." Yet, turning her mind to the influx of immigrants, to the transitional status of western states, she asks, "Who knows how much of old legendary lore, of modern wonder, they have already planted amid the Wisconsin forests?" Just as she began, she finds herself in the end gazing upon a landscape that still seems a territory: "Some seeds of all growths that have ever been known in this world might, no doubt, already be found in these Western wilds, if we had the power to call them to life" (170). Perhaps, in her own inroads to these wilderness states, Fuller invites greater insight into the inward life. Such a journey demands repose in new conceptual spaces. In turning to the works of her friend Lydia Maria Child and examining another layer of the landscape of magnetic speculation, we can offer some final conclusions as to the particular power and truth of animal magnetism to woman in the nineteenth century.

6 . . . .

Exquisite Sensibilities

Lydia Maria Child, Margaret Fuller, and Magnetic Reform

The conviction that woman's present position in society is a false one, and therefore re-acts disastrously on the happiness and improvement of man, is pressing, by slow degrees, on the common consciousness, through all the obstacles of bigotry, sensuality, and selfishness. As man approaches to the truest life, he will perceive more and more that there is no separation or discord in their mutual duties. They will be one; but it will be as affection and thought are one; the treble and bass of the same harmonious tune.

Of what spiritual thing is electricity the type? Is there a universal medium by which all things of spirit act on the soul, as matter on the body by means of electricity? And is that medium the WILL, whether of angels or of men? Wonderful stories are told of early Friends, how they were guided by a sudden and powerful impulse, to avoid some particular bridge, or leave some particular house, and subsequent events showed that danger was there. Many people consider this fanaticism; but I have faith in it. I believe the most remarkable of these accounts give but a faint idea of the perfection to which man's moral and physical instincts might attain, if his life were obedient and true.

Lydia Maria Child, Letters 34 and 35, *Letters from New-York*

WRITING LYDIA MARIA CHILD from her position as editor of the *Dial* in mid-March 1844, Margaret Fuller notes that she has reviewed *Letters from New-York* (1843), a book that her former mentor and friend had forwarded from the city not long after she had relinquished editorship of the *National Anti-Slavery Standard* in May of 1843. Fuller closes her brief letter with what would be a prophecy of future intimacy: "Now, however, that I know you do hold me in friendly regard, I shall come forward to offer the hand, when we meet again, and perhaps circumstances may favor a renewal of acquaintance. In former days, you used to tell me much which I have stored in memory as I have in my heart the picture of your affectionate, generous, and resolute life. *Now,* if we were to meet, we might have more topics in common; At least I ought to have something to impart, now so many pages of the great volume have been opened to my eye."[1] Having lived in New York since she took up her editorial post in May 1841, the forty-one-year-old Child no doubt welcomed a letter from the woman with whom she had studied Madame de Staël in the late 1820s (at one height of her own literary reputation and when Fuller was just in her late teens) and had joined in intellectual conversations during November and December of 1839.[2] As if fulfilling the prediction embodied in her letter, Fuller did find herself in the same city as Child in December 1843 and, as a writer for Horace Greeley's *New-York Tribune,* began traveling to and reviewing some of the same sites and issues as her friend.

Their correspondence inevitably leads the curious reader to wonder if conversations in New York included some consideration of their common interest in animal magnetism. Dated March 19, 1845, one letter from Fuller to James Nathan indicates that she will both dine with Child and visit magnetist Dr. Theodore Leger on the same day. It would seem remarkable if they did not converse over the wonders of this healing science, given the fact that Fuller frequently visited the doctor for her own health and would eventually review his book *Animal Magnetism; or, Psychodunamy* (1846) in the *Tribune.*[3]

---

1. Margaret Fuller, *Letters of Margaret Fuller,* 3:183.

2. In a letter begun November 18 and completed December 12, 1839, Child writes her sister-in-law, Lydia B. Child, that she has been attending "Anti Slavery Committees, and three different courses of lectures" (*Lydia Maria Child: Selected Letters, 1817–1880,* ed. Milton Meltzer and Patricia G. Holland, 125). The first of what became known as Fuller's "Conversations" began on November 6, 1839, and involved many of the prominent women of the Boston area. For an extensive discussion of these events, see "Conversations (1838–1840)" in Capper, *Margaret Fuller.*

3. In her review of Leger's book for the May 30, 1846, *New-York Daily Tribune,* Fuller asserts, "Dr. Leger has become considerably known in this city as a practitioner of Animal Magnetism, and is said to have effected some decisive cures.

Fuller would have been familiar with Child's views on the subject, for, in the essays exploring various people, places, and matters of New York and the age in *Letters from New-York*, Child had included evocative essays on animal magnetism and "electricity."

Considering Child's essays in *Letters from New-York* and her popular fiction of the 1840s in the context of Fuller's and the era's conceptualization of the especial genius of woman provides further insight into the importance of animal magnetism to antebellum narratives. In Child's accommodation of the "evolutionary" implications of woman's finer sensibilities, that is, of woman's apprehensiveness of or special receptivity to the electric or to spiritual laws, we witness an imaginative paradigm that asserts the potential of the "feminine principle" in mediating the effects of outward, or material, forces on the inward life. In fact, in their association of medical findings regarding animal magnetism and their understanding of women's particular sensibilities, both Child and Fuller contributed significantly to the shaping of the era's fictional and nonfictional narratives and thus to the way readers might imagine harmonious resolutions to private and public conflicts.

In Lydia Maria Child's revision and rearrangement of selected essays from her abolitionist newspaper for *Letters from New-York*, we see a clear demonstration of how animal magnetism and notions of "the electric" informed thinking related to the woman question and notions of race. Through choices of which most readers of the selected "letters" would have been unaware, Child reveals the fundamental importance of the new science to her democratic vision. A brief history of the origin and publication of Child's "letters" from New York provides a fuller understanding of the challenges she faced in creating her 1843 collection and thus why notions arising from studies of animal magnetism served a central position in her poetic. From August 1841 to May 1843, Child wrote fifty-eight essays introducing readers to people and places that captured the profound changes of a growing urban setting. Spanning the decade before and during her years in New York, in fact, the city added nearly a half ·

For ourselves, we can only vouch from observation to his possessing a power of transmitting vital energy to those who need soothing or strengthening by this kind of treatment" (*Margaret Fuller, Critic,* C294).

million residents. For a journalist, editor, and reformer, such growth offered not only the opportunity to create copy to help fill the seemingly endless space of four pages of six fine-print columns but also the chance to explore the greater meaning of such flux. New to the place being described or unfamiliar with particular ethnic or cultural traditions, Child negotiates the dynamic between description and reflection by often providing the physical portrayal of the place, person, or context (for example, historical, biographical, social). The letters, however, demonstrate an unwillingness to remain purely descriptive, for they consistently betray the desire for resolution or closure in their return from a venturing out to visit city people and landmarks. Time and again, Child comes "home" to underscore principles that offer stability after exhilarating and sometimes unsettling shifts in perspective.

It is this simultaneous search for and demonstration of a harmonizing vision that led Child to write her "letters." Insight into Child's purpose for creating the essays and the perspective that shaped the form of the columns can be found in the editorial "Farewell" to the *National Anti-Slavery Standard:* "The New-York Letters were inserted upon something of the same principle that the famous Timothy Dexter sent a stock of Bibles to the West Indies, with warming pans, to be used for sugar ladles and trainers. No purchaser was allowed to have a pan, unless he would buy a Bible also."[4] Clearly, through the letters, she hoped to demonstrate the way spiritual laws might enter the material affairs of readers' lives. Without the leavening of transformative stories and metaphors, abolitionist cant promised little fullness and thus less potential to promote lasting private and public change.

In lifting the letters from the *Standard* pages and revising them for the volume *Letters from New-York,* Child further demonstrates her profound concern over the sectarian spirit threatening the voice of conscience, a voice often veiled by the material realities of city life and the incessant bickering within antislavery reform. The opening letter sketches the worldly discord that threatens citizens of the nineteenth century: "You ask what is now my opinion of this great Babylon; . . . Nor do you forget my first impression of the city, when we arrived at nearly dawn, amid fog and drizzling rain, the expiring

4. Lydia Maria Child, "Farewell," 190.

lamps adding their smoke to the impure air, and close beside us a boat called the 'Fairy Queen,' laden with dead hogs." The opening lament soon turns into a litany of urban discord: the juxtaposition of a "blind negro beggar" opposite the mansion of the slave trader, the cool calculations of Mammon on Wall Street ("extracting a penny from war, pestilence, and famine"), the cries of street children selling "hot corn!"[5]

Child follows these sobering reminders of the chaos of city life, however, with a clear pronouncement that her primary aim in the letters lies not in describing material (or finite) facts, but in discerning spiritual truth. "But now," she explains, "I have lost the power of looking merely on the surface. Every thing seems to me to come from the Infinite, to be filled with the Infinite, to be tending toward the Infinite." She continues: "Do I see crowds of men hastening to extinguish a fire? I see not merely uncouth garbs, and fantastic, flickering lights, of lurid hue, like a tramping troop of gnomes,—but straightway my mind is filled with thoughts about mutual helpfulness, human sympathy, the common bond of brotherhood, and the mysteriously deep foundations on which society rests; or rather, on which it now reels and totters" (Letter 1, *Letters from New-York,* 10). Time after time, Child records events or realities that threaten a larger harmony and demand a more acute attention to permanent or eternal values (that is, the Infinite). Such musings reflect neither Pollyannaish simplicity nor sentimental optimism. Rather, Child's eventual assertion in the last of her *Standard* "letters" (and the final essay in her book) that "[m]an is moving to his highest destiny through manifold revolutions of spirit" and that "the outward must change with the inward" (Letter 40, *Letters from New-York,* 178) marks a faith tempered by a contemplation of the inherent violence of American racism, the redemptive power of religious and domestic metaphors, and the findings concerning the healing aspects of magnetic, or electric, forces.

Just as the individual letters revealed the desire of trying to capture the spiritual workings behind material realities, so too did the editing of the collected essays betray an effort to foster an understanding of higher truths—even if through the indirection of

5. Lydia Maria Child, Letter 1, *Letters from New-York,* ed. Bruce Mills, 9–10. All subsequent references to this edition will be cited parenthetically in the text.

a "garland of imagination and taste." In effect, Child faced a larger manifestation of this important artistic challenge. In a letter to long-time friend, lawyer, and fellow abolitionist Ellis Gray Loring, she articulates some of these concerns after asking him to forward a story that she had written for his daughter: "I am hesitating whether or not to print [the story] in the volume of my N. York Letters, to give a little novelty and variety to it. Would you? I shall not print *all* the letters; only the best ones. Would you omit the last two about Women's Rights, or not? I think it best to omit them. Would you publish the one about the execution of Colt, and against Capital Punishment?"[6] Evidently, Loring encouraged Child to include the entirety of the letters and offered to review them on their trek toward publication, thus prompting her response in a letter written March 6, 1843: "I do not agree with you about inserting *all* of them. Some are of a merely temporary and transient interest, and a few more merely written to fill up. The doubt I had about the letter on Colt's execution was that it describes a scene of local and temporary interest, and painful without. As for the letters on Women's Rights, they did not seem to me to amount to much."[7]

The sequence of essays undergoing the most dramatic revision—the pieces entitled "Woman's Rights," "Lightning. Daguerreotype. Electricity. Effects of Climate," and "The Indians"—for *Letters from New-York* appears to indicate that Child had come to see some resonance between the all-pervading force of the electric and the ongoing evolution of relations between genders and races. In her essay on animal magnetism first published in the June 2, 1842, issue of the *Standard,* she came close to articulating this sentiment. While opening the "letter" by acknowledging that she "was ten years ago convinced that animal magnetism was destined to produce great changes in the science of medicine, and in the whole philosophy of spirit and matter" (Letter 19, *Letters from New-York,* 82), Child admits that a great deal of trickery and imposture has sometimes accompanied the public demonstrations of its wonders. Rather than dismiss the whole of animal magnetism, however, she invites readers to question their own skepticism toward the science. "If these things have

---

6. Child, *Selected Letters,* 188.
7. Lydia Maria Child, *The Collected Correspondence of Lydia Maria Child, 1817–1880,* ed. Patricia G. Holland and Milton Meltzer, 16/463.

really happened, (as thousands of intelligent and rational people testify,)" she argues, "they are governed by laws as fixed and certain as the laws that govern matter" (83). Echoing the views of many apologists for animal magnetism, including those asserted by Chauncy Hare Townshend, the essay expresses disbelief that people should accept confirmed demonstrations of sleepwalking and not the state of somnambulism, or magnetic sleep, concluding that animal magnetism

> will come out from all the shams and quackery that have made it ridiculous, and will yet be acknowledged as an important aid to science, an additional proof of immortality, and a means, in the hands of Divine Providence, to arrest the progress of materialism.
>
> For myself, I am deeply thankful for any agency, that even momentarily blows aside the thick veil between the Finite and the Infinite, and gives me never so hurried and imperfect glimpse of realities which lie beyond this valley of shadows. (86)

Interestingly, Child expresses similar convictions in a February 17, 1842, letter to Maria White, confessing that she has been "reading Townshend's [Facts on] Mesmerism," that more recently she sees "in it the explanation of many spiritual mysteries, with which it has not been supposed to have any connection," and that she believes animal magnetism "is the crystal door between the spiritual and the natural."[8] That Child would conceive of the phenomenon of animal magnetism as evidence of laws as fixed as those governing matter prepares the foundation for her later revisions, specifically the repositioning of a discussion of the electric between the essays dealing with such material matters as the physical attributes associated with gender and race.

In its original composition and placement, the *National Anti-Slavery Standard* letter speculating on animal magnetism and the forces of the electric (No. 53) followed remarks on women's rights (Nos. 50 and 51) and the performance of Plains Indians at Barnum's American Museum (No. 52). By adding a section on the effects of climate from her September 22, 1842, *Standard* letter (No. 36) and placing the revised essay between a combination of the "woman"

---

8. Ibid., 13/337.

letters and the piece titled "The Indians," she creates a much more coherent sequence, one that clearly invites readers to see the electric as a force that mediates material and spiritual laws regarding realities threatening the stability of national affairs.

Significant in its assertion that "the present position of women in society is the result of physical force" (*Letters from New-York,* 153) and in its critique of Emerson's failure to see women as "souls" in his address "Being and Seeming," Letter 34 begins to define more clearly the "feminine ideal" and the potential for a higher harmony between men and women. "That the feminine ideal," she argues, "approaches much nearer to the gospel standard, than the prevalent idea of manhood, is shown by the universal tendency to represent the Saviour and his most beloved disciple with mild, meek expression, and feminine beauty. None speak of the bravery, the might, or the intellect of Jesus; but the devil is always imagined as a being of acute intellect, political cunning, and the fiercest courage. These universal and instinctive tendencies of the human mind reveal much" (153). While Child's notions of what constitutes "universal" tendencies certainly strike a disharmonious chord with current conceptualizations of gender, her effort to delineate the features of this higher ideal embodies an attempt to assert the central role of the feminine in understanding and even mediating psychological and social discord.

More than simply expressing a commonplace cognizance of gender differences, Child's revisions subtly communicate her evolving belief that the feminine ideal manifests the presence of a physical agent or energy woven into the very substance of life. By inserting her expanded reflections on electric or magnetic forces between the letters that directly deal with gender and race, she offers a revealing attempt to negotiate those divisions that profoundly threatened the culture. In the feminine, she finds the most dramatic demonstration of these forces and thus the physical energy that seems necessary for spiritual reform. "What *is* this invisible, all-pervading essence," she asks, "which thus has power to put man into communication with all?" To Child, the inexplicable incidents related to mesmerism and clairvoyance suggested the presence of "animal magnetism," a substance connecting all organisms. The implications of these embryonic investigations into the unconscious were not lost on Child: "Is there a universal medium by which all things of spirit act on the soul, as matter on the body by means of electricity? And is that medium the WILL, whether of angels or of men?" Wary that some answers to these questions might lead to ridicule, Child nonetheless refuses to dismiss these psychological insights, insights that suggested the means to enact profound individual and social reforms: "I believe the most remarkable of these accounts [of foresight] give but a faint idea of the perfection to which man's moral and physical instincts might attain, if his life were obedient and true" (Letter 35, *Letters from New-York,* 158–59).

And what might nurture this obedient and true life? Significantly, Child affirms Fuller's notion, expressed in *Woman in the Nineteenth Century,* that woman is the most powerful embodiment and "conductor" of the electric and thus the conduit for greater harmony between the inward and outward, the spiritual and material. In *Woman in the Nineteenth Century,* Fuller had cited an article from the *New-York Pathfinder* on "Femality" that saw "the feminine nature as a harmonizer of the vehement elements" and that forcibly asserted "the lyrical, the inspiring, and inspired apprehensiveness of her being." As Child would have read prior to her review of Fuller's book in February of 1845, Fuller describes women as having a "superior susceptibility to magnetic or electric influence" and as being "electrical in movement, intuitive in function, spiritual in tendency."[9] Woman, then, is not simply a passive harmonizer; her powers, if allowed to flow freely, promise significant social reforms. It is essential to underscore, however, that neither Fuller nor Child saw the feminine as solely that which resides in woman. In other words, the feminine principle characterizes an active power that cannot entirely be understood in terms of biological sex.

9. Margaret Fuller, *Woman in the Nineteenth Century,* in *The Essential Margaret Fuller,* 309. All subsequent references to this book will be cited parenthetically in the text. In a letter to Louisa Loring on February 8, 1845, Child comments: "I have read Margaret's book, Woman in the Nineteenth Century, and I like it much. I procured it in proofsheet, and sent a brief notice of it to the Boston Courier, thinking it might possibly help the sale a little. It is a bold book, I assure you. I should not have dared to have written some things in it, though it would have been safer for me, being married. But they need to be said, and she is brave to do it. She bears a noble testimony to anti slavery principles in several places" (*Selected Letters,* 219). Child's review of *Woman in the Nineteenth Century* was published in the following newspapers: *Boston Courier* (February 8, 1845), *New-York Daily Tribune* (February 12, 1845), and *Broadway Journal* (February 15, 1845).

As Jeffrey Steele confirms in *Transfiguring America: Myth, Ideology, and Mourning in Margaret Fuller's Writing,* we can see in such concepts an effort to delineate woman's harmonizing center. Noting that Fuller sought to expand her "mythic definition of women's creative energies" in part by characterizing them "as the 'electrical, the magnetic element in women,'" he later concludes that her "depiction of women's 'electrical' element begins to play an increasingly prominent part, replacing passive female values with more active and self-assertive qualities that might overcome female idolatry and help create 'harmony' in women's lives." Interestingly, Steele goes on to assert that Fuller's "commitment to reconfiguration of the *inner* self" led her to "reconstruct a new psychological language." For Steele, a central element of this reconstruction involved her use of classical mythology, that is, the configuration of the feminine as encompassing both Muse ("passionate energy") and Minerva ("intellectual discipline").[10] However, such terms and concepts as the "electric" and "magnetism" form the "new psychological language" that reorients an understanding of ancient myths and gender narratives. After all, this psychological language (and the notions of the mind implied by it) provides the lens with which Fuller, Child, and others revisit and revise past myths. Arguably, the fluid and transforming agency of "electricity," or animal magnetism, forms the theoretical center and molds new narratives and myths.

Given the fact that Fuller and Child had reestablished their friendship during their time in New York in the 1840s, it is not surprising that some resonance exists between Fuller's and Child's views. Both shaped their "art" with similar assumptions—and, through direct conversations or indirectly through their writings, they exchanged thoughts on how they understood the peculiar forces being discussed in the writings on animal magnetism. For Fuller, the "Muse is the unimpeded clearness of the intuitive powers which a perfectly truthful adherence to every admonition of the higher instincts would bring to a finely organized human being" (310). For Child, this unimpeded clearness might be seen in the remarkable accounts associated with the electric, accounts that again give the "faint idea" of moral and physical perfection.

10. Jeffrey Steele, *Transfiguring America: Myth, Ideology, and Mourning in Margaret Fuller's Writing,* 129–30, 131, 132–33.

If Child's letter on the "electric" offers an idea as to the transformative power inherent in the feminine principle, then her ensuing reflections upon the Indians at Barnum's American Museum further illuminate the long-term potential of this magnetic presence. In her account, of the Indians, in the *National Anti-Slavery Standard* ("Letter from New-York, No. 52," March 2, 1843), Child focuses on the spectacle of the event. She goes as an observer, and, while she offers some broader philosophical judgments, she remains for the most part in this journalistic rather than editorial (and metaphysical) mode. In the revised letter, however, she incorporates her earlier discussion on "the different races of men" from an article in the *Standard* on January 5, 1842, an article that in part focused on recent studies regarding facial and cranial angles. This antebellum manifestation of scientific racism seemed the material evidence for Caucasian supremacy, for, coupled with phrenological "evidence" that centered moral and intellectual propensities in the forehead, the higher facial angle appeared to indicate a more advanced moral and intellectual state.[11]

Clearly, it seems contradictory to hear an abolitionist apparently leave unchallenged those "facts" of racial difference that seem so obviously informed by racist assumptions (as Stephen Jay Gould has demonstrated in *The Mismeasure of Man*). While problematic in its acceptance of the authority of this information, her letter still resists the popular predilection to center views on race in what her time asserted to be the empirical evidence of an inherent racial hierarchy. Instead, she speculates that the differences in physical appearance and apparent racial characteristics indicate the complex interplay of inward forces and outward influences. Significantly, these forces again seem to signal the primacy of the feminine in human development, for the Caucasian race demonstrated—to use Fuller's terms concerning women—"a superior susceptibility to magnetic or

11. For studies of the era's effort to connect the science of phrenology and animal magnetism, see articles on phrenology and animal magnetism in vol. 4 (1842) of the *American Phrenological Journal and Miscellany,* 184–89, 213–18, 227–29, 308–12. For a book-length study, see J. Stanley Grimes, *Etherology; or, The Philosophy of Mesmerism and Phrenology: Including a New Philosophy of Sleep and of Consciousness, with a Review of the Pretensions of Neurology and Phreno-Magnetism* (1845). As noted later in this chapter, Margaret Fuller reviewed this book for the *Tribune* on February 17, 1845.

electric influence." "That [the Caucasian race] started, *first* in the race," Child speculates, "might have been owing to a finer and more susceptible nervous organization, originating in climate perhaps, but serving to bring the physical organization into more harmonious relation with the laws of spiritual reception" (Letter 36, *Letters from New-York,* 162). Rather than further reinforce the belief in inherent and unchanging biological differences, she emphasizes the happenstance of climatic variations upon "outward" features.

In redirecting readers to what unifies rather than what differentiates, Child distinguished herself from many of her contemporaries. Clearly, however, her own amalgamation of views on the feminine, the electric, and race still betrays the troubling hierarchies that she sought to question. The "congress of ages, each with a glory on its brow" gives little agency to Native Americans and African Americans in the centuries of evolution. Thus, we are left to puzzle through the contradictions inherent in Child's more disturbing assertions:

> You ask, perhaps, what becomes of my theory, that races and individuals are the product of ages, if the influences of half a life produce the same effects on the Caucasian and the Indian? I answer, that white children brought up among Indians, though they strongly imbibe the habits of the race, are generally prone to be the geniuses and prophets of their tribe. The organization of nerve and brain has been changed by a more harmonious relation between the animal and the spiritual; and this comparative harmony has been produced by the influences of Judea, and Greece, and Rome, and the age of chivalry; though of all these things the young man never heard. (163)

At the same time she argues that "[c]limate has had its effect too on the religious ideas of nations" and that "we are all, in some degree, the creatures of outward circumstance," she implicitly accepts the idea that biblical tradition and Greek and Roman literature and philosophy represent the prerequisite influence for this "harmonious relation between the animal and the spiritual." In effect, her notions of the feminine and of beauty drawn from imaginative forms of Western tradition create the terms and the criterion with which to judge the "animalism" of the "Indian" and other "barbarous" civilizations. Child's reflections, then, exist now as an unsettling legacy. Perhaps to Child we could apply Margaret Fuller's critique of her own attempt to articulate a different vision of human relations:

"[S]ome fair effigies that once stood for symbols of human destiny have been broken; those I still have with me, show defects in this broad light" (*Woman in the Nineteenth Century,* 348). And yet, in asserting that the "organization of nerve and brain [of the Caucasian race] has been changed by a more harmonious relation between the animal and the spiritual," Child exemplifies the belief that the human body registers the subtle forces of electric, or magnetic, properties and that, over time, such properties produce finer sensibilities.

In her reflections upon women's rights, the electric, and Indians in Letters 34–36 within *Letters from New-York,* then, Child expanded, revised, and reordered the *Standard* essays in ways that related the feminine principle and its spiritual dimension to central questions of her day. Though Child offered uneasy resolutions in the face of these difficult questions, a central belief remained less equivocal and problematic: in a city and a country marked by profound differences, harmony existed in the paradoxical truth that we might be "the treble and bass of the same harmonious tune" and that "we are all unequal, yet equal" (Letters 34 and 35, *Letters from New-York,* 156, 160). Moreover, it would seem that Child saw in "electricity," or "animal magnetism," the evidence of a harmonizing force.

Child's and Fuller's effort to accommodate the physical and metaphysical properties of animal magnetism suggest that both women could not overlook the consonance between descriptions of animal magnetism and the era's biological and social configurations of the "feminine." For some time, in fact, the medical and cultural discourse had been inviting such speculation. Starting as early as the late eighteenth century, writings on animal magnetism revealed women's special susceptibility to electrical or magnetic forces. And, while men demonstrated the capacity to enter the magnetic state, women increasingly became the subjects of public presentations of its forces. According to Dr. de Mainauduc, one of the individuals who was trained by Charles Nicholas D'Eslon and who brought the new science to England, women are the "most sympathising part of the creation, and most immediately concerned in the health and care of its offspring."[12] Certainly, Mainauduc's desire to attract women to his Hygioean Society and thus increase his own practice may have

12. Quoted in John Martin, *Animal Magnetism Examined: In a Letter to a Country Gentleman* (1790), 8.

influenced his special appeal to the "Ladies." However, even in offi-
cial assessments of animal magnetism, individuals documenting the
findings note the greater prevalence of women's response to mesmeric forces. In "Report of a Committee of the Royal Society of
Medicine," the signers delineate two early conclusions of special
significance: "That the partisans of the animal magnetism do not produce what they call crises, that is, a state of convulsions, but in subjects extremely irritable, extremely nervous, and above all, in women,
whose sensibility has already been excited by the means we have
described." According to the commission appointed by the French
Academy of Science, "many women and few men" actually entered
the state of crisis at D'Eslon's clinic. Prior to this assertion, the report marveled at the manifestation of these crises, that is, convulsions induced by the mesmerist who superintends the process: "[The
onlooker] observes with admiration the various accidents that are
repeated, and the sympathies that are developed."[13]

Women's susceptibility to the operations of magnetic forces would
not have been surprising given conceptualizations of the passive or
receptive nature of the "feminine." It was inevitable that descriptions of animal magnetism should begin to mirror firmly established gender configurations. Whether reinforced in conceptions of
God as the primary mover of physical bodies (that is, as the Being
that set material bodies in motion and thus initiated the reciprocity
fundamental to theories of mesmeric forces), in Judeo-Christian
practices reifying this divine agency in private and public relationships, or in social traditions institutionalizing men as primary dis-
seminators of medical knowledge, the paradigm of male agency and
female passivity could not help but be reflected in mesmeric literature. In *On the Sentient Faculty, and Principles of Human Magnetism*
(1819), Sigismund Ehrenreich graf von Redern, a Swedish nobleman
who was a member of a Paris society "under the presidency of the
Marquis de Puységur," offers a typical rendering of the masculine
nature of the magnetizer and feminine quality of the somnambulist:
"The somnambulist is more passive, than he is active; more influenced upon, than personally exerting any influence. The body is an

13. Benjamin Franklin et al., *Animal Magnetism; Report of Dr. Franklin and Other
Commissioners, Charged by the King of France with the Examination of the Animal
Magnetism as Practised at Paris,* 5, 12.

obedient instrument of his will, and (what is most singular) often obeys also that of the magnetist: volition, in the somnambulist, is not wholly superceded, but in some measure rendered subordinate."[14] Clearly, the male pronoun suggests that the role of somnambulist is not reserved solely for women, and, in fact, in the history of mesmeric practice, men and women were both patients. (The discovery of magnetic sleep, or hypnotic state, that is attributed to Puységur, for instance, arises in his relationship with Victor Race, a young peasant on his estate.) However, in the history of animal magnetism in the United States, the celebrated somnambulists— Jane C. Rider, Cynthia Ann Gleason, Loraina Brackett—were women. Within belief structures that argued women's biological predisposition to such forces and social values that made "natural" the pairing of male magnetist and female patient (and made more difficult an active-passive demonstration of male-male relationships), the public staging of animal magnetism in press, medical study, lyceum, and itinerant performances suggested workings of the world that both limited and liberated women's imagination.

For many, the especial genius of women, their particular sensibility to the electric, suggested a weakness, a propensity for nervous disorders and thus mental and physical disease. In *Remarks on the Influence of Mental Cultivation upon Health,* the text that Fuller had noted in her private journals during the 1830s, Amariah Brigham proposed such a view in reflections on women's education:

> Little attention is given in the education of females, to the physiological differences of the sexes. Teachers seldom reflect, that in them the nervous system naturally predominates; that they are endowed with quicker sensibilities than men, and have imaginations far more active, that their emotions are more intense, and their senses alive to more delicate impressions; and therefore require great attention; lest this exquisite sensibility, which, when properly and naturally developed, constitutes the greatest excellence of women, should either become *excessive* by too strong excitement, or suppressed by misdirected education.[15]

14. Sigismund Ehrenreich graf von Redern, *On the Sentient Faculty, and Principles of Human Magnetism,* 62.

15. Amariah Brigham, *Remarks on the Influence of Mental Cultivation upon Health,* 74.

In many respects, Brigham's characterization of women's special qualities bears a striking resemblance to those depicted by both Child and Fuller. To have an especially responsive nervous system gives a physiological explanation for women's spiritual nature. Moreover, the emphasis on endowments such as "quicker sensibilities," more active imaginations, and receptivity to more delicate impressions represent the same qualities that mark the higher state of mesmeric consciousness. And yet, Brigham clearly implies that such an "exquisite sensibility" requires surveillance that guards against the ill health of excessive stimulation or "misdirected education." In effect, his comments support the predominant hierarchical configuration of male doctor/magnetist and female patient, for, even as they articulate traits central for individual and community change, they implicitly assume the need for masculine strengths to negotiate the harsh realm of the public sphere—traits such as will, intellect, physical strength, and a nervous sensibility less prone to the variances of an unrestrained imagination. Quite literally, magnetists took on this protective role in bringing forth the clairvoyants in their charge.

Within a paradigm aligning men with the public sphere and women with the domestic or private realm, it is not surprising that gendered notions of power should be assigned to the electrical or magnetic forces and that masculinized will should be seen as the conduit for great changes. Witness Samuel Warner's letter to the *American Phrenological Journal*. While written in 1849, it resonates with views voiced throughout the decade and offers a striking juxtaposition to the way Child expressed her own wonder in *Letters from New-York*:

> Is not Electricity the father or begetter of all matter, animate or inanimate, and the immediate and acting cause of all changes and modification of matter, all transformations, vacuums, and pleonasms?
>
> We have always been taught to look upon the earth as a common mother. Is Electricity, under God, to be looked upon in the light of a common father? Look at electric action from the equator to the poles, as connected with vegetation, with animal life, with phrenological and physiological development, with temperaments, habits, dispositions.
>
> Look at its modus operandi; for instance, when we say it strikes a tree, does it, or does it not, do any thing more or less than to follow the tree as the best conductor, and by its force and velocity re-

move for the instant the atmospheric pressure, and thereby suffer
the tree to burst itself? Its partial action in this respect, its passing
down lightning rods, and ploughing deep furrows in the ground,
can, I think, be rationally accounted for upon the theory of atmospheric pressure.[16]

Interestingly, in an enthusiastic tone that Whitman would echo in
"singing the body electric" six years later, Warner renders the features of electricity in overtly masculine terms. Ploughing furrows in
the ground of the common mother earth, this father finds release.
We might ask what in this release changes or modifies matter? What
in this force transforms or reforms?

In the effort to understand the particular nature of this all-
pervading power, antebellum readers would have been inundated
with various "translations" or descriptions of mesmeric forces that
privileged will over receptivity and that betrayed profound uneasiness with the finer "feminine" sensibility. In fact, in *Woman in the Nineteenth Century,* Fuller works up to her speculation on the nature of
the relationship between the feminine and the masculine by responding to cultural attitudes consistent with Brigham's rendering
of women's specific tendencies:

> The electrical, the magnetic element in woman has not been
> fairly brought in any period. Every thing might be expected from
> it; she has far more of it than man. This is commonly expressed by
> saying that her intuitions are more rapid and more correct. You
> will often see men of high intellect absolutely stupid in regard to
> the atmospheric changes, the fine invisible links which connect
> the forms of life around them, while common women, if pure and
> modest, so that a vulgar self do not overshadow the mental eye,
> will seize and delineate these with unerring discrimination. (302)

Recalling Child's notions of the effects of climate on bodily constitution, these thoughts also initiate a critique of a culture that diminishes
rather than elevates the creative genius of those with quickened impulses. In fact, Fuller argues, such natures evoke fear, not sympathy: "Those, who seem overladen with electricity, frighten those

16. Samuel Warner, "Electricity the Great Acting Power of Nature," *American
Phrenological Journal and Miscellany,* 151.

around them. 'When she merely enters the room, I am what the French call *hérissé,'* said a man of petty feelings and worldly character of such a woman, whose depth of eye and powerful motion announced the conductor of the mysterious fluid" (302). This dynamic between the "electric" woman and worldly man outlines potential narratives (real and fictional) within which women were trapped. In many respects, it is the material sensibility ruling over the spiritual. For Fuller, however, another plotting is possible: "Yet, allow room enough, and the electric fluid will be found to invigorate and embellish, not destroy life" (302–3).

Not surprisingly, we see in the writings of Child and Fuller an effort to find a theoretical framework (and language) as well as fictional narratives that envision complementary forces. Fuller's views in her 1845 revision of "The Great Lawsuit" can be traced to earlier characterizations of her own experience with her father and his educational strategies; in these autobiographical fragments, we get insight into this orientation toward harmony, not hierarchy. "Trained to great dexterity in artificial methods, accurate, ready, with entire command of his resources," Fuller describes her father in her "Autobiographical Romance" (1840), "he had no belief in minds that listen, wait, and receive" and "no conception of the subtle and indirect motions of imagination and feeling." Initiating reflections on what has now become well known in Fuller scholarship as the contrasting influences between her father's "Roman" sensibility and "The Garden" of her mother, she notes that everything of Rome "turns your attention to what a man can become, not by yielding himself freely to impressions, not by letting nature play freely through him, but by a single thought, an earnest purpose, an indomitable will, by hardihood, self-command, and force of expression." By the 1840s, Fuller knew enough of the debilitating aspects of this vision (for self-culture and, more broadly, national culture) to resist it. One form of resistance involved helping others conceptualize the nature of its disharmonizing energy: "Man present in nature, commanding nature too sternly to be inspired by it, standing like the rock amid the sea, or moving like the fire over the land, either impassive, or irresistible; knowing not the soft mediums or fine flights of life, but the force which he expresses, piercing to the centre." Such individuals contrasted sharply with the Seeress of Prevorst or other clairvoyants who manifested an ability to let natural energies "play freely through" them; in the language of the era, they were mediums who, though expressing their receptivity to inherent forces in more remarkable ways, exemplified the capacity to achieve a higher state.[17]

So, while some of the magnetic literature and responses to the electric formulated ideas in terms that privileged the masculine, Fuller and Child saw in the new science evidence of the essential contribution of a receptive consciousness or medium to a culture driven by rampant materialism. If, as texts in the 1840s often noted, the nature of magnetic relationships reflected the reciprocity of material and immaterial forces in the universe, then the dynamic between magnetizer and magnetized could be envisioned more positively as a fluid or harmonious relationship rather than a hierarchical one. The masculine and the feminine, then, would represent terms that may be more applicable to complementary forces than antagonistic ones. To acknowledge quite literally a special openness of woman in the nineteenth century is also to infer, given the fundamental principle of reciprocity asserted in the various philosophies of animal magnetism, that receptivity need not imply inactivity or lack of agency. In a model that did not privilege the masculine or the feminine, both sides of the "great radical dualism" could serve central roles; moreover, in a paradoxical but dramatic reframing of the era's gender distinctions, the "feminine" represented an active power when allowed to unfold within the natural interplay with the masculine.

Of course, articulating this harmonious relationship in a culture that tended to translate differences into inequitable power relationships was not easy. With her notion of the "great radical dualism," Fuller does find one way to voice this harmony, for she positions a fluid or dynamic relationship between both forces and underscores the permeability between the active and passive by noting that no single self is wholly masculine or feminine. Unlike Warner's, this framework lends itself to conceptualizing power not as an "acting upon" but as an "acting within." To arrive at these ideas conveys a rejection of the Roman education as a sole or dominant model for developing the self. Significantly, the opening of *Woman in the*

17. Margaret Fuller, "Autobiographical Romance," in *The Essential Margaret Fuller,* 28, 29.

Nineteenth Century confidently asserts this conceptual foundation through a vocabulary that consistently envisions the unfolding of truths in a very "un-Roman" mind. In many ways, we can read Fuller's characterization of artist, philosopher, historian, and man of science as her own rendering of Emerson's "Man-Thinking"—if we understand "Man," as did Fuller, as "both man and woman" or "two halves of one thought":

> Shall we not name with as deep a benediction those who, if not so immediately, or so consciously, in connection with the eternal truth, yet, led and fashioned by a divine instinct, serve no less to develop and interpret the open secret of love passing into life, energy creating for the purpose of happiness; the artist whose hand, drawn by a pre-existent harmony to a certain medium, moulds it to forms of life more highly and completely organized than are seen elsewhere, and, by carrying out the intention of nature, reveals her meaning to those who are not yet wise enough to divine it; the philosopher who listens steadily for laws and causes, and from those obvious, infers those yet unknown; the historian who, in faith that all events must have their reason and their aim, records them, and thus fills archives from which the youth of prophets may be fed. The man of science dissects the statements, tests the facts, and demonstrates order, even where he cannot its purpose. (248)

No matter the calling, it is clear that, if properly understood, the "divine instinct" frees the soul toward what seems an intuitive grasp of preexisting harmonies. To both women and men, there are profound implications of such a state of responsiveness. In effect, because we are all potential mediums of these pervasive energies, we all offer the promise of creating a "new hour in the day of man" (250). In this way, Fuller extends even further the implications of Child's reflections in *Letters from New-York*. Responding to the reality of slavery and the promise of the statement "All men are born free and equal," Fuller asserts, "That which has once been clearly conceived in the intelligence cannot fail sooner or later to be acted out" (254). Rather than a more distant evolutionary vision, Fuller implies that invisible forces can evoke a kind of magnetic action in the short term.

Within this theoretical paradigm, Child and Fuller demonstrate through their work that women have a central role in public crises, especially if we see crises in a mesmeric sense as that which prefaces healing and thus a harmonious "state." In "Thot and Freia: A Romance of the Spirit Land," a story that marked the first of eighteen published in the *Columbian Lady's and Gentleman's Magazine* from January 1845 to May 1847, Child offers a fictional rendering of ideas contained in Fuller's writings as well as a narrative extension of her own notions of the inward. Revising Norse mythology, she creates the story of Freia, "the Goddess of Love, or Feeling," and Thot, whom she notes is "synonymous with Art, Science, or Skill."[18] In effect, Freia embodies the conception of "Femality" that Fuller cites in *Woman in the Nineteenth Century;* the feminine encompasses the "lyrical, the inspiring, and the inspired apprehensiveness of [woman's] being" (309). Thot, on the other hand, is the Roman: he is "[s]trong and sinewy, like a man of iron, with an eye that looked as if he thought creation was his anvil, on which he could fashion all things" (1).

Through these contrasts, Child creates a fable of the dynamic interplay between the masculine and the feminine, the material and the spiritual. Cast out from the glorious valley of Ida and banished to the gloom of Nilfheim, "the world of mist" (1), the exiled Thot still recalls the power of Freia's song and yearns for her presence: "From her harp, I heard the tones to which the trees grow, and the blossoms unfold; and with the tones came to me the primeval words whispered into the heart of each tree, and blossom, and gem, at the moment of its creation; the word which gave them being, and which they must forever obey. I burned with intense desire to press farther into the inmost heart of all being, and learn the one primeval tone, in the one primeval word, from which flowed the universe" (2). Without his knowledge, however, the gods trick Thot into believing that, through his own will, he can seize Freia from the heavens:

18. Lydia Maria Child, "Thot and Freia," 1. This story was originally published as one of Child's "Letters from New-York" written for the *Boston Courier* (July 25, 1844) and was later included as "Letter XX. Genius and Skill. The Romance of Thot and Freia" in *Letters from New York. Second Series* (1845). (After her resignation as editor of the *National Anti-Slavery Standard* in May 1843, Child continued to write her letters for the Boston newspaper.) Child also cut an opening explanation of what prompted the story and published it in the January 1845 issue of the *Columbian Lady's and Gentleman's Magazine.* Subsequent references to the story will be from the *Columbian* version and will be cited parenthetically in the text.

"She came, though reluctantly, at the command of my will. Is Will then the central life?—the primeval word, from which electricity had being?" (2). Instead of Freia, they send a beautiful shepherdess, and, after traveling afar to a "New World across the ocean" (3), Thot seeks from her the word that will give beauty and life to the lifeless forms of his creative powers. In describing his constructions out of earth and stone, Child herself has taken care to suggest that Thot creates through material means, through the geometric and algebraic signs that had formed the basis for originally conjuring up the false Freia.

Inevitably, Thot's enormous powers cannot instill true beauty in their subterranean home nor sustain the life of his companion. All that he has created becomes a tomb that enslaves rather than liberates. Ultimately, the shepherdess dies, initiating Thot's recognition of his own pride as well as the truth of the false Freia's judgment on his creation's superficial beauty. With such a recognition, the true Freia can enter to instruct him: "Me thou couldst not bind for a moment. If thou *couldst* fetter me with thy triangles and squares, the universe would stop its motions. Thou and I, dear Thot, are one from all eternity. Thou hast made this mournful separation, by reversing the divine laws of our being. Thou hast thought to create the outward, and then compel the inward to give it life. But the inward forms the outward and thus only can the outward live" (6). The union of Thot and Freia is essential in this new world, but it is a marriage that can only emerge through an appropriate relationship between active, material energy and inspiration and love. Once Thot humbles himself and thus becomes open to the truths that Freia reveals through dreams, a child is born both strong enough to receive Thot's spirit and "delicate enough" to receive Freia's (6). In this story, then, Child creates one of the era's clearest parables of the proper relationship between the masculine and the feminine. In doing so, she offers her readers a tale that addresses man's desire "to understand the origin of nature and himself, his anxious questioning of the infinite and fearful listening to echoes from the invisible" (1).

In the same month as her publication of *Woman in the Nineteenth Century* and one month after the *Columbian* issue of Child's story, Fuller reviewed J. Stanley Grimes's *Etherology; or, The Philosophy of Mesmerism and Phrenology* (1845). "Man," she remarks in the review, "is always trying to get charts and directions for the super-sensual element in which he finds himself involuntarily moving." She continues with reflections that could have served as a preface to Child's story: "Sometimes, indeed, for long periods, a life of continual activity in supplying bodily wants or warding off bodily dangers will make him inattentive to the circumstances of this other life. Then, in an interval of leisure, he will start to find himself pervaded by the power of this more subtle and searching energy, and will turn his thoughts, with new force, to scrutinize its nature and its promises." As for Fuller (who speaks of her own views in the plural pronoun), "since we became conscious at all of our connection with the two forms of being called the spiritual and material, we have perceived the existence of such an agent, and should have no doubts on the subject, if we had never heard one human voice in correspondent testimony with our perceptions." Confessing that she as well as others seems unable to grasp fully the "laws" of this agent, she still acknowledges the necessity of such inductive and deductive study, for, "[in] metaphysics, in phrenology, in animal magnetism, in electricity, in chemistry, the tendency is the same, even when the conclusions seem most dissonant." As the "mind presses nearer home to the seat of consciousness . . . ," she asserts, "old limits become fluid beneath the fire of thought."[19]

In the next fifteen months, Fuller would also review Catherine Crowe's translation of Justinus Kerner's *The Seeress of Prevorst* (1845), Gibson Smith's *Lectures on Clairmativeness; or, Human Magnetism* (1845), and Theodore Leger's *Animal Magnetism; or, Psychodunamy* (1846). With each, she reveals the same sense that, while perhaps to be questioned in particulars, these works capture aspects of the spiritual world that inform and affect material existence. Confessing that she has read the fourth of Smith's lectures (which, in part, include transcriptions of insights from the clairvoyant Jackson Davis), she

---

19. Margaret Fuller, *Life Without and Life Within; or, Reviews, Narratives, Essays, and Poems,* ed. Arthur B. Fuller, 169, 170, 171. The February 17, 1845, review is also included in *Margaret Fuller, Critic: Writings from the New-York Tribune, 1844–1846.* In presenting a series of seventy-two facts and/or principles that merge eighteenth-century lectures on motion and mesmeric forces with antebellum discourse on physiology, neurology, and phrenology, Grimes's text offers an excellent study on how late-eighteenth-century views had been accommodated in the antebellum period.

reports that it corresponds with "our own impressions as to spiritual facts." Perhaps Fuller has in mind the correspondence between her own "mystical experiences" and the clairvoyant's description of his higher state. According to Davis, an individual situated in a magnetic or clairvoyant state does not receive impressions from external organs: "Nothing is then left but the created mind. It is, then, like a stone that is thrown into the water;—the wave from the origin swells, extends, expands, until it reaches the distant shore. The mind is so situated that it expands, extends, reaches and searches, until its wave has battered against the regions of space!"[20]

The particular truths embodied in animal magnetism continued to inform Child's stories and her life. In April of 1845, the *Columbian* published "The Children of Mt. Ida," a tale that plots the tragic relationship between Corythus and his clairvoyant lover, Oenone. Drawn to material power and external beauty, Corythus abandons his lover and his pastoral life on Mt. Ida for the glories of Priam. (In a clairvoyant trance, Oenone reveals that Corythus is the heir to the king of Troy.) Interestingly, the *Broadway Journal* opines that this tale "is the most simple and perfect story that any American woman has yet produced." In the tragic heroine, the review continues, Child "has, unconsciously we suspect, drawn the portrait of a perfect woman, a wife and mother, in Oenone, a very different being from the Glumdalclitches who form the ideal of Miss Fuller's women." Moreover, "in the disguise of a fiction Mrs. C. has introduced one of the marvelous psychological developments, which have become too common in our day, to be laughed out of countenance by our wise men who will receive no truths less than a century old." Clearly, in positioning Oenone as the ideal woman (and Corythus "as near an approach to as perfect a man as our imperfect nature has yet developed"), the reviewer fails to discern the moral of the story. Only together in Mt. Ida, the story appears to assert, are the peculiar beauties of the feminine and the masculine realized. That the reviewer also juxtaposed Child and Fuller betrays an ignorance of both their relationship and their sympathetic views—though it does suggest that, much more than Child, Fuller had directly and extensively addressed the "woman ques-

20. Fuller, *Margaret Fuller, Critic*, C163:4; Jackson Davis, quoted in Gibson Smith, *Lectures on Clairmativeness; or, Human Magnetism*, 35.

tion" in terms that may have reserved a less tragic role for ideal womanhood.[21]

For both Child and Fuller, the deeper significance of divine electricity and woman's "exquisite sensibility" emerged in its promise to reform the hearts and minds of citizens diminished by material forces. Recalling in her review of Grimes's *Etherology* an unexpected meeting with a clairvoyant who, seven years earlier, had responded to her suffering, Fuller hints at this promise of new states of consciousness. Having failed to recognize Fuller and reflecting a loss of her magnetic powers, the woman nonetheless pens two lines that seem to evoke earlier sympathies: "The ills that Heaven decrees / The brave with courage bear." Fuller concludes the review with final reflections on the clairvoyant's penciled message:

> Others may explain this as they will; to me it was a token that the same affinity that had acted before, gave the same knowledge; for the writer was at the time ill in the same way as before. It also seemed to indicate that the somnambulic trance was only a form of the higher development, the sensibility to more subtle influences—in the terms of Mr. Grimes, a susceptibility to etherium. The blind girl perhaps never knew who I was, but saw my true state more clearly than any other person did, and I have kept those penciled lines, written in the stiff, round character proper to the blind, as a talisman of "Credenciveness," as the book before me styles it, Credulity as the world at large does, and, to my own mind, as one of the clews granted, during this earthly life, to the mysteries of future states of being, and more rapid and complete modes of intercourse between mind and mind.[22]

---

21. Review of "The Children of Mt. Ida. By Mrs. Child." Though Burton R. Pollin's *Edgar Allan Poe: Writings in "The Broadway Journal"* does not confirm authorship, one suspects that the reviewer might have been Edgar Allan Poe, then coeditor of the *Broadway Journal,* whose own views of sublime poetry involved the death of a woman character. See Edgar Allan Poe, "The Philosophy of Composition," in *Edgar Allan Poe: Essays and Reviews,* 17, 18–19. See Steele, *Transfiguring America,* for an extensive exploration of the way that Fuller resists and reconstructs the alignment of women with cultural representations of death.

22. Fuller, *Life Without and Life Within,* 173. In his merging of mesmerism and phrenology, Grimes hypothesizes an "organ of *Credenciveness*" that marks the "propensity to act upon testimony or assertion." In effect, he seeks to explain the phenomena, witnessed in the interaction between magnetist and patient,

For Fuller, these reflections recall the yearning for the intercourse between mind and mind that remains possible for those of exquisite sensibilities. For both Fuller and Child, it is a yearning that arises from more than women in the nineteenth century; it is a desire that marks the peculiar urge of a harmonious, democratic state.

---

of susceptible subjects being controlled by simple assertions of the mesmerist: "Assert to the subject, in a decided tone, for instance, '*You cannot open your eyes,*' and if his eyes were shut when you made the assertion, he cannot open them afterwards until you again say, '*Now you can open them,*' or something to that effect" (Grimes, *Etherology,* 188, 186).

Conclusion

Singing the American Body Electric
Whitman and the Mesmeric Turn

> He . . . learns that in going down into the secrets of his own mind
> he has descended into the secrets of all minds. He learns that he
> who has mastered any law in his private thoughts, is master to that
> extent of all men whose language he speaks, of all into whose lan-
> guage his own can be translated.
>
> Ralph Waldo Emerson, "The American Scholar"

> I celebrate myself,
> And what I assume you shall assume,
> For every atom belonging to me as good belongs to you.
>
> Walt Whitman, "Song of Myself"

IN THE SPRING OF MY first year of graduate school, I took
a Walt Whitman seminar from Ed Folsom. In my files, I still have
blue-stencil copies of Whitman's doggerel verse of the 1840s. When
I teach *Leaves of Grass,* I bring out this early poetry and let students
take turns reading from "The Inca's Daughter":

> Before the dark-brow'd sons of Spain,
> A captive Indian maiden stood;
> Imprison'd where the moon before
> Her race as princes trod.[1]

---

1. Walt Whitman, *Walt Whitman: The Early Poems and the Fiction,* ed. Thomas
Brasher, 6.

Just as I did in the spring of 1983, my class wonders at the profound disparity between the voice and form of the 1855 "Song of Myself" and the conventional rhythms of the uninspiring juvenilia. Inevitably, someone asks the obvious question: How could the person who sung of a "Peruvian monarch's child" also compose the opening lines of "Song of Myself"?

In these closing reflections on how the era's notions of mesmerism and the mind cultivated the kind of consciousness that led to such dramatic shifts in sensibility and form, I offer an indirect response to this query. Whereas the preceding chapters focusing on Poe and Fuller carefully trace the confluence of what they wrote and said within the context of the magnetic literature, this conclusion more narrowly (but, I hope, suggestively) applies the implications of the culture's mesmeric turn to a transformative American text. Though arising from a complex set of influences and circumstances, *Leaves of Grass* and its central poem, "Song of Myself," arguably reconstitutes historical and cultural materials through a mesmeric consciousness, that is, through an epistemology rooted in the science of animal magnetism. This is not to say that Whitman knowingly applied the concepts and vocabulary of magnetic philosophies—though evidence indicates this possibility. Rather, it is to suggest that his ability to break spatial-temporal boundaries and reconfigure gender, class, and cultural relationships depended on a new psychological orientation. Unlike his predecessors, ruled by rigid models, Whitman did not conform thoughts to things or even simply conform things to thought. Ultimately, he absorbed the law of thought itself and allowed its form to unfold.

In an overlooked March 1963 article entitled "Whitman's Debt to Animal Magnetism," medievalist scholar Edmund Reiss ventured from his primary area of research to explore the poet's "indebtedness to the contemporary fad of animal magnetism, especially concerning its appearance in the phraseology and nature of many of his poetic images and his conceptions of the poet and the leader." Calling attention to one of Whitman's obscure tales, the May 1848 story "Samuel Sensitive," Reiss notes the author's brief reference to mesmerism. According to Reiss, however, the first edition of *Leaves of Grass* "shows a development over the technique of 'Samuel Sensitive,' for now both his mind and imagery have assimilated the mesmeric terms." In a suggestive overview of Whitman's poetry and private writings, Reiss brings forward telling evidence of the bard's cognizance of the language and concepts of animal magnetism. He concludes: "Not only does [Whitman] frequently portray all life joined in a magnetic bond, but the nature of much of his imagery affords a startling resemblance to much in the language and techniques of animal magnetism. Many of the roles assumed by his 'I,' such as hypnotist, clairvoyant, prophetic leader, and healer, are the most important practical manifestations of the theories of animal magnetism."[2]

In *Walt Whitman and the Body Beautiful,* Harold Aspiz offers a definitive consideration of the relationship between the era's writings on mesmerism and Whitman's work. His chapter "The Body Electric" recalls one of the poet's most obvious references to the era's discourse on animal magnetism ("I Sing the Body Electric") and probes a range of other poems, including "Song of Myself," "Song of the Answerer," "The Sleepers," and "Salut au Monde!" As we have seen in Lydia Maria Child's *Letters from New-York,* Fuller's *Woman in the Nineteenth Century,* and the era's literature on animal magnetism, the "electric" could be seen as synonymous with the magnetic and was often explored in relation to the vital fluid from which the mind partook in times of higher consciousness. As Aspiz documents in his book, "Whitman used electrical concepts to illustrate the dynamism and intuition that qualified him to be his nation's poet. He admitted his personal attraction to those whom he found 'physically and mentally magnetic,' and he preserved a clipping on 'Personal Magnetism' which stated that 'the large magnetic power which every person may well covet is a *birthright*' and that those who lead unhealthful or dissipated lives 'squander and exhaust this "capital stock" of power.'" As did Poe, Fuller, Child, and others, Whitman drew some of his understanding of the electric or mesmeric consciousness and of the psychological underpinnings to artistic and reform principles from Chauncy Hare Townshend's *Facts in Mesmerism.* Reviewing the book in the August 14, 1842, *New York Sunday Times,* he declares that it "reveals at once the existence of a whole new world of truth, grand, fearful, profound, relating to that great mystery, in the shadow of which we live and move and have our being, the mystery of our Humanity."[3]

---

2. Edmund Reiss, "Whitman's Debt to Animal Magnetism," 80, 81, 88.
3. Harold Aspiz, *Walt Whitman and the Body Beautiful,* 150–51, 154.

Over the course of the 1840s and early 1850s, then, Whitman absorbed the philosophical and scientific discourse on mesmerism. Further evidence that mesmeric thought informed the concepts and language of his artistic vision arises in one of his notebooks. In a description of his poetic inspiration and power, Whitman employs words and images that clearly resonate with the literature on animal magnetism: "a trance, yet with all the senses alert—only a state of high exalted musing—the tangible and material with all its shows, the objective world suspended or surmounted for a while, and the powers in exaltation, freedom, vision—yet the *senses* not lost or counteracted."[4] In the mesmeric literature, similar reflections and terminology occur in sections that most directly address the somnambulant state. According to Joseph Philippe François Deleuze, individuals in this trance-like state reveal a "developement of sensibility, of which we can have no conception. They are susceptible of receiving influence from every living thing that surrounds them, and principally from living beings. They are not only affected by physical emanations, or the effluvia of living bodies, but also, to a degree much more surprising, by the thoughts and sentiments of those who surround them, or who are busy with them." Significantly, sensation shifts from the sense organs to an internal faculty. Admitting that somnambulists "exhibit very different phenomena," Deleuze ultimately declares that "the only distinctive and constant character of somnambulism is, the existence of a new mode of perception." In *Human Magnetism,* William Newnham asserts that "the somnambulist knows nothing beyond what he knew before in his natural condition" but adds that "the exaltation of his memory, and powers of comparison, produces intellectual combination which render his manifestations of mind superior to themselves in his ordinary state."[5]

For Reiss and, to a lesser extent, Aspiz, however, the emphasis seems to be on how Whitman's mesmeric "phraseology" and "poetic images" illuminate content rather than form. At the same time, their

4. Quoted in F. O. Matthiessen, *American Renaissance: Art and Expression in the Age of Emerson and Whitman,* 539–40.

5. Deleuze, *Practical Instruction in Animal Magnetism,* 77, 91; Newnham, *Human Magnetism,* 225.

insights into the nature of Whitman's poetic persona and how it illustrates the higher-order consciousness of clairvoyants point toward another compelling truth: in embodying the sensibility of the magnetic mind, Whitman discovered a democratic ("American") poetic form. Given the period's effort to distinguish between the limitations of passive fancy and the expansive potential of a constructive imagination, it is not surprising that the "laws" of the imagination arising from insights into elevated modes of perception and transition states influenced democratic poetics. Within such a theoretical framework, things (that is, content) must be peripheral to thought(s) (that is, epistemological orientation); how one knows conditions how one writes.

To develop the implications of these insights, it is again useful to turn to the era's association between the outward world and the nature of mind. Just as the universe offers evidence of counteracting forces of attraction and repulsion, of the centripetal and the centrifugal, so too does the mind encompass such polarities. Moreover, just as studies in the nature of electric and magnetic forces suggest a harmonizing agent in divine creation, so too does the individual mind—in its highest state of awareness—reflect the influence or effect of this invisible and all-encompassing power. The vital "I," then, can be seen as a fluid embodiment of oppositions mediated by a harmonizing magnetism.

"Song of Myself" can be examined as an emblematic manifestation or unfolding of this dynamic. From the very beginning, Whitman envisions the self as the interplay between centripetal and centrifugal pulses. The individual represents a consciousness through which sensation finds order; it is the conscious self that experiences or perceives the world with a narrow and narrowing singularity. In many ways, to echo Poe's cosmic vision in *Eureka*, the self is the originating or simple "Unity" that contains within the laws of its inevitable expansion:

> I celebrate myself,
> And what I assume you shall assume,
> For every atom belonging to me as good belongs to you.
>
> I loafe and invite my soul,
> I lean and loafe at my ease . . . . observing a spear of summer
> grass.

> Houses and rooms are full of perfumes . . . . the shelves are
>   crowded with perfumes,
> I breathe the fragrance myself, and know it and like it,
> The distillation would intoxicate me also, but I shall not let it.[6]

This unifying force of the "I" coexists with the pulse of constant expansion. Further developing the full implications of his opening
lines, Whitman expresses the centrifugal dimensions of the self and
the present age in canto 3: "Urge and urge and urge, / Always the
procreant urge of the world" (lines 36–37). Moreover, in canto 6, the
single blade of grass quickly transforms into a hieroglyphic of seeming oppositions: black folk and white, young and old, woman and
man, death and life. Ultimately, however, this canto articulates not
an affirmation of limiting antipathies or the threat of irreconcilable
differences, but a co-presence of centripetal and centrifugal forces.
The single entity—whether a blade of grass or the individual self—
contains the one and the many. Significantly, the rhythm of the one
to the many, this coexistence of the centripetal and centrifugal can
be read in terms of the self-conscious act of mind. The "electric"
presence of the perceiving, interpreting consciousness is the poem
itself. As readers, we join in this way of knowing, this harmonizing
pulse of the poetic imagination.

As the poet, Whitman embodies the laws of such rhythms and
pulsings in the poetic innovations that guided the form of the poem.
In canto 24, the section that announces the poet's identity, we again
see the assertion of the "I" alongside lines that underscore the expansive nature of the individual self. Hence, the poet is at once a
single, speaking presence as well as a "kosmos." Even more dramatic,
the momentary narrowing into a named identity gives way to the
centrifugal forces breaking the house of the self wide open: "Unscrew the locks from the doors! / Unscrew the doors themselves
from their jambs!" (lines 502–3). This movement inward and outward embodies a recurring dynamic of the entire poem: that which
gets named as me receives a balancing naming of that which is not
me. To be whole is to enact the idea that the self contains body and
soul, life and death, the "me" and "not me." Metaphorically, Whitman
embraces the attraction and repulsion of seeming oppositions. And,

---

6. Walt Whitman, *Leaves of Grass*, ed. Malcolm Cowley, lines 4–8. Subsequent
references to this 1855 edition will be cited by line number parenthetically in
the text.

not surprisingly, he contains these counteracting impulses in the language of the electric: "Through me the afflatus surging and surging. . . . through me the current and the index" (line 506). As Harold Aspiz underscores in his look at the same section (and the poet's later description of the "threads that connect the stars—and of wombs and of the fatherstuff" [line 514]), Whitman envisions the poetic persona's "electro-spermatic ejaculation" as conduit for the larger forces of the universe: "Just as the 'father-stuff' represents the electrical source of human life, so the stars represent the electrical sources of universal life." In fact, noting his earlier drafts of these lines, Aspiz calls attention to how Whitman "had associated these 'threads' with the electrical cores" that some of the era's literature had "located in various parts of the body."[7]

Whitman's catalogues represent further poetic innovations that arise from mesmeric consciousness. In them, we see the kind of receptive state or "apprehensive genius" that Fuller describes before turning to her consideration of the Seeress of Prevorst in *Summer on the Lakes*. That Whitman's persona can be seen as a medium again is examined in Aspiz's text. "There is a notable resemblance," he points out, "between the nineteenth-century trance mediums who experience a 'superior state' of clairvoyance and the visionary persona of *Leaves of Grass*." Interestingly, Aspiz compares the "persona's mystical experiences" to the Seeress of Prevorst's transition state, that is, her position between life and death, waking and sleeping, that Justinus Kerner explores in some detail:

> During her trances, she reportedly entered into a somnambulistic state in which she saw herself "out of her body and sometimes double." At such times, she beheld her body from the outside through the eyes of her other self, the supersensory faculty which she called the "nerve-spirit"—the immortal companion of the soul in life and death and the guide on her dream-journeys to the dead. In "sleep-waking" or "clairvoyance," she said, "the inner-man steps forward and inspects the outer, which is not the case either in sleep or dreaming."

According to Aspiz, while Whitman's visionary poetry shares affinities with "what James E. Miller calls 'the traditional mystical experience,'"

---

7. Aspiz, *Walt Whitman and the Body Beautiful*, 149. Aspiz quotes from the 1892 "deathbed" edition of *Leaves of Grass*.

its "structural and thematic elements" connect it to other "mesmeric dream poems" such as "The Sleepers." He concludes that "[s]ection 33 also contains the poem's second great panoramic catalog of sensory perceptions" and that, "whereas the catalog in section 15 merely dramatizes the persona's newly expanded powers of observation, this later catalog reveals a quantum growth in his perceptual-clairvoyant faculties." In capturing the magnetic consciousness harmonizing an ever-widening receptivity *and* an ever-narrowing, sensual particularity, cantos 15 and 33 explicitly manifest a higher mode of perception.[8]

While "Song of Myself" and many other poems and narratives of the period can lose their vitality if read through a single critical perspective, a mesmeric interpretive paradigm offers a way of opening up broader understandings by calling attention to affinities between seemingly disparate writers. Such a paradigm, after all, is rooted in the period's efforts to assimilate medical, scientific, and psychological "truths," to theorize the fluidity of life and artistic endeavors, and to encompass the transitional nature of individual and national identity. Without being reductive, then, it may be possible to characterize the "becoming" and "journeying" of "Song of Myself" alongside a tradition of antebellum texts that defy rigidity, that experiment within various genres and forms, and that critique an inability to reflect the laws of creation in the paradoxical oppositions that mark a vital life and imagination. In the context of this mesmeric turn, it is possible to understand Poe's unifying and annihilating collapse to the One and Whitman's dissolution of the poetic "I" within the continuum of the science of transition states. Though their creative and critical dispositions favored the centripetal and the centrifugal, respectively, the two writers shared common psychological principles.

In the beginning of *Woman in the Nineteenth Century,* Margaret Fuller indicates her orientation to such principles when underscoring the kind of "unfolding" of form that marks her text and a democratic tendency:

> Poets and priests have strung the lyre with the heartstrings, poured out their best blood upon the altar, which, reared anew

8. Ibid., 162, 166, 174, 175.

from age to age shall at last sustain the flame pure enough to rise to highest heaven. Shall we not name with as deep a benediction those who, if not so immediately, or so consciously, in connection with the eternal truth, yet, led and fashioned by a divine instinct, serve no less to develope and interpret the open secret of love passing into life, energy creating for the purpose of happiness; the artist whose hand, drawn by a pre-existent harmony to a certain medium, moulds it to forms of life more highly and completely organized than are seen elsewhere, and, by carrying out the intention of nature, reveals her meaning to those who are not yet wise enough to divine it. . . .[9]

Fuller would later add that "human beings are not so constituted that they can live without expansion" (260). With such speculation, it becomes clear that, whether in relation to social or literary reform, artists must endeavor to construct their chosen forms in ways that mirror the energetic flux of "love passing into life." Moreover, Fuller consistently reminds readers of the necessity to remove those visible and invisible constraints that inhibit a complete realization or embodiment of harmonious forces. The possibility of achieving such artful forms (and social change) demanded an aesthetic cultivation of the notion of an organic "unfolding" of forms rather than an imitative conforming to past literary models. In short, artists needed to conceive of "medium-moulding" and self-construction as an unfolding or flowering of "pre-existent" and inner harmonies. To understand such underlying principles or harmonies, writers of the period turned to some of the most evocative efforts to combine philosophical idealism with new and exciting insights into the material workings of human and planetary bodies. When Fuller speaks of the "intention of nature" unfolding within an artistic medium, then, she imagines the microcosm of the human mind as embodying the macrocosm of larger magnetic attractions and repulsions. Thus, the faculties of the mind (for example, Reason, Intuition, Imagination)—and the neurological wiring that conduct and construct sensation, thought, and memory—provide the inherent models for literary and social reforms.

Whitman's and Fuller's unique contribution to the literature of

9. Margaret Fuller, *Woman in the Nineteenth Century,* in *The Essential Margaret Fuller,* 248. All subsequent references to this book will be cited parenthetically in the text.

transition states is to make more explicit the relationship between a mesmeric consciousness and democratic art. As Townshend underscores in his study and as Whitman embodies in his writing, "In mesmerism the mind recurs to its native character and fundamental endowments, seeming to cast aside the accidental differences induced by education, circumstances, and neglect of moral discipline."[10] Fuller, too, visibly links the onward progress of the principles of liberty to "woman in the nineteenth century." Both writers recognized that the constitution of the mind transcended the boundaries of region, race, class, age, and gender and thus their decision to employ aesthetic choices consistent with the principles of inner states followed a democratic plan. Moreover, they demonstrated a belief that the imagination, properly nurtured, prepares individual readers for the work of democracy. To develop what might be termed sympathetic or electric forms contributed to democratic citizenship by inculcating a new way of knowing. In the mind, after all, we dwell in possibility.

Poetry and narratives that elevated the centrality of the "I" risked misinterpretation. By emphasizing the unit before union (*Woman in the Nineteenth Century,* 312), for example, Margaret Fuller invited the possibility of seeing her ideas as antagonistic to community. The many efforts to delineate the particular nature of transition states by examining the self (or representative individuals such as the Seeress of Prevorst), however, were never meant to foster unchecked individualism. On the contrary, the ultimate end of works ranging from "Self-Reliance" to *Walden* to *Woman in the Nineteenth Century* was not isolation, but return to a larger community threatened by division forces. Repeatedly, these works and others demonstrated the possibility of ideal union through fostering a willingness to act with the knowledge that the individual mind represents the imprint of divine laws. Thus, while seeming to overstate the centripetal energy of the independent self in order to combat a cultural deference to England and Europe, Emerson consistently directed readers of essays such as "The American Scholar" to focus on inward faculties or qualities such as intuition and self-trust: "He then learns that in going down into the secrets of his own mind he has descended into the secrets of all minds."[11] Given her period's em-

<hr />

10. Townshend, *Facts in Mesmerism,* 351–52.
11. Emerson, *Selections from Ralph Waldo Emerson,* 74.

phasis upon marriage as the seemingly sole means of achieving identity or worth, it is also not surprising that Fuller seemed to cut off the self from "relations": "If any individual live too much in relations, so that he becomes a stranger to the resources of his own nature, he falls, after a while, into a distraction, or imbecility, from which he can only be cured by a time of isolation, which gives the renovating fountains time to rise up. Many minds, deprived of the traditionary or instinctive means of passing a cheerful existence, must find help in self-impulse, or perish. . . . Union is only possible to those who are units" (312).

Through this study's extensive look at the history of this mesmeric turn and its role in the works of Poe and Fuller, however, we have come to see that "mind" means more than "self" or "individual soul." In other words, references to the mind call forth richer associations for readers steeped in the era's physiological and psychological investigations. "Mind" literally and figuratively signifies the site of a vital fluid and its harmonizing potential. That so many writers could point with such confidence to the capacity of the individual mind to generate change goes beyond faith and philosophy. Too many studies were documenting and personal experiences affirming the physical effects of invisible causes. In bringing together the material and the spiritual, the mesmeric literature appealed to unifying laws in an age of profound divisions.

Readers, then, must remain vigilant to antebellum writers' efforts to address the destructive disequilibrium that comes from failing to acknowledge counterbalancing oppositions and the unifying nature of magnetic forces. The primary or active imagination, after all, manifests this encompassing vision. Again, as Coleridge notes in *Theory of Life,* "Infinite repulsion, uncounteracted and alone, is tantamount to infinite, dimensionless diffusion, and this again to infinite weakness; viz., to space. Conceive attraction alone, and as an infinite contraction, its product amounts to the absolute point, viz., to time."[12] Such assertions should be understood in their relation to Nature and to Art, that is, to the laws that govern the universe and the perceptual orientation that guides narrative and lyric.

In "Circles," Emerson further illustrates concepts that get "writ large" in "Song of Myself." Starting with an emphasis on the "eye" or I that resonates with the spirit if not the letter of "Self-Reliance," the

---

12. Coleridge, *Theory of Life,* in *Shorter Works and Fragments,* pt. 1, 522.

essay finds form in the centripetal-centrifugal dynamic of the first lines: "The eye is the first circle; the horizon which it forms is the second; and throughout nature this primary figure is repeated without end." Such imagery exhibits the expanding and contracting energies so prevalent in a wide range of the era's philosophic and scientific literature. It would not be unreasonable for readers to worry over a vision that seems to emphasize fluidity, volatility, and impermanence and that imagines the toppling of institutions with but a "thought" or the transformative force of the next new generalization. We seem caught between the apparent isolation of the single soul and the potential chaos of an expansive idea. In short, it seems a vision of disorder, not ultimate order. (Not unlike Poe's vision in *Eureka,* it seems as if the One initiates ever-expanding circles that threaten to contract with destructive consequences.) In the end, however, Emerson introduces what might be termed a "magnetic" or "electric" turn: "Yet this incessant movement and progression which all things partake could never become sensible to us but by contrast to some principle of fixture or stability in the soul. Whilst the eternal generation of circles proceeds, the eternal generator abides. That central life is somewhat superior to creation, superior to knowledge and thought, and contains its circles."[13] In short, the essay reminds readers that individual thought and creation never stray from the informing influence of a higher consciousness. For many, an attention to the guiding direction of this central life invites an education in the nature of thought and of the mesmeric consciousness.

Just as we might consider the literature of the period in the context of mesmeric principles, so too can we understand the era's criticism in light of magnetic concepts and vocabulary. Thus, we can more fully see why Margaret Fuller offers a veiled critique of Emerson in *Summer on the Lakes* in terms of his limited embodiment of the electric. For Fuller, the Emersonian Self-Poise requires "more of love, or more of apprehensive genius, (for either would give you the needed expansion and delicacy)"—with more of these, she remarks, "you would command my entire reverence."[14] In Emerson's work, Fuller heard a sensibility that would deny her and others their "full,

---

13. Emerson, "Circles," in *Selections from Ralph Waldo Emerson,* 168, 176.
14. Fuller, *Summer on the Lakes,* in *The Essential Margaret Fuller,* 149–50.

free life." As the receptive writer must allow form to unfold or be molded from "divine instinct" or the electric nature of one's apprehensive being, the ideal critic must foster a literary practice and reading sensibility that elicits an elevated consciousness. Through criticism, Fuller (and Poe) discerned the central features of their own or others' forms within a framework that emphasizes the concentration necessary for more profound effects and the unity implicit in "transition states."

Returning to Whitman, it is clear that he had absorbed this aesthetic of the transition state. Within and between cantos, "Song of Myself" follows the ebb and flow of the movement between particularity of the individual soul and its expansive nature. For this poem and others in *Leaves of Grass,* readers must ultimately resist the desire to come to final explanations and accept the uneasiness of an "in-between" or "fluid" position. The "answer" is in movement, because motion is the nature of thought and thus of a vital and electric life:

> Every condition promulges not only itself . . . it promulges what
>   grows after and out of itself,
> And the dark hush promulges as much as any.
>
> I open my scuttle at night and see the far-sprinkled systems,
> And all I see, multiplied as high as I can cipher, edge but the rim
>   of the farther systems.
>
> Wider and wider they spread, expanding and always expanding,
> Outward and outward and forever outward. (lines 1180–85)

If we are to take the poet at his word at the beginning of canto 44 and see the ensuing sections as his effort to stand up and "explain [him]self" (line 1133), we might learn something about the nature of this explanation through the poet's choice of the term *promulge.* "To promulge" is to publish or proclaim a law or decree. So what is this law that declares "not only itself" but that which "grows after and out of itself"? If one understands *law* as rules or codes imposed by some authority and/or articulated in legal or religious custom, then the final lines must remain confusing. The poet does not come down from the mountain to deliver a list of principles or commandments. However, if one sees *law*—or has come to view *law* through the exercise of reading the poem—as a way of being or knowing the world, then the final cantos offer a consistent and understandable message. In other words, the answer emerges in the closing effort to assert form and plan in the nature of this journey to and from the self. Anchored in and with the singular pronoun, the "I," the poem remains the site of coexisting energies unified through the electric will of a poetic voice.

In "The Mesmeric Medium," the final chapter of *Facts in Mesmerism,* Chauncy Hare Townshend offers a gesture that would have been especially striking to an American readership during the age of Manifest Destiny; he confesses that the "last and most important point of view" relates to "the future prospects of man, considered as an improvable being, capable of immortality." In effect, he invites a consideration of the self and society as transition state: "That man is improvable and capable of a development, the limits of which have not yet been ascertained, is his high prerogative which distinguishes him from the brute creation. . . . Mesmerism is no miracle, but a development of faculties inherent in man." For a generation of writers who had come to see how we know as constituting what we know—that is, to understand that, in Foucault's terms, "knowledge has anatomo-physiological conditions"—Townshend's concluding reflections further reinforce the central role of art and writing for a democratic culture. In an age of social and literary reform, literature is nothing if not a manifestation of the "phasis of our nature."[15] For those artists who remain true to the fundamental life and its laws, text is transition state.

Not surprisingly, Townshend allows himself to voice (with more optimistic zeal) the broad-reaching implications of the mesmeric medium: "As regards our future state . . . there is the greatest reason to believe that mesmerism is a boon granted by God to confirm our faith and to cheer us on our way. All its phenomena combine to identify it with that which Coleridge has called the 'fundamental life.'" He goes on to define the fundamental life as "the *body* (for what is life, in our case at least, but mind incorporate!) that we are to retain throughout eternity." In effect, the body or "organic life" of-

---

15. Townshend, *Facts in Mesmerism,* 350, 351; Foucault, *The Order of Things,* 319; Townshend, *Facts in Mesmerism,* 351.

fers the means of "communicating with matter" and represents a "temporary development" of some other, more permanent state. According to Townshend, all of nature points to the fact that the "fundamental body" existing beyond death inevitably retains "something physically from [its] actual condition" in the present. Moreover, "[e]verywhere we behold that one state includes the embryo of the next, not metaphysically, but materially; and entering on a new scene of existence is not so much a change as a continuation of what went before."[16] Clearly, then, all of life betrays evidence of a transition state and, as such, contains the laws of its future form. It would take the cultural circumstances of the 1830s and 1840s—the broad public attention on somnambulants, the translation and/or publication of key mesmeric texts, a fascination with the philosophies of Kant, and a preoccupation with the dynamic nature of democratic realities—to lead antebellum writers to ponder the social and literary implications of such ideas.

In Edgar Allan Poe's "Mesmeric Revelation," the magnetized Vankirk echoes Townshend's assertions. Distinguishing between our present, rudimental body and an ultimate, complete form, he states that our "present incarnation is progressive, preparatory, temporary" and our "future is perfected, ultimate, immortal." He continues: "When I say that [the mesmeric state] resembles death, I mean that it resembles the ultimate life; for when I am entranced the senses of my rudimental life are in abeyance, and I perceive external things directly, without organs, through a medium which I shall employ in the ultimate, unorganized life."[17] If in fact a mesmeric consciousness represents a glimpse into the condition of the ultimate life and if this viewpoint provides insights into the nature of higher perception, then it does more than provide a revelation into what is to be. It illuminates the higher laws that shape a higher art.

16. Townshend, *Facts in Mesmerism,* 352, 354, 355.
17. Poe, "Mesmeric Revelation," in *Collected Works of Edgar Allan Poe,* 3:1037.

Bibliography

IN ORDER TO DISTINGUISH more clearly between primary and secondary materials as well as between the era's literary and mesmeric sources, I have divided the bibliography into four sections: primary sources, secondary sources, journal sources on mesmerism/animal magnetism and related subjects, and additional sources on mesmerism/animal magnetism. The primary sources include nineteenth-century poetry, fiction, essays, criticism, and correspondence; the secondary sources, of course, represent texts that illuminate these primary works and their authors, antebellum literature and culture, and the science of animal magnetism. Following these categories, I include two sections listing writings on mesmerism/animal magnetism. The first focuses on articles from literary and medical journals, arranging citations alphabetically by journal and chronologically by article. For those who wish to explore this material in more depth, I feel that such an arrangement facilitates research in the journals and, potentially, the tracing of changing attitudes toward mesmerism. The sources here are the most eclectic, including stories and essays as well as medical studies on animal magnetism, electricity, and notions of the mind. The final section contains an extensive listing of book studies in English. Though some material is from the seventeenth and eighteenth centuries, the texts are primarily from the first half of the nineteenth century.

Primary Sources

Child, Lydia Maria. "The Children of Mt. Ida." *Columbian Lady's and Gentleman's Magazine* 3 (April 1845): 145–54.

———. *The Collected Correspondence of Lydia Maria Child, 1817–1880.* Ed. Patricia G. Holland and Milton Meltzer. Millwood, NY: Kraus Microform, 1980.

———. "Farewell." *National Anti-Slavery Standard,* May 4, 1843 (vol. 3, no. 48, p. 190).

———. *Letters from New-York.* Ed. Bruce Mills. Athens: University of Georgia Press, 1998.

———. *Letters from New York. Second Series.* New York: C. S. Francis, 1845.

———. *Lydia Maria Child: Selected Letters, 1817–1880.* Ed. Milton Meltzer and Patricia G. Holland. Amherst: University of Massachusetts Press, 1982.

———. Review of *Woman in the Nineteenth Century,* by Margaret Fuller. *Boston Courier,* February 8, 1845, 2.

———. Review of *Woman in the Nineteenth Century,* by Margaret Fuller. *New-York Daily Tribune,* February 12, 1845, 1.

———. Review of *Woman in the Nineteenth Century,* by Margaret Fuller. *Broadway Journal,* February 15, 1845, 97.

———. "Thot and Freia: A Romance of the Spirit Land." *Columbian Lady's and Gentleman's Magazine* 3 (January 1845): 1–7.

Clarke, James Freeman. *The Letters of James Freeman Clarke to Margaret Fuller.* Ed. John Wesley Thomas. Hamburg: Cram, de Gruyter, 1957.

Coleridge, Samuel Taylor. *Biographia Literaria, or Biographical Sketches of My Literary Life and Opinions.* Vol. 7 of *The Collected Works of Samuel Taylor Coleridge.* Ed. James Engell and W. Jackson Bate. Princeton: Princeton University Press, 1983.

———. *Poetical Works.* Vol. 16 of *The Collected Works of Samuel Taylor Coleridge.* Ed. J. C. C. Mays. Princeton: Princeton University Press, 2001.

———. *Shorter Works and Fragments.* Vol. 11 of *The Collected Works of Samuel Taylor Coleridge.* Ed. H. J. Jackson and J. R. de J. Jackson. Princeton: Princeton University Press, 1995.

———. *Specimens of the Table Talk of the Late Samuel Taylor Coleridge.* Vol. 14 of *The Collected Works of Samuel Taylor Coleridge.* Ed. Carl Woodring. Princeton: Princeton University Press, 2000.

Dall, Catherine W. Healey. *Margaret and Her Friends; or, Ten Conversations with Margaret Fuller upon the Mythology of the Greeks and Its Expression in Art.* 1895. Reprint, New York: Arno Press, 1972.

Emerson, Ralph Waldo. *The Collected Works of Ralph Waldo Emerson.* Ed. Alfred R. Ferguson et al. 6 vols. Cambridge: Harvard University Press, 1971– .

———. *The Early Lectures of Ralph Waldo Emerson.* Ed. Robert E. Spiller et al. 3 vols. Cambridge: Harvard University Press, 1966–1972.

———. *The Essays of Ralph Waldo Emerson.* Cambridge: Belknap, 1979.

———. *The Journals and Miscellaneous Notebooks of Ralph Waldo Emerson.* Ed. William H. Gilman et al. 16 vols. Cambridge: Harvard University Press, 1960–1982.

———. *Selections from Ralph Waldo Emerson.* Ed. Stephen Whicher. Boston: Houghton Mifflin, 1957.

Fourier, Charles. *The Utopian Vision of Charles Fourier: Selected Texts on Work, Love, and Passionate Attraction.* Trans. and ed. Jonathan Beecher and Richard Bienvenu. Boston: Beacon Press, 1971.

Fuller, Margaret. "Bettine Brentano and Her Friend Günderode." *Dial* 2 (January 1842): 313–57.

———. "Canova." *Dial* 3 (April 1843): 454–83.

———. "Entertainments of the Past Winter." *Dial* 3 (July 1842): 46–72.

———. *The Essential Margaret Fuller.* Ed. Jeffrey Steele. New Brunswick: Rutgers University Press, 1992.

———. "Festus." *Dial* 2 (October 1841): 231–61.

———. Fuller Manuscripts and Works. Houghton Library, Harvard University.

———. "Goethe." *Dial* 2 (July 1841): 1–47.

———. "The Great Lawsuit. MAN *versus* MEN. WOMAN *versus* WOMEN." *Dial* 4 (July 1843): 1–47.

———. "'The Impulses of Human Nature': Margaret Fuller's Journal from June through October 1844." *Proceedings of the Massachusetts Historical Society* 102 (1990): 38–126. Ed. Martha L. Berg and Alice de V. Perry. Boston: Massachusetts Historical Society, 1991.

———. "Leila." *Dial* 1 (April 1841): 462–67.

———. *The Letters of Margaret Fuller.* Ed. Robert N. Hudspeth. 6 vols. Ithaca: Cornell University Press, 1983–1994.

———. "The Life of Sir James Mackintosh." *American Monthly Magazine* 7 (June 1836): 570–80.

———. *Life Without and Life Within; or, Reviews, Narratives, Essays, and Poems.* Ed. Arthur B. Fuller. Boston: Brown, Taggard, and Chase, 1859.

———. *Margaret Fuller, Critic: Writings from the New-York Tribune,*

1844–1846. Ed. Judith Mattson Bean and Joel Myerson. CD-ROM. New York: Columbia University Press, 2000.

———. "Menzel's View of Goethe." *Dial* 1 (January 1841): 340–47.

———. "Meta." *Dial* 1 (January 1841): 293–98.

———. "Modern British Poets." *American Monthly Magazine* 8 (September 1836): 235–50.

———. "Modern British Poets." *American Monthly Magazine* 8 (October 1836): 320–33.

———. "Present State of German Literature." *American Monthly Magazine* 8 (July 1836): 1–13.

———. "Richter." *Dial* 1 (July 1840): 135.

———. "Romaic and Rhine Ballads." *Dial* 3 (October 1842): 137–80.

———. "A Short Essay on Critics." *Dial* 1 (July 1840): 5–11.

———. "Yuca Filamentosa." *Dial* 2 (January 1842): 286–88.

Hawthorne, Nathaniel. *The Blithedale Romance.* Vol. 3 of *The Centenary Edition of the Works of Nathaniel Hawthorne.* Ed. William Charvat, Roy Harvey Pearce, Claude M. Simpson, et al. Columbus: Ohio State University Press, 1971.

———. *The House of the Seven Gables.* Vol. 2 of *The Centenary Edition of the Works of Nathaniel Hawthorne.* Ed. William Charvat, Roy Harvey Pearce, Claude M. Simpson, et al. Columbus: Ohio State University Press, 1965.

———. *Mosses from an Old Manse.* Vol. 10 of *The Centenary Edition of the Works of Nathaniel Hawthorne.* Ed. William Charvat, Roy Harvey Pearce, Claude M. Simpson, et al. Columbus: Ohio State University Press, 1974.

Poe, Edgar Allan. *Collected Works of Edgar Allan Poe.* Ed. Thomas Ollive Mabbott. 3 vols. Cambridge: Harvard University Press, 1979.

———. *The Complete Works of Edgar Allan Poe.* Ed. James A. Harrison. 17 vols. New York: Crowell, 1902.

———. *Edgar Allan Poe: Essays and Reviews.* New York: Library of America, 1984.

———. *Eureka: A Prose Poem.* New York: G. P. Putnam, 1848.

———. *The Letters of Edgar Allan Poe.* Ed. John W. Ostrom. 2 vols. Cambridge: Harvard University Press, 1948.

———. "Mesmerism 'In Articulo Mortis.' An Astounding and Horrifying Narrative, Shewing the Extraordinary Power of Mesmerism in Arresting the Progress of Death." London: Short and Co., 1846.

———. *The Science Fiction of Edgar Allan Poe.* Ed. Harold Beaver. New York: Penguin, 1976.

Whitman, Walt. *Leaves of Grass.* Ed. Malcolm Cowley. 1855. Reprint, New York: Penguin, 1959.

————. *Walt Whitman: The Early Poems and the Fiction.* Ed. Thomas Brasher. New York: New York University Press, 1963.

Secondary Sources

Alterton, Margaret. *Origins of Poe's Critical Theory.* 1925. Reprint, New York: Russell and Russell, 1965.

Ambrose, Stephen E. *Duty, Honor, Country: A History of West Point.* Baltimore: Johns Hopkins Press, 1966.

Aspiz, Harold. *Walt Whitman and the Body Beautiful.* Urbana: University of Illinois Press, 1980.

Austin, Robert B. *Early American Medical Imprints: A Guide to Works Printed in the United States, 1668–1820.* New Haven, CT: Research Publications, 1961.

Beecher, Jonathan. *Charles Fourier: The Visionary and His World.* Berkeley: University of California Press, 1986.

Brown, Lee Rust. *The Emerson Museum: Practical Romanticism and the Pursuit of the Whole.* Cambridge: Harvard University Press, 1997.

Bruner, Jerome. *On Knowing: Essays for the Left Hand.* Cambridge: Belknap, 1962.

Capper, Charles. *Margaret Fuller: An American Romantic Life; The Private Years.* New York: Oxford University Press, 1992.

Charters, Ann. "A Brief History of the Short Story." In *The Short Story and Its Writer: An Introduction to Short Fiction.* 5th ed. Boston: Bedford/St. Martin's, 1999.

Coale, Samuel Chase. *Mesmerism and Hawthorne: Mediums of American Romance.* Tuscaloosa: University of Alabama Press, 1998.

Colbert, Charles. *A Measure of Perfection: Phrenology and the Fine Arts in America.* Chapel Hill: University of North Carolina Press, 1997.

Crabtree, Adam. *Animal Magnetism, Early Hypnotism, and Psychical Research, 1766–1925: An Annotated Bibliography.* White Plains, NY: Kraus, 1988.

————. *From Mesmer to Freud: Magnetic Sleep and the Roots of Psychological Healing.* New Haven: Yale University Press, 1993.

Darnton, Robert. *Mesmerism and the End of the Enlightenment in France.* Cambridge: Harvard University Press, 1968.

Davidson, Edward H. *Poe: A Critical Study.* Cambridge: Harvard University Press, 1957.

Dickerson, Vanessa D. *Victorian Ghosts in the Noontide: Women Writers and the Supernatural.* Columbia: University of Missouri Press, 1996.

Ellenberger, Henri F. *The Discovery of the Unconscious: The History and Evolution of Dynamic Psychiatry.* New York: Basic Books, 1970.

Forman, Sidney. *West Point: A History of the United States Military Academy.* New York: Columbia University Press, 1950.

Foucault, Michel. *The Birth of the Clinic: An Archaeology of Medical Perception.* New York: Vintage, 1994.

————. *The Order of Things: An Archaeology of the Human Sciences.* New York: Vintage, 1994.

Fuller, Robert C. *Mesmerism and the American Cure of Souls.* Philadelphia: University of Pennsylvania Press, 1982.

Gould, Stephen Jay. *The Mismeasure of Man.* 1981. New York: W. W. Norton, 1996.

————. "Poe's Greatest Hit." *Natural History* 102 (July 1993): 10–19.

Harris, W. C. "Edgar Allan Poe's *Eureka* and the Poetics of Constitution." *American Literary History* 12 (Spring–Summer 2000): 1–40.

"Hartley, David." *Encyclopaedia Britannica.* 2003 ed. *Encyclopaedia Online.* July 30, 2003. < http://search.ed.com/eb/ article?eu = 40213 >.

Hoagland, Clayton. "The University of Eureka." *Southern Literary Messenger* 1 (May 1939): 307–13.

Hudspeth, Robert N. "Margaret Fuller's 1839 Journal: Trip to Bristol." *Harvard Library Bulletin* 27 (October 1979): 445–70.

Jordanova, L. J., ed. *Languages of Nature: Critical Essays on Science and Literature.* London: Free Association Books, 1986.

Kennedy, J. Gerald, and Liliane Weissberg, eds. *Romancing the Shadow: Poe and Race.* New York: Oxford University Press, 2001.

Krutch, Joseph Wood. *Edgar Allan Poe: A Study of Genius.* New York: Knopf, 1926.

Lind, Sidney E. "Poe and Mesmerism." *PMLA* 62 (December 1947): 1077–94.

Lohafer, Susan. *Coming to Terms with the Short Story.* Baton Rouge: Louisiana State University Press, 1983.

Lohafer, Susan, and Jo Ellyn Clarey, eds. *Short Story Theory at a Crossroads.* Baton Rouge: Louisiana State University Press, 1989.

Matthiessen, F. O. *The American Renaissance: Art and Expression in the Age of Emerson and Whitman.* New York: Oxford University Press, 1941.

Myerson, Joel. "Margaret Fuller's 1842 Journal: At Concord with the Emersons." *Harvard Library Bulletin* 21 (July 1973): 320–40.

Nelson, Roland W. "Apparatus to Poe's *Eureka.*" In *Studies in the American Renaissance, 1978,* ed. Joel Myerson. Boston: Twayne, 1978.

Nordstedt, George. "Poe and Einstein." *Open Court* 44 (March 1930): 173–80.

Osowski, Judith Marie. "Structure and Metastructure in the Universe of Edgar Allan Poe: An Approach to *Eureka,* Selected Tales, and *The Narrative of Arthur Gordon Pym.*" PhD diss., Washington State University, 1972.

Pannapacker, William A. "A Question of 'Character': Visual Images and the Nineteenth-Century Construction of Edgar Allan Poe." *Harvard Library Bulletin* 7, no. 3 (1996): 9–24.

Pattie, Frank A. *Mesmer and Animal Magnetism: A Chapter in the History of Medicine.* Hamilton, NY: Edmonston Pub., 1994.

Pearce, Roy Harvey. *The Continuity of American Poetry.* Middletown, CT: Wesleyan University Press, 1987.

Pollin, Burton R. *Edgar Allan Poe: Writings in "The Broadway Journal," Nonfictional Prose, Parts 1–2.* New York: Gordian Press, 1986.

Quinn, Arthur Hobson. *Edgar Allan Poe: A Critical Biography.* 1941. Reprint, Baltimore: Johns Hopkins University Press, 1998.

Reiss, Edmund. "Whitman's Debt to Animal Magnetism." *PMLA* 78 (March 1963): 80–88.

Review of "The Children of Mt. Ida. By Mrs. Child." *Broadway Journal,* March 29, 1845.

Reynolds, David S. *Beneath the American Renaissance: The Subversive Imagination in the Age of Emerson and Melville.* New York: Knopf, 1988.

Roob, Alexander. *Alchemy and Mysticism.* Köln: Taschen, 1997.

Silverman, Kenneth. *Edgar A. Poe: Mournful and Never-ending Remembrance.* New York: HarperCollins, 1991.

Steele, Jeffrey. *Transfiguring America: Myth, Ideology, and Mourning in Margaret Fuller's Writing.* Columbia: University of Missouri Press, 2001.

Stern, Madeleine. "Margaret Fuller and the Phrenologist-Publishers." *Studies in the American Renaissance* (1980): 229–37.

Swirski, Peter. *Between Literature and Science: Poe, Lem, and Explorations in Aesthetics, Cognitive Science, and Literary Knowledge.* Montreal: McGill-Queen's University Press, 2000.

Tatar, Maria. *Spellbound: Studies on Mesmerism and Literature.* Princeton: Princeton University Press, 1978.

Thomas, Dwight, and David K. Jackson. *The Poe Log: A Documentary Life of Edgar Allan Poe, 1809–1849.* Boston: G. K. Hall, 1987.

Versluis, Arthur. *The Esoteric Origins of the American Renaissance.* New York: Oxford University Press, 2001.

Weiner, Philip P. "Poe's Logic and Metaphysics." *Personalist* 14 (October 1933): 268–74.

Winter, Alison. *Mesmerized: Powers of Mind in Victorian Britain.* Chicago: University of Chicago Press, 1998.

Yolton, John W. *Perception and Reality: A History from Descartes to Kant.* Ithaca: Cornell University Press, 1996.

———. *Thinking Matter: Materialism in Eighteenth-Century Britain.* Minneapolis: University of Minnesota Press, 1983.

Zwarg, Christina. *Feminist Conversations: Fuller, Emerson, and the Play of Reading.* Ithaca: Cornell University Press, 1995.

Journal Sources on Mesmerism/Animal Magnetism and Related Subjects

American Phrenological Journal and Miscellany

"The Phrenological Organs Excited by Means of Magnetism.—No. 1." 4 (July 1842): 184–89.

"Phrenology and Animal Magnetism.—No. 2." 4 (August 1842): 213–18.

"Phrenology and Animal Magnetism.—No. 3." 4 (September 1842): 227–29.

"Phrenology and Animal Magnetism.—No. 4." 4 (December 1842): 308–12.

Warner, Samuel. "Electricity the Great Acting Power of Nature." 11 (May 1849): 151–52.

American Quarterly Review

"Animal Magnetism." 44 (December 1837): 388–415.

The Boston Medical and Surgical Journal

"Mesmerism." 2 (August 11, 1829): 411–13.

"Mesmerism." 2 (August 25, 1829): 446–47.

"Mesmerism." 2 (October 27, 1829): 584–87.

"Mesmerism." 2 (December 15, 1829): 698–99.

"Paracelsus." 3 (March 16, 1830): 82–83.

"Magnetism, a Remedy in Various Diseases." 4 (May 17, 1831): 231–32.

"Identity of the Nervous Fluid and Electric Fluids. By Dr. David." 4 (July 5, 1831): 336–38.

"Mental Alienation." 8 (May 8, 1833): 197–202.

"Anatomical Pathology of Mental Alienation—Concluded." 8 (May 15, 1833): 213–17.

"Animal Magnetism." 9 (September 4, 1833): 62–65.

"The Laws of Nature Inviolable." 9 (January 1, 1834): 330–32.

"The Springfield Somnambulist. Letter from Thomas Miner, M.D. to L. W. Belden, M.D." 10 (March 12, 1834): 73–74.

Belden, Lemuel W., M.D. "An Account of Jane C. Rider, the Springfield Somnambulist." 11 (September 10, 1834): 53–84.

Barnard, Joseph H., M.D. "Case of Somnambulism." 10 (November 5, 1834): 203–9.

Colby, M. F., M.D. "Additional Observations on the Case of Mrs. Cass, the Stanstead Somnambulist." 11 (December 17, 1834): 297–304.

North, Elisha, M.D. "Remarks on Somnambulism, Etc." 11 (January 6, 1835): 352–53.

"Medical Philosophisings: Remarks on the Senses, Somnambulism, and Phrenology." 12 (March 4, 1835): 58–62.

Belden, Lemuel W., M.D. "The Springfield Somnambulist." 12 (April 29, 1835): 192.

"The Uxbridge Somnambulist." 13 (September 2, 1835): 66–67.

P. "Physical and Moral Evils of the Present System of Female Education in the United States." 13 (January 13, 1836): 357–61.

"Animal Magnetism." 13 (February 3, 1836): 418–19.

"Mr. Poyen's Lectures on Animal Magnetism." 14 (February 10, 1836): 8–12.

Nichols, Thos. I. "Effects of Animal Magnetism." 14 (March 2, 1836): 56–57.

"Animal Magnetism." 14 (March 23, 1836): 114.

"Animal Magnetism." 14 (April 6, 1836): 141–45.

"Animal Magnetism." 14 (April 27, 1836): 192–95.

"Magnetical Experiments." 14 (June 22, 1836): 322.

West, Benj. H. "Experiments in Animal Magnetism." 14 (July 6, 1836): 349–51.

Poyen, Charles. "Institute of France." 14 (July 13, 1836): 364–66.

———. "The Report from the French Academy." 14 (July 20, 1836): 382–84.

———. "Animal Magnetism in Bangor." 15 (November 2, 1836): 205–6.

"Popular Lecture on Animal Magnetism." 15 (January 4, 1837): 349–52.

Haskell, Benjamin D. "Bell's Eclectic Journal." 17 (January 10, 1837): 366–68.

"Animal Magnetism." 15 (January 25, 1837): 403.

"Case of Somnambulism." 16 (June 14, 1837): 293–302.

Haskell, Benjamin D. "Identity, Sleep, and Dreaming." 17 (August 9, 1837): 12–17.

———. "Identity, Sleep, and Dreaming." 17 (August 23, 1837): 39–43.

"Animal Magnetism." 17 (August 30, 1837): 66.

"Deleuze's *Practical Instruction in Animal Magnetism.*" 17 (September 6, 1837): 98.

"Animal Magnetism." 17 (September 13, 1837): 89–92.

H., D. "Animal Magnetism." 17 (September 20, 1837): 104–11.

"New Theory." 17 (September 20, 1837): 113.

"Practical Instruction in Animal Magnetism." 17 (September 20, 1837): 113–14.

Mesmer [pseud.]. "Mesmerism." 17 (September 27, 1837): 125–28.

"Psychodinamist." 17 (September 27, 1837): 131.

Mesmer [pseud.]. "Mesmerism." 17 (October 18, 1837): 171–73.

"Progress of Animal Magnetism." 17 (October 18, 1837): 177.

Mesmer [pseud.]. "Mesmerism." 17 (October 25, 1837): 185–87.

"Propositions on the Nervous System, and on the Formation of Animals." 17 (October 25, 1837): 181–85.

"Practical Instruction in Animal Magnetism." 17 (November 1, 1837): 209.

Haskell, Benjamin D. "Functions of the Brain." 17 (November 29, 1837): 261–72.

"Progress of Animal Magnetism." 17 (December 13, 1837): 303–5.

"Animal Magnetism in London." 17 (January 3, 1838): 344–47.

"Deleuze." 17 (January 10, 1838): 370.

Zoroaster [pseud.]. "Animal Magnetism." 17 (January 24, 1838): 395–98.

Haskell, Benjamin D. "On Inflammation." 17 (January 31, 1838): 407–16.

"Dr. Bell's Select Medical Library and Eclectic Journal." 18 (July 11, 1838): 371.

"Animal Magnetism." 18 (July 25, 1838): 403.

"Animal Magnetism." 18 (August 1, 1838): 418.

Haskell, Benjamin D. "On the Evolution of Organic Existences." 19 (December 19, 1838): 309–16.

————. "On the Evolution of Organic Existences." 19 (December 26, 1838): 328–32.

Clough, John, M.D. "The Influence of the Mind on Physical Organization." 21 (January 29, 1839): 410–15.

"Animal Magnetism." 19 (January 30, 1839): 414–15.

"Dr. Elliotson and Animal Magnetism." 20 (March 6, 1839): 66.

"Animal Magnetism." 20 (June 26, 1839): 322.

Allen, N. H. "Ultraism." 21 (December 4, 1839): 270–73.

"Connection of Mental Philosophy with Medicine." 24 (April 21, 1841): 179.

"Connection of Mental Philosophy with Medicine." 24 (April 28, 1841): 193.

"Animal Magnetism." 24 (May 26, 1841): 257–58.

Review of "Prof. Smith's Select Discourses—No. II, 'Functions of the Nervous System.'" 24 (June 30, 1841): 337–44.

"Animal Magnetism in Boston." 24 (July 14, 1841): 380.

Candidus [pseud.]. Review of "Prof. Smith's Select Discourses—No. IV, 'On the Functions of the Nerves.'" 24 (July 14, 1841): 404–10.

"Dr. Poyen." 24 (July 28, 1841): 414.

"The Mesmeric Epidemic." 24 (August 4, 1841): 428–29.

"Animal Magnetism in Salem." 25 (August 18, 1841): 37–38.

"Progress of Epidemic of Animal Magnetism." 25 (September 8, 1841): 86.

"The Philosophy of Mesmerism." 25 (November 17, 1841): 237–42.

"Baltimore Animal Magnetism Report." 25 (December 19, 1841): 341.

"Manual of Magnetism." 27 (August 10, 1842): 18.

"Swedenborg's Knowledge of Physiology." 27 (October 19, 1842): 193–94.

Lafarque, M. Jules. "On the Locations and the Functions of the Brain." 27 (December 14, 1842): 309–17.

"Imagination." 27 (December 21, 1842): 328–30.

Lafarque, M. Jules. "On the Locations and the Functions of the Brain." 27 (December 21, 1842): 325–28.

Mansfield, J. D., M.D. "Mesmerism." 27 (December 21, 1842): 332–33.

Lafarque, M. Jules. "On the Locations and the Functions of the Brain." 27 (December 28, 1842): 348–51.

———. "On the Locations and the Functions of the Brain." 27 (January 4, 1843): 364–68.

———. "On the Locations and the Functions of the Brain." 27 (January 11, 1843): 375–79.

"Amputation during Mesmeric Sleep." 27 (January 11, 1843): 386–87.

Lafarque, M. Jules. "On the Locations and the Functions of the Brain." 27 (January 18, 1843): 393–98.

———. "On the Locations and the Functions of the Brain." 27 (February 1, 1843): 423–34.

Burton's Gentleman's Magazine

Review of *Vandeleur; or, Animal Magnetism.* 2 (February 1838): 138–39.

"The Real Animal Magnetism." 4 (February 1839): 135.

"Book of Miracles." 4 (April 1839): 251.

"An Opinion on Dreams." 5 (August 1839): 104.

The Magnet

Sherwood, Henry Hall, M.D. "The Magnetic Forces." 1 (June 1842): 3–6.

Sunderland, La Roy. "Preliminary." 1 (June 1842): 1–2.

Southern Literary Messenger

G., H. J. "Influence of Free Governments on the Mind." 1 (April 1835): 389–93.

"Remarkable Dream and Prediction, with Their Fulfilment." 1 (August 1835): 658–60.

"The Somnambulist." 3 (February 1837): 152–54.

"The Animal Magnetizer." 4 (April 1838): 253–56.

"Theory of Animal Magnetism." 5 (May 1839): 319–25.

"Humbugs of New York." 5 (June 1839): 380–83.
"Catalepsy." 5 (July 1839): 433–38.
"Catalepsy." 5 (December 1839): 834–35.

Additional Sources on Mesmerism/Animal Magnetism

Abernethy, John. *Lectures, Anatomical and Physiological.* London: Longman, Hurst, Rees, Orme and Brown, 1819–1823.

Belden, Lemuel W., M.D. *An Account of Jane C. Rider, the Springfield Somnambulist: The Substance of Which Was Delivered as a Lecture before the Springfield Lyceum, Jan. 22, 1834.* Springfield, MA: G. and C. Merriam, 1834.

Bell, John, M.D. *The General and Particular Principles of Animal Electricity and Magnetism, etc. In Which Are Found Dr. Bell's Secrets and Practice, as Delivered to His Pupils . . . Shewing How to Magnetise and Cure Different Diseases; to Produce Crises, as Well as Somnambulism, or Sleep-walking, [etc.].* London: printed by the author, 1792.

Braid, James. *Neurypnology; or, The Rationale of Nervous Sleep, Considered in Relation with Animal Magnetism. Illustrated by Numerous Cases of Its Successful Application in the Relief and Cure of Disease.* London: John Churchill, 1843.

Brigham, Amariah. *Remarks on the Influence of Mental Cultivation and Mental Excitement upon Health.* 2nd ed. Boston: Marsh, Capen, and Lyon, 1833.

———. *Remarks on the Influence of Mental Cultivation upon Health.* Hartford: F. J. Huntington, 1832.

Bush, George. *Mesmer and Swedenborg; or, The Relation of the Developments of Mesmerism to the Doctrines and Disclosures of Swedenborg.* New York: John Allen, 1847.

Collyer, Robert H. *Psychography; or, The Embodiment of Thought.* Philadelphia: Zieber and Co., 1843.

Colquhoun, John Campbell. *Isis Revelata: An Inquiry into the Origin, Progress, and Present State of Animal Magnetism.* Edinburgh: Maclachlan and Stewart, 1836.

Colquhoun, John Campbell, trans. *Report of the Experiments on Animal Magnetism, Made by a Committee of the Medical Section of the French Royal Academy of Sciences; Read at the 21st and 28th of*

June, 1831. Translated, and Now for the First Time Published, with an Historical and Explanatory Introduction, and an Appendix. By J. C. Colquhoun. Edinburgh: Cadell, 1833.

Crumpe, M. G. S. *Letters on Animal Magnetism.* Edinburgh: W. H. Lizars, 1845.

Deleuze, Joseph Philippe François. *Critical History of Animal Magnetism.* London: W. Wilson, 1816.

———. *Practical Instruction in Animal Magnetism.* Trans. Thomas C. Hartshorn. New York: D. Appleton, 1843. Reprint, New York: Da Capo, 1982.

Dickerson, K. *The Philosophy of Mesmerism, or Animal Magnetism.* Concord, NH: Morrill, Silsby and Co., 1843.

Digby, Sir Kenelm. *Of Bodies, and of Mans Soul. To Discover the Immortality of Reasonable Souls. With Two Discourses of the Powder of Sympathy, and of the Vegetation of Plants.* London: printed by S. G. and B. G. for John Williams, 1669.

Dods, John Bovee. *The Philosophy of Electrical Psychology: In a Course of Nine Lectures.* New York: Fowler and Wells, 1850.

———. *The Philosophy of Electrical Psychology: In a Course of Twelve Lectures.* New York: Fowler and Wells, 1852.

———. *Six Lectures on the Philosophy of Mesmerism, Delivered in the Marlboro' Chapel, January 23–28, 1843.* Boston: Redding and Co., 1843.

Du Commun, Joseph. *Three Lectures on Animal Magnetism.* New York: Berard and Mondon, 1829.

Dupotet, Jules. *Introduction to the Study of Animal Magnetism; With an Appendix Containing Reports of British Practitioners in Favour of the Science.* London: Saunders and Otley, 1838.

Franklin, Benjamin, et al. *Animal Magnetism; Report of Dr. Franklin and Other Commissioners, Charged by the King of France with the Examination of the Animal Magnetism as Practised at Paris.* 1784. Translated from the French. Philadelphia: H. Perkins, 1837.

Gibbes, Robert Wilson, M.D. *A Lecture on the Magnetism of the Human Body. Delivered before the Apprentices' Library Society of Charleston.* Columbia, SC: Dubose and Johnston, 1843.

Grimes, J. Stanley. *Etherology; or, The Philosophy of Mesmerism and Phrenology: Including a New Philosophy of Sleep and of Consciousness, with a Review of the Pretensions of Neurology and Phreno-Magnetism.* New York: Saxton and Miles, 1845.

Herwig, H. M. *The Art of Curing Sympathetically, or Magnetically, Proved to Be Most True Both by Its Theory and Practice, Exemplified by Several Cures Performed That Way. With a Discourse concerning the Cure of Madness and an Appendix to Prove the Reality of Sympathy.* London: printed for Tho. Newborough at the Golden Ball in St Pauls Church-yard . . . , 1700.

Jackson, Seguin Henry. *A Treatise on Sympathy, in Two Parts.* London: J. Murray, 1781.

Jones, Henry. *Animal Magnetism Repudiated as Sorcery;—Not a Science. With an Appendix of Magnetic Phenomena, by William H. Beecher, D.D.* New York: J. S. Redfield, 1846.

Kerner, Justinus. *The Seeress of Prevorst: Being Revelations concerning the Inner-Life of Man, and the Inter-Diffusion of a World of Spirits in the One We Inhabit.* Trans. Catherine Crowe. New York: Harper and Brothers, 1845.

King, John. *An Essay of Instruction on Animal Magnetism; Translated from the French of the Marquis de Puységur, Together with Various Extracts upon the Subject, and Notes.* New York: J. C. Kelley, 1837.

Lang, William. *Animal Magnetism; or, Mesmerism; Its History, Phenomena, and Present Condition; Containing Practical Instructions and the Latest Discoveries in the Science. Principally Derived from a Recent Work by William Lang. With a Supplement Containing New and Important Facts Never before Published in the U. States, by Rev. Chauncy Hare Townshend, Author of "Facts in Mesmerism, Etc."* New York: James Mowatt and Co., 1844.

Lawrence, Sir William. *An Introduction to Comparative Anatomy and Physiology; Being the Two Introductory Lectures Delivered at the Royal College of Surgeons, on the 21st and 25th of March, 1816.* London: Callow, 1816.

Lee, Edwin. *Animal Magnetism and Homoeopathy; Being an Appendix to Observations on the Principal Medical Institutions and Practice of France, Italy, and Germany.* London: Churchill, Princes Street, Soho, 1835. Edinburgh: Maclachlan and Stewart, 1835.

Leger, Theodore. *Animal Magnetism; or, Psychodunamy.* New York: D. Appleton and Co., 1846. Philadelphia: G. S. Appleton, 1846.

Macpherson, John. *Lectures on Moral Philosophy.* Philadelphia: Zachariah Poulson, 1791.

Martin, John. *Animal Magnetism Examined: In a Letter to a Country Gentleman.* London: printed for the author, 1790.

May, Alexander. *An Inaugural Dissertation on the Unity of Disease, as Opposed to Nosology: Submitted to the Examination of the Rev. John Ewing, S.T.P. Provost; the Trustees and Medical Faculty, of the University of Pennsylvania, on the Thirty-first of May, 1800, for the Degree of Doctor of Medicine.* Philadelphia: Way and Groff, 1800.

May, Arthur. *An Inaugural Dissertation on Sympathy: Submitted to the Examination of the Rev. John Ewing, S.T.P. Provost; the Trustees and Medical Faculty, of the University of Pennsylvania, on the Sixth Day of June, 1799, for the Degree of Doctor of Medicine.* Philadelphia: Way and Groff, 1799.

Mesmer, Franz Anton. *Mesmerism: The Discovery of Animal Magnetism.* Trans. Joseph Bouleur. Edmonds, WA: Holmes Pub. Group, 1998.

———. *Mesmerism: A Translation of the Original Scientific and Medical Writings of F. A. Mesmer.* Trans. and ed. George Bloch. Los Altos, CA: William Kaufman, 1980.

Morley, Charles. *Elements of Animal Magnetism; or, Process and Application for Relieving Human Suffering.* New York: Fowler and Wells, 1847.

Newnham, William. *Human Magnetism; Its Claims to Dispassionate Inquiry. Being an Attempt to Show the Utility of Its Application for the Relief of Human Suffering.* New York: Wiley and Putnam, 1845.

———. *The Reciprocal Influence of Body and Mind Considered; as It Affects the Great Questions of Education, Phrenology, Materialism, Moral Advancement and Responsibility, Man's Free Agency, the Theory of Life, the Peculiarities of Mental Property, Mental Disease, the Agency of Mind upon the Body, of Physical Temperament upon the Manifestations of the Mind, and upon the Expression of Religious Feeling.* London: Hatchard and Son, 1842.

Osler, Sir William. *Sir Kenelm Digby's Powder of Sympathy: An Unfinished Essay.* Introduction and notes by K. Garth Huston. Los Angeles: Plantin Press, 1972.

Pearson, John. *A Plain and Rational Account of the Nature and Effects of Animal Magnetism; in a Series of Letters, with Notes and an Appendix.* London, 1790.

The Philosophy of Animal Magnetism Together with the System of Manipulating Adopted to Produce Ecstasy and Somnambulism— The Effects and Rationale. By a Gentleman of Philadelphia. Philadelphia: Merrihew and Gunn, 1837. Reprint, Philadelphia: Press of Patterson and White, 1928.

Poyen, Charles. *A Letter to Col. Wm. L. Stone, of New York, on the Facts Related in His Letter to Dr. Brigham, and a Plain Refutation of Durant's Exposition of Animal Magnetism, &tc. By Charles Poyen. With Remarks on the Manner in Which the Claims of Animal Magnetism Should Be Met and Discussed. By a Member of the Massachusetts Bench.* Boston: Weeks, Jordan, 1837.

————. *Progress of Animal Magnetism in New England. Being a Collection of Experiments, Reports and Certificates, from the Most Respectable Sources.* Boston: Weeks, Jordan, 1837. Reprint, New York: Da Capo, 1982.

A Practical Display of the Philosophical System Called Animal Magnetism, in Which Is Explained Different Modes of Treating, with Some Medical Observations on the Diseases of the Human Body, Which Is Peculiarly Adapted to Relieve; Together with the Manner and Reasonableness of Absent Treatment: the Whole Calculated to Instruct Every Capacity, in the Rational Principles of the Mysterious Science. London: 1790.

A Practical Magnetizer [pseud.]. *The History and Philosophy of Animal Magnetism, with Practical Instructions for the Exercise of This Power.* Boston: J. N. Bradley, 1843.

Puységur, Armand Marie Jacques de Chastenet, Marquis de. *An Essay of Instruction, on Animal Magnetism.* New York: J. C. Kelley, 1837.

Redern, Sigismund Ehrenreich graf von. *On the Sentient Faculty, and Principles of Human Magnetism.* London: printed for Sherwood, Neely, and Jones, 1819.

Romer, Isabella F. *Sturmer; A Tale of Mesmerism.* 3 vols. London: Richard Bentley, New Burlington Street, 1844.

Sherwood, Henry Hall, M.D. *The Motive Power of Organic Life, and Magnetic Phenomena of Terrestrial and Planetary Motions, with the Application of the Ever-Active and All-Pervading Agency of Magnetism, to the Nature, Symptoms, and Treatment of Chronic Diseases.* New York: Chapin, 1841.

Sibly, Ebenezer. *A Key to Physic and the Occult Sciences: Opening to Mental View, the System and Order of the Interior and Exterior Heavens; the Analogy betwixt Angels and the Spirits of Men; and the Sympathy between Celestial and Terrestrial Bodies.* 5th ed. London: printed by W. Lewis for G. Jones, 1814.

Smith, Gibson. *Lectures on Clairmativeness; or, Human Magnetism. With an Appendix.* New York: Searing and Prall, 1848.

Stearns, S. *The American Oracle. Comprehending an Account of Recent Discoveries in the Arts and Sciences, with a Variety of Religious, Political, Physical, and Philosophical Subjects, Necessary to Be Known to Families, for the Promotion of the Felicity and Happiness.* . . . New York: Hodge and Campbell . . . , 1791.

————. *The Mystery of Animal Magnetism Revealed to the World, Containing Philosophical Reflections on the Publication of a Pamphlet, Entitled: "A True and Genuine Discovery of Animal Electricity and Magnetism. . . ."* London, 1791.

Stone, William L. *Letter to Doctor A. Brigham, on Animal Magnetism: Being an Account of a Remarkable Interview between the Author and Miss Loraina Brackett While in a State of Somnambulism.* New York: George Dearborn, 1837.

Sunderland, La Roy. *Pathiesm; with Practical Instructions. Demonstrating the Falsity of the Hitherto Prevalent Assumptions in Regard to What Has Been Called "Mesmerism" and "Neurology," and Illustrating Those Laws Which Induce Somnambulism, Second Sight, Sleep, Dreaming, Trance, and Clairvoyance, with Numerous Facts Tending to Show the Pathology of Monomania, Insanity, Witchcraft, and Various Other Mental or Nervous Phenomena.* New York: published for the author by P. P. Good, 1843.

Teste, Alphonse. *A Practical Manual of Animal Magnetism; Containing an Exposition of the Methods Employed in Producing the Magnetic Phenomena; with Its Application to the Treatment and Cure of Diseases.* London: Hippolyte Baillière, 1843.

Townshend, Chauncy Hare. *Facts in Mesmerism, with Reasons for a Dispassionate Inquiry into It.* New York: Harper and Brothers, 1841. Reprint, New York: Da Capo, 1982.

Wilson, John. *Trials of Animal Magnetism on the Brute Creation.* London: Sherwood, Gilbert, and Piper, 1839.

Winter, George. *Animal Magnetism: History of; Its Origin, Progress, and Present State; Its Principles and Secrets Displayed, as Delivered by the Late Dr. De Mainauduc. To Which Is Added, Dissertations on the Dropsy; Spasms; Epileptic Fits; St. Vitus's Dance; Gout; Rheumatism; and Consumption; With Upwards of One Hundred Cures and Cases.* . . . Bristol: printed by George Routh, 1801.

Index